Extraordinary

Stephen Gillen:
The Search For A Life Worth Living

STEPHEN GILLEN

This book is autobiographical, reflecting the author's present
recollections of experiences over time. Some names and characteristics
have been changed, some events have been compressed, and some
dialogue has been recreated. Memory can be a fickle thing, so the
Author trusts that any minor errors in times, dates and details of
particular events will be understood. Some names and identifying
details have been changed to protect the privacy of individuals.

Cover Design by Danji Designs
Cover Image by Pat Lyttle
Business & PR Photography Daphne Deluce

What People Are Saying About The Author

Stephen is an amazing individual who has really shown us that we can change. It was an honour to work with him and his story is certainly unique, one that has and will continue to touch many people for many years to come.

Ross Kemp, Actor & Presenter

Stephen's story stands alone in the annals of transformation and resilience. I've fought many world champions, known many tough and highly capable men who had to go through the fire to claim their greatness. It is a journey of great courage that always tests the best of us. In Stephen we have a fine example of someone who went through the raging fire to be forged for greatness. His story is a must read and is a testament to how no matter how challenging our road, everything can be overcome.

Joe Egan, Irish Champion x 4,
Actor & sparring partner to the great Mike Tyson

Stephen's story is amazing, unputdownable. Rarely do people escape gang life in one piece, and even rarer do they turn their life around into an inspirational story equal to Stephen's. This book is a game-change for the reader!

Anton Brisinger, Lifestyle Editor at Esquire

'I have had the honour of working with Stephen over the past two years. To think at one point, we were on opposite sides of the legal spectrum, with me as a senior police officer, is just incredible. His insight into his life and the revelations that came from his enlightened thinking should be shared far and wide. Stephens's story is a testament to the fact that your past does not have to define your future...'

Kul Mahay, Former Senior UK Police Commander - Leadership Development Specialist

Malala Yousafzai once said, 'Let us remember: One book, one pen, one child, and one teacher can change the world.' Here is a book that is sure to change the world. Utterly Exhilarating!

Mariett Ramm, Founder and Editor in Chief 'The Billionaire Chronicles'

'It matters not what someone is born, but what they grow to be... A must-read!'

Andy Loveday, Producer & Director of the 'Rise of the Foot Soldier' franchise

'Thanks, Stephen for guiding us through an extraordinary, and incredibly inspiring life-journey. Hard, gritty, pacey, and riveting. A remarkable transformation.'

Steve Frew, Scotland's first Gymnastics Commonwealth Games Gold Medallist

'This book inspired me to write mine. Now, Stephen is a mentor and friend...'

Darren Hamilton, Former British
Light welterweight Champion

'I've known, Stephen since we were tearaways. I'm proud to call him my friend. His book is an amazing example of dark turning to light against all the odds. His book is a true gift to the world.'

Jack Ramdan, Founder of Factory East Community
Project/Charity (in the East End nominated for
the QAVS Queens Award for Voluntary Services)

'Stephen Gillen, an incredible man. His story will take your breath away. It is truly inspirational that he come out of it the other end to be the people's champion. If he can overcome those obstacles, anything is possible. He is simply extraordinary.'

Nana Akua
GB News Presenter & Anchor

Acknowledgements

I must thank many friends, business partners, collaborators, and most importantly my 'inner circle' who, diligently supported me throughout everything I faced in the world, truly they are my greatest strength. They know who they are and in many areas of media, entertainment, broadcasting, publication/public relations, self-development, public speaking, sport and diverse industries in business.

A special thank you must be given to Daphne, my partner in life and business who, forever seeing the real me and the massive global vision I have in the world, is with her unique and special talent forever behind me and working hard towards all that we are creating.

To Lucia, Stevie, Sophie, Sydney, Mikie, Dustin, and the rest of the family and friends who, in their many colourful ways support and enrich my life more than they know.

To Delroy my childhood friend/family, and his family who, for all these years, has been forever my shadow in support. And especially for all those who, being faced with hardship, challenges and doubts, nevertheless believed, supported, and stood beside me on my journey and to build and develop the wonderful things in the world we do today.

I must also thank Taryn my diligent publisher and friend and Rick my Literary agent for their great work and continued professionalism on this massive project.

For all the heroes in the world who inspire me the most, you are, and always will be the finest. A Special dedication to the Howie family, Gerard, Margret, Tom, Jack, Tony, Geraldine, David & family – forever in my thoughts and gratitude for a chance at life

Table of Contents

Foreword..1

Introduction..3

Prologue...7

Chapter 1 – Living Through The Troubles 11

Chapter 2 – Across the Sea, A New Life 31

Chapter 3 – Bethnal Green And A New Family.................115

Chapter 4 – A Life Of Crime 163

Chapter 5 – Organised Crime and Serious Offences..........199

Chapter 6 – Sentencing 245

Chapter 7 – Inside Hell...267

Chapter 8 – New beginnings, The Same Mistakes 349

Chapter 9 – Breakdown & Rehab 377

Chapter 10 – Building a Life 421

Foreword

In the intricate journey of life, few stories unfold as compellingly or undergo such profound transformation as that of my friend, Stephen Gillen. His story, a testament to the resilience of the human spirit, unfolds across the pages of this book, revealing a journey that transcends the darkest depths of adversity to reach the pinnacle of redemption and purpose.

Abandoned as a baby, thrust into the unforgiving realm of brutal care homes, and navigating the treacherous paths of borstal and criminality, Stephen's early life was marked by challenges that would have extinguished lesser spirits. Yet, within this crucible of hardship, a remarkable transformation was brewing—a metamorphosis that would see him emerge from the shadows of a Category A prisoner to become a beacon of hope and change.

Stephen's life is a compelling narrative of redemption, not just in the legal sense but in the most profound human sense. His journey from the streets of Belfast and London, where survival meant embracing the harsh codes of gangster life, to his current stature as an international peace prize nominee, global CEO, TV presenter, and author, is nothing short of miraculous. It is a story that speaks volumes about the power of change, the importance of second chances, and the unyielding capacity of the human heart to seek and create a meaningful existence.

I have had the unique privilege of walking a path that mirrors Stephen's in many ways. Having also known the life of organized crime, and having made my own journey towards redemption and contribution, I see in Stephen's story a powerful affirmation of the possibility of change. It is a narrative that resonates deeply with me, not just for its parallels to my own life but for its universal message of hope.

Stephen Gillen is indeed the real deal. His authenticity shines through in every chapter of this book, not only chronicling his past as a formidable figure in the underworld but also highlighting his extraordinary transformation into a man dedicated to making a positive impact on the world. Through his work in prisons, with gangs, and in his various roles beyond, Stephen embodies the essence of true leadership and the profound impact one individual can have on the lives of many.

To call Stephen Gillen my friend is an honor. His latest literary work is more than just a book; it is a manual for anyone seeking to overcome their circumstances and aspire to a life of significance and fulfillment. I wholeheartedly recommend you immerse yourself in these pages and allow Stephen's remarkable journey to inspire you to pursue the best possible version of your own story.

Michael Franzese
A former caporegime of the NY Colombo Crime Family,
Motivational Speaker & Author

Introduction

As I recount the story of my life, I question how I will manage to do so and remain alive. If someone had forewarned me at birth of what lay ahead, would I have mustered the courage to persevere?

What I am about to divulge is akin to galloping through hell on horseback. It involves brutal, violent narratives about deaths and individuals who have committed, and continue to commit, unspeakable acts. Some of these individuals persist in their heinous ways, while others are no longer alive. Grudges linger; some believe I harbour them still.

Even now, I find certain events difficult to articulate; some tales seem too dark to drag into daylight. It is only with the support of others that I can bear to see these words in print. I question the value of recounting such tales, wondering if they serve humanity. Yet, I am convinced that others are essential in aiding human progress and addressing the burdens we carry. You will find fragments of our shared humanity throughout these pages, especially in the emotional turmoil and the pain. Through the struggles and challenges, there is an understanding that life is about surmounting insurmountable odds and scaling seemingly unscalable heights.

This narrative is ultimately about triumphing over the impossible, about becoming something I was never destined to be. It is a tale of transformative inspiration, of journeying from profound darkness into the light, of rediscovering myself.

Today, I am not the person I once was. Today, I am human.

I have penned this book for numerous reasons. To document the truth, to serve as a testament that might not only facilitate change in others but also act as a cautionary account of how not to live.

Part of my intent was to delve into the past and decipher it, making sense of the history that once confounded me. To examine the bones of past extremities and finally lay to rest the ghosts that linger. I believe these spectres, the echoes of a person's past, remain eternally. The demons we battle in silence can only be subdued and kept at bay.

They also serve as a stark reminder not to revert to old ways. If we strive to comprehend them on a profound, knowledgeable level, we might muster the bravery to transform and impart our insights to future generations, empowering them with newfound wisdom to avoid repeating our errors.

I am convinced that both this planet and its inhabitants have a definitive purpose. Once the past is woven, it takes a colossal effort to unravel it. This tumultuous push and pull of life is designed for learning and growth, to stretch our capabilities, to not revert to past mistakes. Through these trials, we forge a path and become something more.

I now understand that, like many others, I was both blessed and cursed. Cursed with a volatile human condition capable of horrors, which I recognise as far from normal. Yet, I am blessed to have discovered that on the flip side of immense anger, hatred, destruction, loneliness, and rejection lies the capacity for immense kindness, forgiveness, love, bravery, honour, and hope.

Bound by this paradox, I realised I needed to comprehend these conflicting traits, that perhaps I was always meant to wade through darkness until I found the light.

Prologue

Ireland, 1969

Kathleen surveyed the cramped lounge, her gaze resting on Jesus on the cross. His expression of disappointment seemed to echo how everyone felt about her. This house, this life - despite being loved, she felt imprisoned, and she loathed every moment.

Shrugging into her coat, Kathleen headed for the bus in search of a few hours of pleasure and freedom. She needed to escape before it was too late.

As the front door slammed shut, Madge watched her departure from the upstairs window. Kathleen was a tempest of anger, resentment, and desperate longing for something that eluded her here. Madge sensed trouble on the horizon.

Five hours later, Madge found herself at the bus stop, hands wringing with anxiety. The final bus of the night approached, its belly empty of passengers. As it drove past without pausing, Madge's resignation set in; this wasn't the first time Kathleen hadn't come home, and she doubted it would be the last.

At eighteen, Kathleen was the epitome of rebellion. Young and striking, she harboured a fiery spirit. The world wronged her, and so had her mother's death, leaving her adrift.

Madge, who had sacrificed her own prospects to care for her siblings, looked like a martyr. But Kathleen wouldn't follow that path; the dawning of the seventies promised women opportunities, and she was determined to seize them.

Walking in the back door, Kathleen braced herself for the barrage that was surely to come. As expected, Madge stood in the kitchen, worry and annoyance plain to see in her face.

'Where have you been, Kathleen? I was up half the night worried for you. When you weren't on the last bus I feared the worst.'

'Oh don't tell me you were waiting at the bus stop again? Jesus, Madge, we've been through this.'

'How many times must I tell you not to take the Lord's name in vain in this house?'

Kathleen rolled her eyes, slipping effortlessly into rebellious teenager mode.

'Oh here we go. Just let me live my own life. You've made your choice, you want to be stuck here, that's up to you, but don't try to enforce it on me.'

'I just want you to be safe, Kathleen. These streets are dangerous and the Brits are just looking for an excuse. You're lucky you didn't get yoursel' arrested.'

'Ach don't be daft. And anyway, they can frisk me any time they like, they might find something sharper than my tongue waiting for them!'

'Kathleen you stop such talk right now!' Madge looked horrified, the back door was open and their conversation could be heard outside. 'And keep your voice down. You know what would happen if,' Madge hesitated, lowering her voice to a whisper, 'the wrong people heard you say that.'

Kathleen sneered. 'You're just jealous that I can go out and have a good time, whilst you're here praying for a better life! Well you know what? You're not my Ma. She's gone and I'm going too, soon enough!'

Madge took a backward step. The impact of Kathleen's words fell hard on her. 'Where do you think you're going?'

'I don't know yet, but I'm no' staying here so I'm not. I've been offered a job in London. I might go there.'

'London? Doing what? Why would you want to go there? To England?'

'Why? Are you nuts? The question is, why not. Why would I want to stay here? It would be a new life for me Madge, don't you see that?'

Madge was still reeling from the shock and hurt of Kathleen's throw away comment about their mother. 'Well if that's how you feel, go on and pack your bags now. I won't stop you.'

'You couldn't anyway.'

With that last snarled comment and a glare over her shoulder, Kathleen went off to pack for her new life across the water.

A few hours later, aboard the Belfast to Liverpool ferry, Kathleen stared into the tumultuous waters of the Irish Sea, apprehension about the future gnawing at her. She inhaled the bracing sea air. Her fears were inconsequential; she was free now and had no intention of ever returning.

CHAPTER ONE

Living Through The Troubles

*"There is no instance of a nation benefiting
from prolonged warfare."*

— Sun Tzu, The Art of War

I have cheated death a hundred times. I have been in the company of princes, kings and queens, and I have touched the stars. But I've also been to the very depths of the human soul, where darkness, death, cruelty, pain and torture lie. I was there for many years.

It can be said that numerous things can trigger a man's demons. I know now what initiated mine. For me, it was a constant sense of feeling different. Of being abandoned in this world, looking to belong whilst filled with the fear of what was coming next. Throughout my life, I have seen death, destruction and suspicion around me, wondered how I would survive and what skills I would need to make a life for myself.

I was brought up in Belfast in the early 70s in the centre of the troubles where a civil war raged between the Republicans and the loyalists and British forces, living in a warzone.

I was born in England in 1971, but as a baby, some months old, I was taken back to Belfast by my mother, Kathleen, to the place of her birth. She left me with my aunt and uncles while she returned to England, aiming to forge a life for herself. I didn't know it then, but this one act was to be the catalyst for who I was to become.

My life in Ireland as a child, though, was magical. I could navigate six streets and be close to the Mourne Mountains or the rich wild greenery of the forest by the Antrim Road. The people there were the salt of the earth. They loved nothing better than good food, a great laugh, banter and a decent drinking session. They were also very tough, hard and loved to fight, they did not shy away from confrontation.

Then there was the war. The divide. Everywhere, the brightly painted paramilitary murals demanded attention. The green of the Tricolour clenched fists and balaclava figures on gable walls. Two streets later, the red, white and blue of the Union Jack, kerb stones painted to match and slogans like 'No Surrender'.

I lived with four people in the house. The focal point and my stability was my surrogate mother, Madge. She and her brothers were my family. Jack, Gerard and Tom. They were bricklayers, decent, God-fearing people. Every Sunday, like clockwork, I would journey up the Antrim Road to church. They were well known in the community for helping, for their kindness, for their honesty. The community was very tight knit there in those days, introverted and insular. Everyone seemed to know everyone. My uncles were the go-to people if the neighbours wanted an extension or good quality bricklaying work; there wasn't a house that they hadn't had some part of the building.

Times were tough. There was no money, no luxuries, and people neither had nor cared for anything extravagant. They were simple, humble, more focused on day-to-day survival, and more grateful. Madge was a robust and steely woman with a loving and engaging manner that set everyone at ease. She was wise with a giving and kind nature that changed people. She was the boss of her brothers but let them think they were in charge. Together, they made space to nurture this young baby from England. Looking back, I now understand their many sacrifices to give me an upbringing.

I felt I was cocooned in that little three-bedroom house in Belfast. A place of calm, safety and normality. It had a small kitchen extension my uncles had built before I was born and I remember the colours being drab but comforting. Everyone congregated in the front room around the coal fire, prepared early every morning, burning bright all day and late into the evening.

My uncle Thomas was a quiet, soft man; he had once been caught in a bombing and suffered terribly with his nerves. He smoked Embassy cigarettes constantly and went nowhere apart from his boxing club to watch the sport he loved. My Uncle Jack was a tall and silver-haired man, always busy and talkative. He had been in the navy and had travelled the world. He had fantastic stories and smoked the strong Players' cigarettes. Gerard was my father figure. He was central amongst the brothers and seemed to be the dominant hand in most affairs. I can see now that they had agreed and defined roles in my life while I growing up. Madge would be my mother, and Gerard, my father. Together between them, they guided my life and managed all my affairs.

At this time, I didn't understand that I had another mother. Kathleen had grown up in this environment, this swirling anger and fear; she'd come and gone again in a short space of time, perhaps looking for something that didn't exist. Kathleen had been seeing a man in Belfast called Bobby Gillen. He was a good man, someone to be trusted. He was solid and stable. I guess, though, that wasn't what Kathleen wanted. She came back to Belfast briefly, telling the family that she was working as an Au pair for a family and was looking after a baby. Kathleen showed

Madge a picture, I now know it was of me. She returned with me shortly after and tried to make things work. Perhaps she hoped to convince Bobby that I was his son, and she gave me his name. I know this wasn't true; my father was a man named Tommy. Not a good man by all accounts, I've been told this, and Kathleen needed to get away. Always wild of heart, I now know that she thrived on going against the grain; I found out later in life that she would hid guns in my pram during the troubles, to take through check points. That may sound terrible to you, but one person's terrorist is another's freedom fighter; it was all she really knew, and in that hard, confusing and brutal landscape of war everyone was leveraged in one way or another.

Kathleen tried to make things work with Bobby but left for London again. Over time, she came and went. She had another child, Martin, who is eighteen months younger than me, but the fire in her soul was too strong, and she left for the final time. Martin stayed with his father. I knew nothing of him until some years later when I would inevitably get into trouble whilst playing with him; I vividly recall him parroting what he'd heard from an adult: ' Stephen, you're always in trouble.'

I had been left there as a small child who didn't understand the world. I can't even remember Kathleen being there; if she visited me, I have no memory, so the only mother I knew was Madge. I was very happy with her; she was my reality. My daily rituals were built by this beautiful, kind soul. She had a kind, knowing oval face with dark, greying, wavy hair that would always be hidden by a blue patterned silk headscarf tied at the chin. She was my world, and like clockwork, I would be washed down twice a day with the imperial leather soap in the sink or the little yellow plastic basin under the bathroom sink. She was my sweetness in the world, my protection. Together with her three brothers, they created a wonderful, safe haven inside that house that contained the horrors outside. They were solid figures in my life. There was a calm security as long as I stayed close.

There was love, and above all that, there was protection, wise instruction and principles, and consistency. Looking back now, it was the fundamental lessons at this formative age that created my solid principles of family.

Outside the door was a raging inferno of death, civil war, paramilitaries, suspicion, finger pointing and cruelty. Everywhere were the checkpoints. You would walk through, and bags, people, faces, and demeanours would be scanned, checked and searched. I pointed once at the soldiers who weaved in and out of house doorways.

'Look, guns, soldiers!'.

Gerard smacked me around the head quick and hard. 'Shhhh, don't point, Stephen. Never point. They may think you're holding something and fire!'.

Even as a child, as far back as I can remember, I knew there was suspicion everywhere. That you always had to be careful of bombs going off, of the riots. It was imprinted on me that the authorities were not to be relied on, trusted, or talked to. You always had to be careful what you said and who you spoke to. It was the strangest thing, but it set me up with excellent insights and a keen eye; I could usually tell the difference between a catholic and a protestant at a hundred paces. It was in the look on the face, in the eyes. The way they stood and moved. The way they spoke, even the clothes they wore. This was something that, looking back, set me apart from others in the criminal world; I never lost that ability; I honed it over time. A sixth sense and instinct that kept me in front, always.

The soldiers would arrive in armoured cars anytime and jump out with rifles and machine guns. They would weave in and out of doorways, moving all in their path, and they would bring an attitude of wrath and fear with them. Snipers, helicopters, and cold stares combined with frightened and cautious movements. Some of them would be nice to us kids. They would throw a smile or even give sweets. But I would always be cautious.

'Hey, mister, why you here?'

'…Go back to your home.

'What's the gun for mister?'

Silence.

People talked in hushed tones. People always worried about what they would say and who was listening.

One of my earliest memories is of being around five and having a bright little yellow Tonka truck. Just outside the front door and over to the left of the street was a little hill that used to go down to the next junction. I wasn't allowed too far at that age, but one of my greatest joys was riding it down the hill. At five years old, I knew nothing about my environment, the people, the horrors, or the deeds that were a part of daily life. I just knew you had to be careful, forever watchful. Not to trust anyone outside your family home and to keep your mouth shut. In a child's mind, it is not strange that you would have to watch travelling from one street to the next. You have no fundamental understanding that there is any difference. That one street would be friends, and the other deadly enemies - it just was.

It's only when you become older that you realise and know more about other cultures and the world beyond your own environment that you realise that there is something very terrible, very unique, that you have grown up with. It's a shame because the people needed to prosper and be together in such hard times, not divided.

The pain the war caused was appalling. The people had to be brutal. Over a thousand years of religious war had kept this beautiful island in continuous bloody turmoil.

Brother turned against brother.

Community turned against community. Family turned against family.

It was two opposites of hell that made no sense. There were always conflicts, riots and dangerous hair-trigger movements. They would just appear, usually at night, but they could also come in the day. They would always be accompanied by gunshots, bottles and fire. Roads being cordoned off, shouting, smashing of windows and stones being thrown.

Our back garden, about eight meters by six meters, had a little slim concrete path with two short steps up to the next level. To the left was a little bit of grass, and at the back, two little coal bunkers, which we used to use for the coal fire in the front room. Just at the back of the bunker was the monkey puzzle tree.

As a tiny child, I would always go out there. It was where I used to play because I wasn't really allowed out because of the trouble. More often than not, I would stand at the front room window and watch the other kids of the street play. They would laugh, shout, push and pull each other, play on their bikes, and I would just watch. I would yearn to be part of it, to be involved and play. I was too young then; my time would come.

My world was the back garden. Behind the monkey puzzle tree was the Nocher's family garden. They were a big family, four boys and one girl, and they would always be climbing up on their shed roof, throwing things and fighting. One of those boys, David, would be shot dead later on as he went to buy breakfast for his children. My family knew the mother well, and so did I, but they were different to me. They also seemed to have a freedom I didn't.

The monkey puzzle tree stood proud, unmoving and alone. My uncle used to tell me wonderful fantasies as a child, how curved streets had giants buried under them, how you couldn't go out at night because of banshees, and how certain places were dangerous because of giant praying mantis. They were ridiculous yarns – and I loved them.

I asked him one day, in the back garden in Belfast, 'What is that spikey tree?'.

'The what?'.

'Tell me about that, the tree that's always there?'.

'That's a monkey puzzle!'

'A Monkey Puzzle?'.

'Never speak in front of a monkey puzzle tree. Be careful of what you think when you are close to it, especially what you say! They can live to be a thousand years old. As old as some of the mountains in these parts. They have a secret language. But they are truly magical. It is said that Monkey Puzzle Trees hold all the secrets of the land... but beware, for they are so loyal, so silent that whoever they hear speak loses the gift of speech and can never speak again!'

I looked at the spikey arms of the tree, its armoured tallness, and I looked at how alone it was and how strong it looked. I felt it could never be moved, climbed even. Resilient. It looked lucky and independent in this place of suspicion and spirits. I was always in awe of it and intrigued. I felt frightened of it in some little way as well.

During the day, I thought of cowboys and Indians and the brown plastic fort I constantly played with. I had my cars, plastic soldiers, generals and armies. Making camps and hiding in dugouts. Building things, and when I was old enough, going with the other children and running away free, no longer cocooned. Playing with toy guns and on my bike. I would hear the excitement, riots, and gunshots at night and want to be with the big boys. I would want to be doing what they were doing, to be part of their excitement, and I had no fear.

Until one night, the deafening noise is the first thing I recall, shouting, crashing, loud swearing. The shattering of glass, of armoured police and army vehicles accelerating. Gunfire peppered the night somewhere close, the deafening barrage of rhythmic volleys quickening, stopping, then erupting again. Then the fire lit the night sky like burning rainbows as petrol bombs arched. I could see a coach on its side as a roadblock; flames ravished it, crackling, sending embers into the darkness.

I could feel the heat of the flames and see their glow dancing in the night. My heart was beating in my chest. I was 7 and wiped sweat and dirt off my hands onto my trousers, searching for comfort. I was out alone. I was lost; the riot had emerged from nowhere, and I was cornered. I ran. I felt the fear of danger course through me of being in the darkness lost. Bodies ran in all directions as there was the crack of rubber bullets.

These impressions have stayed with me throughout my life. Locked away, I have been unable to speak of them with clarity. This memory has, at times, haunted me. It has held me in depression, made me question things, and it has spurred me to act in the worst, most dangerous of circumstances.

The daylight had dissipated quickly, but the dark evening coldness had returned quicker. I knew my aunty Madge and family would be worrying now.

Everyone was throwing stones at the police and armoured vans. The army pigs (green armoured vehicles with riot mesh & hatches) crashed into the burning bus. The barricade started to swing open. People scattered. The gunfire elevated. My eyes widened in panic, and I ran. I was unaware of the people that ran and dispersed behind and beside me. But I could feel them. I thought only of a place to hide and escape the noise and the gunfire. Without conscious thought, I found one. My face was in the damp earth, in a front garden under a hedge, and my breathing rattled in my ear. I tried to be invisible from the gaps in the bottom of the hedge.

Stiffening with fear and cold, I watched.

The armoured vans roared up the street. There was an eerie silence, then full-out gunfire again. The main crowd had been directed to the next street, but the battle continued. I had been there a while, rooted to the spot and afraid to move. Then, the Republicans started shooting from the flats near me. It was a strategy to draw the security forces in. Gunfire was traded.

Then I saw him. There were two at first, but the other took up a crouched firing position and with his self-loading rifle he fired. They both had on jeans, their faces covered. The one who drew closer to me zig zagged, rifle in hand in a dark duffel coat buttoned against the night. I was sure his eyes met mine for a moment, that he was aware of me. A child cowering in the hedgerow. But he raised the rifle as if to take a shot up the road where the wreckage of the bus was. The street lay desolate, a stark silence suddenly shattered by the sporadic vibrancy of gunfire, the billowing smoke, and the frantic running of those caught in the turmoil.

Then it happened. I watched it all. The shot the boy took to the chest flung him backwards. The wind was squeezed from his lungs. I watched, terrified, as he hit the ground in front of me and winced. He gasped for breath and spluttered, coughing blood. I could see the blood run from the side of his mouth as he rolled in pain. The gunfire continued close by.

I wanted to say something but could not talk. He was mumbling to himself. I couldn't understand it.

Then, 'Mother, God Mother. Help me. Father.'

The tears were rolling down my cold cheeks. I was frozen in terror but could not move. I tightened the grip of my little fingers on the earth and felt the dampness of the mud. I was sure he saw me now as I managed to say, 'Sorry. I'm sorry. Are you okay?' I stretched out my hand through the gap in the bottom of the hedge to try and comfort him.

He didn't answer. I watched him. I felt his pain. It was over twenty minutes; his movements were slowing as he was dying. He still called for his mother and his family. Minutes stretched on, each one feeling longer than the last, as if time itself was weighed down, moving with the lethargy of protracted, heavy hours.

I travelled this time with him in terror and pain, and I felt it deep inside me like a stain I couldn't remove.

Two of his comrades appeared from the darkness. One pointed his rifle. Together, they pulled him back, hopefully to safety. I saw his legs drag along the pavement lifelessly, and I saw the black Doc Martin boots he wore. They did not see me cower in the darkness or that I had tightly closed my eyes.

Across the road, on the fourth-floor balcony of the high flats, a man with binoculars watched the balaclava figure twisting on the floor from the gunshot wound and shuddered. He stood, eyes focusing through the highly intensified lenses, unable to express the feeling he was experiencing. A pavement being stained by running blood.

The chaos was about him. It stained the night; he thought in the vantage point he had chosen. Hammering his ears. In the drilling sound of the bullets and the running crowds and the bricks and the bottles, he was transfixed with the boy who was dying in front of him. He paused as he saw a small hand appear from under the hedge row, the private exchange as the dying boy turned toward it, and his lips moved.

They pulled him back now, his comrades, the boy who bled, out of the line of fire towards cover. The gunshot had slowed the movement of his struggles. The man with the binoculars studied the garden and the bottom of the hedge where the hand had appeared. He saw the young boy crawl back. Saw him, face stamped with terror and patchiness of tears on his face, climb the gardens to the side of him and get to safety at the end of the road.

From his high and hidden vantage point, the man known in Belfast as 'The Gardener' watched as the boy turned toward his line of sight one more time. The sharp black hair, small frame, jeans and coloured jumper, he saw it all, imprinted the memory before he lowered the binoculars. On his right hand, he had only three fingers. A wound that had come years after his birth, his ring and little finger were missing.

Icy Fear still gripped me. I could smell the earth and undergrowth as I crawled through the garden to save myself. Although cold, my little body was sweating inside my ripped, dirty jeans, top, and heavy jumper. I still felt the fear of the boy who reached for his mother while he died. My mind screamed that I must find a way out of here, but to use the road was death. The next garden had a small brick wall. I vaulted across it quickly, feeling exposed and rushed to the next hedge.

The shooting was further away now, fainter. But the road remained empty and looked more dangerous than ever. I listened intently, trying to trace movement for the lost sounds of gunfire.

What should I do?

My mind was filled with my front room at home. The fire burned healthily, and my Uncle Tom sat deep in the chair watching the news. Jack was on the couch beside him smoking a Player, Gerard read his big double-sized paper, and my aunt Madge washed the dishes preparing for dinner.

I forged a way through the next garden.

I was at the corner of the road, and my eyes peered suspiciously down and along three stretches of street. The small tenement houses were barred and quiet. Not a soul. Lights were on. There was an ominous feeling hanging in the air.

I realised everyone would be worried about me.

The pain and horror of what I had witnessed lingered and couldn't be moved from my mind. I thought of him. The gun, the hidden face in the mask. The impact. A figure that pleaded. Why did they go? I had to move.

Sprinting across the open stretch of road. My target was the slim concrete alley separating the tenement houses' backs.

'What are you up to, wee man?' She stood there, a young but towering figure face hidden by a hood and scarf. The dog she controlled pulled hard on its leash and snarled and barked. A strong, healthy Alsatian type that was big for its size.

'Stop', she bellowed and pulled on the lead.

I pulled back.

'She's okay.' She gave a tight smile, and her eyes narrowed. 'As long as you're not a Brit'?

There was waning light in the ally, cover. She pulled me quickly by the hand.

'Quick', she forced a rapid break forward down the concrete. 'I know you. You're the Gillen boy, aren't ye?'

Silence.

'Margaret? Gerard, Serpenton Parade?

'Yes', my voice cracked in a battered voice that stretched into a whisper.

'No worries, wee man. I'll get you home. You got some blacks to be out and about here tonight!'

Her hand had tightened in a vice-like grip around mine. In the cold air, I watched the dog's breath. It pulled us into a back garden. There was a tin bath, and the enclosed walls of the garden illuminated the back-door kitchen window. It opened in a burst, and people passed us carrying a box.

'Don't mind them.' she said as we went through the tiny kitchen into a small front room. The aged curtains were drawn, and a dim light burned in the corner. There were three of them. Two with rifles and one with a revolver. They wore green jackets, jeans and balaclavas. One stroked the barrel of the gun stretched across his knee. The one near the window pointed his rifle. The one with the short had his finger on the trigger guard.

Everyone looked.

'Jesus', they sighed. 'What the fuck. You not see it's brutal here tonight?'

The room was dirty, littered with old furniture, tins and bottles. A safe house. The TV squawked. I realised it was tuned into the security force frequency as I heard the crackle of walkie-talkies.

'I found the wee man.' We stood there, me, her and the panting dog. 'I know the family he's from up the road. I'm going to take him back.'

'Well, go on then. Fecks sake.'

The dog was made to heel and told to quieten down. I was pulled quickly behind her again, fast in the cold evening air. Marching quickly, no talk, brisk strides. Up the alley and over the road. I kept turning behind me as if someone were chasing us. The air remained menacing as we marched, and in my mind was the boy.

Six months later…

The morning ritual had started at 7am. In a cold bathroom, as the coal fire was being built, I had stood tall in the yellow basin and been washed down briskly with the flannel. I dressed in my school uniform, and Margret fixed my black and white tie. I was fed as the house struggled to wake up, and my uncle Gerard escorted me out the door. We went down the path and up the road. Around the corner at the top of Serperton Parade and up the steep hill to Antrim Road. The boy still stayed in my thoughts. The visions of the night would creep back unannounced and spoil my moments, stealing my joy. Streets were on either side of us as we climbed upwards, near the church. I was never the same after the boy. The gunshots still rang in my ears to remind me of the imminent danger. I had become more sullen since that evening. More aware of the world. Nothing had been said on my return. I was hugged tightly and scolded a little for being out so late, but sensing something was wrong, I was bathed and bundled to bed with a snack. In those days, they did have long conversations and feelings, and what I saw never came up.

A place of fun and pranks had restructured into lurking dangers and moving shadows.

Gerard carried a paper rolled up in his hand. It swung as we walked, the same route clockwork since as far back as I could remember. School was on my mind now, the Christian brothers and the nuns that ran it. The school, Park Lodge, was a two-story building on Antrim Road. It was for infants and primary and held about one hundred and fifty children. I had been through infants there, and I struggled now through primary. We got close to the school, and I buttoned my little blazer, and tidied my short grey trousers. My satchel was at my shoulder, and I felt dread.

It was the usual feeling I always got drawing near to the school. Even before I arrived, I saw my teacher. The Christian brother in charge of our class. A large man, he towered above all of us. His black flowing robes would dance when he moved, and always, he seemed to glower at us through round spectacles. The nuns were not much better, sometimes even worse. Brutally strict, it was a brave soul who forgot his homework. Being disrespectful was suicidal. They would line the class up for one misdemeanour and punish us all with the strap. They made us learn. They had a class full of high achievers in the making because of it. I was no different; I liked school but feared the punishments. I was a bright child with a clear intellect and enquiring inquisitiveness. I excelled in most things and was a great reader interested in history. Nearly there. My hands recoiled, and their muscle memory remembered the painful stinging of the leather strap.

At break time, we would kick the ball in the fenced playground, and the time would stretch out there until I yearned to get home. On a good day, just further down was

Cave Hill, and there were mountain goats there which would climb the rocky grey side of the sheer rockface by the two caves in the mountain. We would watch them and their aerobatics and then play soldiers on the way back down the hill through the woods.

I was at the front entrance, and kids rushed in past me. I saw Gerard's smile; he raised his clenched fist, pointed the rolled paper towards me, and then nodded. I gave a small smile. He was gone, and I watched him walk back the way we came. I steadied myself to settle in class; I was a changed boy. My stomach had a different feeling, unrecognisable notions in my head. I walked slowly in, unaware that my little reality would soon be changed beyond anything I could have imagined…

CHAPTER 2
Across the Sea, A New Life

"Anger may in time change to gladness; vexation may be succeeded by content. But a kingdom that has once been destroyed can never come again into being; nor can the dead ever be brought back to life."

— Sun Tzu, The Art of War

Ireland, 1980, Age 9

I stood looking at the dock, the great ship, the depth and green-blue vastness of the swelling and moving water. I had never known so much loneliness, so much anxiety. Fear was a close second to the sadness in my heart. I couldn't put a solid shape to it, but it was in the unknown, the going into alien places where I had never been before, that the terror lived. I was buttoned up against the early morning cold in my heaviest coat and held tight to my little blue suitcase. I watched the men of the ferry work with the massive ropes that anchored the ship, and inside, I shivered as I tried to steel myself for what was to come.

Beside me, Gerard, his hair sparse, thinning and grey, stood with his shoulders bowed. He had always looked vital to me, a champion who would always win through. I saw a difference in him now. He fixed a face against the world, but I knew inside he screamed. He gazed more those days as if he was there but was not there. As if things had become less important or exciting. He looked across the docks occasionally, glancing sideways to check on me. It was my feelings he experienced. My worry and anxiousness pained him.

I had been a happy child, joyous against the sharp edges of life. Always curious to engage in the next adventure. That boy had gone, though, changed forever. A numbness had crept into my soul, insidious in how it had suffocated my joy. I looked across the far water, out into the great ocean that stretched as far as my eyes could see, and my thoughts returned to the crying. The words that hadn't made sense.

The words I'd thought could not be real.

We had stood in the house's little, green main bathroom downstairs. We had held each other, adult and child, and cried hard. Madge had died. She had been in hospital with what I now knew was aggressive cancer. She had been in there for six weeks as she fought to the end. I had missed her. I had continuously called for her, for her warmth and the comfort she gave me. They had kept me away. They had mourned away from my sight, keeping the brutality of her dying from me and concluded that it was no place for a child. They could hardly bear it themselves, and as it had looked certain, the end was there; this wonderful woman, a sister, a matriarch, and a mother would be remembered the way she was last seen.

The seagulls hung in the air, and I watched them glide free. It had been decided that the Irish troubles were becoming too dangerous with an escalation in activities, especially riots and bombings. The sectarian cauldron had been boiling over into all-out war as the tit-for-tat killing fields were primed for complete annihilation. It had been further discussed and decided that the little house in Belfast was broken without Madge's influence. That although it was not spoken of or voiced clearly, it was the beginning of the end for the brothers. That the pain they held would translate into a lengthy and dark mourning.

It was best that the little bundle, brought from England as a baby, should return across the Irish Sea. Gerard had looked for weeks to locate my mother. He had searched every avenue he could, and finally, my new home was found. I would live with a woman I did not know but to whom I belonged. I know the decisions Gerard and his brothers made were out of necessity, not choice.

People lined up to board the ferry, and we joined the queue. Gerard looked at me again to check. I imagine now what he must have thought. *That he felt the worst he'd ever have. That the future looked bleak for us all. He said that he was sorry, but it was for the best that I needed a woman's hand. Behind me, everything I had known was crumbling and deteriorating. That there was nothing left there that I would recognise.* He tried a smile; I knew he would miss me terribly, the warmth of my innocence, the responsibility that focused him and helped his health and purpose. He would miss the moments of family love shared.

Also, I knew he would worry. He would sit in the chair by the fire with his brother, smoking a cigarette, making the best of it while people killed each other outside the door. He would think of the decisions they had made, and he would consider if they had been right. He would put a brave face on, get up earlier, do extra work and build the fire. He would think of his sister Margret and imagine the child in England.

He had already had one mild heart attack. He would take care of himself. He would pay more attention to these things because, with his sister gone, he felt responsible for the other two.

They checked the passports and the faces and scrutinised the baggage.

'Go through,' and we were waved onto the steel bridge up to the ship's deck. The wind had picked up, and I glanced around. Way beyond the smooth hills at the back of the docks were the winding roads that stretched like tree branches. Belfast and the little house in Serpenton Parade had to be somewhere over to the left behind the hills.

'Come on, son. Let's get settled; we can get a cup of tea. He hadn't turned. I was somewhere else. Everything was changing too fast; I had no control. I had left everything. No toys. No need for toys, or soldiers, or the fort, or the bike. Only the need for the case. I didn't know what was in it, just my few meagre belongings. I hoped that my mum would have new toys for me, that I'd have many things to look forward to if I could just let go of the fear.

I had a strange picture of my aunt Madge in front of me. It was the back of her. I'd seen the headscarf, the silhouette, the movement that she had, but she'd walked away from me, and I'd pointed and called her name. I moved to get close to her, but the figure, the back of her, had continued to move away from me.

'Stephen. Stephen!' Back there on the deck, our luggage tight beside us. Gerard grasped my little shoulders and shook me again, 'Stephen, can you hear me? God, son, you're daydreaming. You ok?'

We started moving, and I heard the ship's horn bellow as it prepared to carve its path. I looked down as the water swelled, rippled and was pushed by the movement of the great ship. One hand grasped the smooth iron railing tightly; the other sought comfort and held my uncle's hand. I could see, far in the distance, the makings of a new land, a strange place of unknowing. My nervousness played with my fear and with a slight excitement.

The ship moved beneath our feet, and I looked at him, deep into his eyes, for the first time that morning. 'I am, Uncle Gerard', I whispered. 'I'm fine'.

We had travelled through the night from Belfast by coach to Larne. We would then cross the Irish Sea to Stranraer in Scotland, then on to the mainland of the United Kingdom, where we'd take the waiting coach through the night to Victoria Station in London.

Back in the port of Larne, as the rain had lashed through the blowing wind, the man with three fingers had looked far into the mighty ocean. He'd had a ball of strange feelings rising and falling inside him. A central anger that taunted him, a torturing, searing sensation like the twist of a long knife. He had left his home in the Divis flats part of West Belfast early when the night still held back the light, and the dampness of the morning positioned itself. With solid feelings driving him, he had trailed the desolate and dirty streets and then driven to the port in his tweed jacket, with his matching cap pulled tight at his ears.

A well-known figure in Northern Ireland, it had been vital for him to travel to his destination unseen, un-tracked, and invisible. The sea had swelled in front of him. A ginormous, untameable soup that had twirled and turned with the fierceness of the rain. He had arrived in good time to see the boy. A young slip of a thing with a small suitcase stumbling along with an air of fear and uncertainty. The man known as the Gardener had held far back, hood covering his features as he'd sipped a coffee and studied hard the tiny boy with his suitcase, holding tight to his uncle's hand.

He had done the checks. He knew the boy, his uncle, and his family. He had confirmed he had the right target.

The Gardner watched as they entered the ticket office, sat in the waiting room with the other departing passengers and boarded the ferry. From his clandestine vantage point, he had watched closely.

He'd taken a last look out into the vastness of the rough and troubled waters of the Irish Sea. With the wind hitting him from the east and the lashing rain attacking the phone box, he'd rang the number given to him on a piece of white paper.

He'd said in a calm, steady, sure voice, 'Yes, it's him, alright. I saw him and had a good look. It's definitely him…'

Send Youth Detention Centre aged 14

The prison officer's sharp voice cut through the air, 'Come on, get your kit squared away. Those bed-packs up in the dorm are a bloody disgrace.'

My first time in prison, a lean and slight fourteen-year-old, I hastened to fold my kit to match the size of the blue tiles on the floor, just like the other young inmates in the changing room. The narrow space was often a hotspot for violence. A row of sinks bisected the room, lined with open dark grey lockers that housed our drab prison attire. The air was thick with the bark of orders. Glancing around, I saw a motley collection of undeveloped bodies, some tall and gangly, others short and pudgy, with diverse skin tones and awkward expressions.

The officers' ire was directed at a black-haired lad, unperturbed as he methodically laced his boots and fastened the gaiters around his ankles. The intensity of their rage surged. I observed the boy, slight for his age yet emanating a certain vivacity. A singular streak of grey cut through his otherwise pitch-black hair. Sleep had eluded me; our dorm housed thirty beds with thin mattresses, starched sheets, and a solitary thin green blanket each. The nights were bitterly cold, filled with restless tossing and turning - children fraught with anxiety, far from the familiar comforts of home, others paralysed by the stark reality of their circumstances.

A scuffle broke out at the back. My eyes caught sight of a white boy; his face flushed with terror. He was outnumbered by a group of black boys who had cornered him.

'You lot at the back! Get back in line!' bellowed the most formidable officer, tall and rigid, with a scarlet burn scar marring half his face and neck.

'Now you will do as you're told,' his voice thundered like a sergeant major's, echoing through the corridors.

'Attention,' he commanded, and we snapped to, standing upright. Then, from behind, a voice broke through.

'Having a laugh, are we? Since when did we sign up for boot camp?'

I turned towards the voice. It belonged to the boy with the grey streak, his smile broad, his eyes scrutinising yet playful.

'When God made me, they broke the mould. Even my mum says so. I'm Connie Slaney, from Bermondsey, South London. Nice to meet you. And you are?'

'Stephen Gillen. I'm from East London,' I replied, shaking his firm hand.

Connie's steely grey-blue eyes sparkled with mischief, betraying an air of the unpredictable. The kind of look that suggested hidden depths of turmoil, yet capable of great mirth.

The prison officer's shout cut through the tension, 'Quick march!'

Our sniggers were suppressed, a shared secret behind our disciplined façade.

'Look at old Red Neck,' Connie whispered, barely containing his mirth. We marched on, young conscripts led by a scarred veteran. Out of the shadows, through the doors, we emerged into the courtyard's sunlight, passing the grey, single-storey education block.

'He got that burn on a bombed ship,' Connie snickered. 'I just call him Red Neck.' He was deliberately coaxing laughter from me - a risky game in this unforgiving place.

We circled the field inside the tall green fence, marching to the cadence of 'Left, left, left, left, left, left, left, left, left, left, left, left, right, left... Right wheel.'

The sun shone in the clear sky, a brilliant orb promising a scorcher of a day. The chirping of birds and the hum of summer enveloped us.

Connie continued, 'Feel like a right plonker, marching about. It's like following the lead in one of those old war films.'

I struggled to contain the bubbling laughter, guarded, still unsure if Connie was a friend or just another adversary. The giggles burst through our disciplined exterior. We marched on, arms swinging, a pair of comrades bound by shared amusement amidst the rigid order of our surroundings.

England, 1980, Age 9

We had gone deep into the Irish Sea. We had put the cases safe, had tea and a sandwich, and the bad weather had swept in. We sat inside the ship on the top level, and the metal walls and ferry windows were crashing against spraying water. It was okay. It was customary in this water that weather like this could suddenly appear out of nowhere. I was reassured. I always believed everything my Uncle Gerard told me.

'How you feeling, Stephen?' He had forced the words out slowly, low as if it hurt him to speak.

I felt his day was hard. I could see the tiredness around his eyes. The haggard energy that draped around him. There was no strength in his eyes now, no brightness.

'Everything's going to be alright, Stephen. Okay, son?

I watched the red metal floor of the ship sway and heave. I kicked my little legs under my seat and fiddled with my hand in my lap. 'Yes'.

He told me of England; it was better, a good life. My family were grand people. Kathleen was a fine woman with a good man who would be my new father. I was not to worry; I would have great friends, and the schools were okay.

He stopped a moment. I watched his furrowed brow search for the next sentence. The ship went right and left, and the floor rolled in an uncertain sea. I stopped swinging my legs under the chair.

'I know it's hard, he continued,' his hands tightened together in front of him.

I sat there, and England, although drawing closer, seemed an unreal picture in my imagination. A place I could not see in my mind.

'I so wish it were different, Stephen. I wish your Aunt Madge was still here.' His face had turned then, slightly betraying his still raw feelings. 'It is better this way. We've decided... You need a woman's hand... I can't give you that.'

The water splashed violently outside against the windows of the boat. My uncle Gerard was saying something else in a soft tone. It continued, a further description of the difference of a better England...

My focus had strayed. My mind was taken against my will, and there was a mixture of sadness and panic in my stomach. I was remembering. I was in the back garden again; it would not be three years past. I had a little green plastic soldier in my hand, I had been in the mud and earth and stones of the back garden playing with it, and I had been angry about not being allowed out into the front road where it was busy with children I knew playing. The monkey puzzle tree had covered my back with the shadow of a midday sun, and Aunt Madge, in her head scarf, scowled through the back kitchen window at me as she washed dishes.

I felt the rebellion inside me as I watched the Nocher kids play on the tin roof of their shed. I thought I was too protected. I was big, the other children ran wild, I saw them do it. I had stamped my feet. I had closed my face to Madge and my uncles, and I had run and thrown one of my plastic soldiers in the open hearth of the fire. I had stood there a moment as it burned to reinforce my point. My Uncle Tom, perched in the armchair next to the chimney breast, looked at me with soft, confused eyes. I had run again out into the garden in anger.

Madge still watched behind the window from the kitchen sink. One of the Nochers at the back started smashing the tin corrugated iron off his roof with a stick. The green soldier was clasped in my hand. It had cast dark green, legs rooted in a standing firing position from the shoulder. I was still troubled by frustrating anger. Margret was there; she had come out from the kitchen by the side door. She dried her hands on a checked tea towel, and love and mischief were in her eyes. She smiled knowingly, and my anger slid as my love rose…

'Please get ready to embark. All passengers with cars go down to be ready to embark!' the bark and vibration of the ship's speaker cut my thoughts. My memories were stolen back, and my mind recoiled. My little hand rested in Gerard's, and people moved. The ship turned, still unsteady. We joined the activity stuck waiting with our cases in a slowly moving queue to the lower decks. There was an uncertain future ahead of me that was sure, but the trust was with my Uncle Gerard. I clung to his hand tightly. There was dread in my chest. It had found a place there, and removing it was difficult. I had memories of the little house back behind us. The people and places I had left behind. England. Faceless people who were strange to me and who I must settle and make a life with. I tried hard to imagine her, this Kathleen, her love, her smile. There was nothing to anchor to. No photograph, no letters, no phone calls. My trust was with Gerard.

My hope was that this new mother was lovely. In my mind, she was like my Aunt Madge; they were sisters, so they must be alike. Hopefully she would be all I could wish for and more. Would I be safe? Would I be looked after? Would I have a great crack? Would I have great new toys and better soldiers? Would the garden be grand and big with greenery, and would I run wild with the other children?

In my heart was a perfect image of what it would be like to be with my mother, that she had left me behind. It didn't matter; she wanted me now and would be home for me.

We had navigated the ship's lower levels and then stood on the hard concrete of the dock with our cases. We were in Scotland, the Cairn Ryan Port of Stranraer. It was a day of predicted lashing rain. The wind was picking up. Grey clouds gathered, and rain threatened. Half directed by one of the stewards, we walked towards where the coach would soon depart. It was a long journey, many hours, slow and cost-effective. It would hit the motorways towards London, and the roads would stretch into the late evening.

We would arrive at Watford Gap Services, and everyone would get a stop to eat and use the toilet, stretch their weary legs that were stiff and full of pins and needles.

We were in the holding room now, the wind blowing and tearing at our jackets. We sat in a drab, faceless room for commuters without energy or personality. Gerard guided me to a chair, a comforting hand on my shoulders. I saw his features. He smiled. I trusted the smile as we settled on the wooden seats to wait. The grey skies outside reminded me of the darkening concern inside me. I had been brave since it had been explained to me.

The wind steadied itself and clashed into another reconfiguration. I settled deep into the depth and safety of my blue padded jacket collar, and the uncertainty spread through me...

Woodside Children's Home Aged 13

The night wrapped around us like a cloak. I looked at Tony beside me, who was trying to drive the old blue Ford Escort. He was a year older than me at fourteen. A rebel with short blond combed hair, a strong, quiet youth with scarred cheeks from acne. It was the early hours; a bright moon hung high and clearly broke the blackness with its ghostly yellow glare. The gears rattled unhealthily, jammed again, then found a correct position. The car shot forward, climbing wildly in speed. We peered out of the windscreen into the rushing darkness that rose to meet us, Tony turned, made a slight movement, gave an unsure grin, and then returned his attention to the blackness in front of us.

It was a quiet road in North London, and a small roundabout with a grassed hill beckoned ahead. I had stolen cars with Tony a few times, coming out with the big bunch of car keys jiggling locks, unlocking steering columns, accelerating at high speeds in stolen vehicles and getting chased by the police.

We came too fast as we hit the silent roundabout. Tony had mistimed the gear change again, his hand struggled to find an appropriate gear, and the gear stick kicked back, rattling.

'Oh Jesus God!' I had my hands on either side of me. They gripped hard the edge of the black leather passenger seat.

Tony tried to turn the steering wheel in a last-ditch attempt to control the car, to slow down and stop the impending doom. The vehicle lunged forward, sixty miles an hour, with no brakes. It cut into the road of the roundabout, threw and jolted our bodies upwards as it mounted the kerbs of the small mound. My eyes widened, fear and panic advanced with breakneck certainty to the centre of me. It was a split second, but it stayed with me, wildly hitting my mind and body with one explosion. The car raced over the grassed mount of the hill and I could only hold on looking at what was in front of me. The car smelt old, oily, damp and rusty. The tapping of fast-moving undergrowth against the car's bodywork filled my ears and a crackling, snapping, tinkling mesmerised me.

'Holy Shit,' I spoke loudly.

Although slowed slightly by the mount, the car still moved with increased pace. Down the other side of the mount, we hit a road sign, then the curved tarmac of the other side of the roundabout. The car jumped from the ground and jolted, vaulting the linear concrete kerbs of the footway. We flew leaping over a grass verge and hit a slim concrete post that steadied a wired fence.

Our bodies shook for a moment with the impact. We looked at each other quickly, blank faces that had realised how close they had come. We had hit the fence post with such force that the front of the car was buckled. Steam rose from the engine, hissing.

Tony was out of the car door in a second.

I was out just as fast and ran around the car to join him. We ran in spurts, and the cold moonlit air hit our lungs. It mingled with the spiked body chemicals and the gratitude of our close shave. We sprinted from the scene. We were lucky, no one had seen us or had been hurt. I was thankful. Down a house lined street, sprinting as fast as we could, our breathing, deep gulps, recreated into mist before us. We swung a left into another similar road, then a right to the lights of a row of closed shops.

We continued running through the moonlight until we felt safe from capture. Hurriedly, we had zigzagged through old streets. They were lined with houses and flats and ran beside the high, black wrought iron railings of a tree bordered park. We climbed over the closed park gates and fell to the other side. It was late, darkness ruled with silence in these hours, but traffic from the busy road arterials on either side of us still appeared. We quietened our pace, relieved, as we covered the outer grass verge of the park towards the inner darkness, silence, and the cover of the tall trees. The wind rose. The swaying arm branches of the fern trees shifted together as if in an orchestra.

Tony's head was down as he walked.

'We should be fine now. The accident is far behind us…' I noticed my clothing. Only jeans, trainers, a tee-shirt underneath a worn thin jumper and a black tracksuit top. 'It's cold here.' I continued. 'It'll be freezing later!'

He was slightly ahead, head still down. No sound, still walking.

'Over there, Tony,' I pointed to a slim winding man made path.' Let's sit at the benches a while…'

He turned a moment in the shadow of the trees, a grin on his face.

I followed behind him. I thought he was in the same kind of clothes as me and wouldn't fare much better in the coldness of this night.

The trees surrounded us, tall, cloaking, swaying creatures, ancient and whispering. Resting birds in the treeline shuffled. A large bird bolted from the tree blackened interior. A sudden flapping rush that scraped and moved leaves and branches.

'I don't know what happened. One minute I had it, then lost the car completely,' Tony said. He didn't turn, kept his head in front as he spoke. We were coming into the tree bordered pathway.

'The gears were tough,' he continued.

'Your legs weren't long enough to touch the pedals. Your problem, Tony, is you need to get a driving licence, I stated.

He turned. In the dark moonlight. A silence. Our eyes locked, and I had a light in my eyes, a creased brow and the sarcasm was clear on my face.

Tony looked at me, eyes blinking, and he laughed. A deep, genuine, long, hearty sound that vibrated through the bench. I was with him. We looked at each other, our eyes watering with laughter, structured giggles rolling across us as we gasped for more air.

We found one of the wooden benches that lined the pathway and sat. Tony had his hand on my shoulder; the relief was needed. The laughter was a tonic to our pain and worry, and we wished it could go on forever. I had always liked Tony. I took to him the first time they had taken me to the children's home. He had stood there in the reception area, a cap on his head, looking older and more mature than the rest, more alone, and with a quiet strength that singled him out.

The local authority ran Woodside Children's home as a Children's Home for vulnerable children. In reality, behind the closed doors of the two buildings that held about 40 children, it was the last stop before prison for many. Holding a Secure Unit for special cases, which had the corners of every room rounded, and twenty-four-hour-a-day surveillance in case of suicide, it was a place of violent containment for small children who were treated like adults. The jarring impact of a high-speed car accident seemed nothing in comparison to the physical abuse by the 'staff'.

On the bench, we looked ahead into the dark shrubbery on the far side of the trees. The wind had picked up, and my exposed skin was reacting to the dropping temperature, my shivers were increasing.

'What we gonna to do?' Tony sat, legs swinging below the bench, hands clasping the bench framework either side of his knees.

'I don't wanna go back,' he continued. I'd rather stay here. He moved his head and indicated the space around us.

'We won't have to. Don't worry,' At that moment, a great pain in my shoulder and arm began.

'We need food, Stephen. What we going to do. I'm hungry?'

'We'll find something, we're not going back.' I answered. The pain had moved; it travelled now down the right side of my body. I felt the anger rise to a peak in me.

I had been in the dining room at the care home. Sat at one of the little wooden tables that each held six children and one or two staff members on a wooden chair. Mr Windmill, a big, tall barrel of a man with wispy, thinning, black, greasy hair, had been at the table growling his orders. There were a few nasty bullies in there. In my opinion, he was right at the top of the list.

One of the smaller girls, a tiny little thing with slight sandy hair, had sat and cried. The pain of her sniffles had mixed with her running tears chapping her face, and he had forced her to eat. Slammed the plastic cup filled with orange on the table in the middle of us, and my anger erupted. He had pushed and pushed the girl, who we had heard had been abused and kicked and thrown out by a dysfunctional family. My eyes had filled, my heart going out to help her, and my little fists had hurt as I clenched the silver cutlery in my hands with seething rage.

'How's your arm,' breaking my chain of thought, Tony looked concerned with pained eyes.

'Windmill... I was just thinking of him... It's okay, a bit of a sharp pain at the top of my shoulder,' I moved my arm as if to confirm the words. Pain shot through my side again. A twisting, stabbing fire that disappeared then resumed.

My mind was back to the girl. The rage. The place where terrible things were done and no one helped.

The little girl had sat there in her creased dress printed with bright flowers, and he had forced her to a silent torture that saw her gasp for breath, choke back her pain and control her sniffles. The kids on the table had kept their heads down, not wanting to be involved or draw attention to themselves. I had watched his treatment of the girl, her lonely desperation, and the curl of his cruel mouth, and I had jumped up and flung my whole plate of dinner in his face. Fish, gravy, carrots and mashed potatoes had been my shout in the dark.

The whole dining hall was aware of it. Heads turned, jaws dropped, and eyes glazed. I had the silver fork in my hand. Small and thin for thirteen, I stood to face him as tall as I could. The people at my table had moved back. The little girl widened her tear-filled eyes.

The sound of the chair screeching back assaulted the air as Windmill stood from the table. Mash potatoes mixed with brown gravy slid down the side of his neck. His eyes were wild. They stared daggers at me as his large frame moved in one movement around the table. He claimed me like a big black bear with a freshly caught deer salmon. Wiped me from my feet. I punched out and tried to use my slight weight and kicked.

I pulled at him at the elbow of his jumper. He had me round the neck in a vicelike grip with one arm. He squeezed and held me tighter, twisting his arm, and my body was lifted as we walked backwards, his body and arm dragging me behind him. I choked, tried to breathe, and fought him with all my strength. We were out of the dining room into the pale white walls of the slim corridor that led further into the centre of the main building.

He dragged me, still struggling for breath. My trainers twisted on the light blue lino floor tiles. I tried to get a position of leverage. To gasp, breathe, find needed air, to hurt him back, I twisted my body hard. He tightened harder his firm grip. He pulled and dragged me. Words were on my lips. I cursed him, swear words, spoken in broken and strangled syllables. We were up the hall. I looked back, and I saw the face of the girl. She had left her little chair, and she no longer cried. She hugged the doorframe of the dining hall. There was no expression on her face as she watched.

We had navigated the corner, out of sight of everyone, and he now tightened his vice-like grip till I couldn't breathe. He pulled me, more lifeless, through a communal area, and he said something, threats. Flecks of spit sprayed the side of my face, and stale, unkept breath filled my nostrils as he shouted his anger. I pulled at his hair and clawed at his ears. He let go, and I clawed at him again before his big hands found me again. They grappled, held, pulled, and swung me forcefully into the wall. My head hit the corner of the brickwork, and the pain soared through me, crippling my resistance. In a pathetic motion, my hands were up, but it was a token defence as his weight covered me. I was on the floor; he manhandled me, dragging and wrenching me out onto the concrete of a space behind the building. My face was black and blue, and my cheeks puffed by the beating. He dragged me along the uneven floor, and I lost consciousness.

'Come on. Let's go, Stephen... Let's move. We need to find somewhere; it's so cold!' Tony was up and looking at where to go in the tree line.

My teeth were chattering beneath my lips. The wind battered the trees faster now and summoned a freezing cold early morning air with its quick movement into the night. It had helped to remove the terror of not wanting to go back. The waiting, walking, sleeping nightmare and the constant violent daily battles that we would have to endure. I thought of the other children left behind. Some would run away from time to time like us - most would stay. I thought of the little ten-year-old girl… I wondered if she was okay. If they left her alone, if she played with dolls and glitter, if she had started eating and if she was happier.

The rising winds crashing in from the east of the city had moved the cloud cover. Tempered by fast-moving dark clouds, the moonlight shone intermittently high behind the treeline. We walked together into the blackness, following the slim, winding path. We shivered against the night. We were silent. We were together, though alone with the turmoil of our thoughts.

London, 1980, Age 9

'She stood there… Her back to the silver kitchen sinks with the soft afternoon light to her side, cutting the room in half shadow. A young-looking, attractive woman with a hard face, tidy, short blond hair, engaging hazel/green eyes that searched, and her arms were out. It was on the third floor, in a small flat, and the kitchen was tight. She wore jeans and a simple pale cream patterned jumper that clashed with the coloured plates that hung on the walls.

Her smile beckoned. Gerard was looking on, and I had gone close to the outstretched arms, the embrace. I had felt the warmth. I had felt the strangeness of her and the little kitchen we all stood in. I had met my mother… and I hoped all would be okay. There was talk, and there was happiness in the air. Tea was poured, and smiles followed questions. Eyes rolled and searched and enquired. Kathleen and Gerard parked in soft chairs, continuing to catch up and I sat there. I felt awkward and looked around the place, the tidiness of it, and the newness. It was different to what I had known, what I had expected...

I studied the room. Open, not cluttered, clean. A grey settee, a chair, a TV and a few prints were on the wall. A corner cupboard with glass that housed plates and glass ornaments. There were no toys. A fresh, clean set of spaces easily scrubbed.

'You look well, Son'. She smiled, still with the searching eyes. 'How was the boat. Good enough, the journey, I hope. Glad to see you, Son.'

Gerard nursed his tea.

He was getting ready to leave for the trip back to Ireland.

I could see from the window the wooden nets of a large climbing frame on a small green. Tall grey claustrophobic flats tightened in clusters everywhere I looked. I watched the strange woman who was my mother. It was a funny feeling, all was alien, strange. My mother's accent had the Irish in it, I knew. People outside spoke the clear English I had heard sometimes in Belfast as soldiers would speak.

I had a little room next door. Slim and tight, I liked its smallness. The case and the little clothes I had brought had been unpacked, Kathleen had helped me. She had said I would be great, showed me the small bathroom, asked what food I liked and said we would sort everything out.

Gerard's departure was hard. Everyone smiled and hugged, a brave face was put on and kisses were exchanged. We had stood and held each other, and I had felt the moment was somehow similar to when he had told me of Madge's death, that she was gone. He was going down the stairwell outside the flat when I saw him last. He held onto the iron railings and clasped his bag. He looked older and tired. He hid his true feelings, I know now. He was away down the stairs, and I was struck by my loneliness.

In the background, the Roberts rambler stuck in the kitchen played 80's Patti LaBelle and Michael McDonald's 'On My Own...'

A big bear of a man with broad shoulders and massive, strong hands entered the room, a slight grin on his face. Michael. He was Kathleen's boyfriend. He spoke with the same Irish accent as hers although he was a man of few words. He was from the old country back home near Dublin. His family had been farming people who had dairy cattle and other animals and land and like Kathleen, he had come to England for work and in search of making a life.

He was an honest man. He built houses and ran gangs of men in all-weather as a foreman. He tried to do his best and be fair. His moods were terrible and controlled the house. Looking back now, with my own children and the significant challenges life would bring, I understand more and hold no judgments. They were a young family starting out in the world. Times were brutal, cold. The guns, the bombs, the fears and suspicions had gone from my life. So, too, had the great warmth I knew. They had been replaced with the isolation of being in a strange environment.

Everything new. All was alien. People, places and things were fresh to my eyes. There was no anchor, no point of recollection or similarity. No comfort, no easy transition. Only coldness, worry, strange places and unrecognisable people.

My mother tried. There was no money, and every penny was spoken for. She had worked as a receptionist but now had to look after me. Michael worked every day he could hard and fast as if there was no tomorrow. He had an old Rover 3500, which he would park in the communal bay at the front of the flats. He would come home from work, settle in and eat. Boiled bacon, cabbage, potatoes. Or there would be mincemeat. The anxiousness of everything ruled me. I had little understanding of the world and how things worked in England.

Like England, Northern Ireland in the 1970s and early 80s was a place of great pop music and new romantics. The technological age had not yet arrived; music and fashion were big, Margaret Thatcher was the British Prime Minister and digital mobile phones were invented. Times were different then and the war in Northern Ireland had shaped people's perceptions. Judgement reigned unjustifiably in many ways amongst and between different era groups. People had one goal: to survive and make a life in the best way possible. The people who had made the exodus from the Emerald Isle had imported with them the behaviours and ways of looking at the world taught to them by their parents in Ireland.

Many of those ways had been successfully translated to the UK and worked well. Others did not.

I had explored the neighbouring flats on the council estate. I had played football with a few of the kids my age. I had gone in goal and gave a great show. They had tried from every angle to score and strangely couldn't. They thought I was a great goalie and they had a strange look in their eyes at the way I spoke. A few had asked questions; it was difficult to answer. I had made excuses and ran home, back from the far side school field that backed onto the estate, through the flats and up the stairs holding my football. I tried, but I was just so different, I couldn't tell you what it was; I just couldn't fit in with the life now presented to me.

The TV threw moving images. I sat cross-legged on the front room floor and watched. There were ships and troops, the sea, helicopters were in the background, and the war correspondent talked about the invasion of Argentina. Kathleen was behind me.

She touched me on the hair, a loving gesture. 'How was it out, Son? I want you to eat now…'

I turned to her, smelling soap on her skin.

It was a little plate of sandwiches, ham, cucumber and tomato. I was a small child, really. I was about the right height for my age but very thin. Anxiety and fear robbed me of my appetite, and I was just skin and bones.

'You need to eat, Son. You want to fill out now, don't you? Too thin you are. Get it ate!'

She had turned on her heels and was away back into the small kitchen with the woven wooden blind at the window. I ate as best I could, like a mouse. Following my arrival, I had not felt well. I tried and played; I could not sit still, but I could not eat. Most of the food my mother would cook would make me sick, I would force the food in and it would not stay. Mealtimes were an ordeal. They would look at me strangely. Their trying would wear thin, annoyance would overtake my mother and she would turn. 'You'll fuckin' get it ate. It's hard enough. Lucky you have food to eat.

The worst time would be when Michael was there at the end of the evening. My mother would change; the radio would be replaced by the TV and the noise of the pots and pans of the kitchen making dinner. She would float in and out like a maid, and I would feel like I shouldn't be there but was unsure what to do. They would try. There was silence as Michael watched the evening news. I would be rooted to the chair, careful of my behaviour and what I said, as the speed and strictness of my punishments frightened me. He had a cushion behind him, at the back. A massive man too big for the chair. A tray of food was on his lap and a glass of fresh milk on the ledge beside him.

He looked at me, I thought he had goodness in him. He worked hard but paid the price for the brutal daily work that translated into foul moods. I saw a terrible temper. Knew it was always there and never far beneath the surface. He had the knife and fork in each hand and looked at me with balanced eyes. I saw his large hands; I was no stranger to the belt. It would leave red welts that would mark, and at times, even my mother would intervene to lessen it, which says a lot as her temper was as raw as his at the time. He knew only the brutality his dad had shown him, that was how he thought you had to be as a father, here I was a cuckoo in his nest, a scrawny child, ungrateful, whiny and just one more thing he had to deal with. He hadn't wanted me; I wasn't his child for him to be saddled with. He would try deep inside himself, but he would usually lose, and the strength of his angry moods would change things. My mother watched me from the kitchen doorway, a tea towel in her hand. I saw they loved each other, Kathleen and Michael, and they would survive against the everyday worries of that era. At times, when the guilt ate at him, he would do something nice or bring a gift home for me; it wasn't from love tough; it was pure guilt, and I wasn't a stupid child; I soon saw through those more pleasant times.

I went to my room, sat on the bed, and looked out of my window into the falling evening light. There were sounds of people and children outside somewhere. I was alone here. An alien, a stranger, who spoke differently. Apart from, not a part off. Different.

Further along the road in the single tiny houses by themselves was the O'Shea family. Tony and Saoirse lived there, then the kids Roisin and Tommy. I was told they were close cousins of Michaels, and because it wasn't far, it was okay to sleep over. Tommy was my age, and we played at all sorts. We had bikes and marbles, and we would play fight and roam close to the house within watching distance from his mother, Saoirse, at the back of the house.

I thought of the other kids on the estate. I had had a few silly fights already. I had held my own and felt I was being tested and poked. Because I was different, I stuck out from the rest and, because of it, got special treatment.

I loved the sleepover with Aunt Saoirse and Tommy. I loved the warmth and love that shone from Saoirse. A calm presence, she smiled at everything she touched. A tiny woman with a warm face, wavy fair hair and patterned skirts who smoked.

She was a kind and gentle soul with bright eyes full of mischief, and when Tommy and I would play, she would spoil us. She brought light every time I saw her, and I wished I could stay.

I heard my dad Michael's voice through the thin walls. He was stuck in his ways, I had heard my mother say. He had been treated with the same strictness back home. He had been taught that way; he didn't know any different; it hadn't done him any harm... My mother said something, it was mumbled, incoherent through the walls. I had become known amongst the other kids in the flats, and I had already gained a reputation. I had more freedom now and would run wild up the road at the shops and over the flats. A few times, I was brought back home for throwing stones and smashing things and being caught in places where I shouldn't have been...

She had a stern look on her balanced face, 'I need to take you to the school tomorrow, Stephen.' She explained the trouble to get me into the right school. The paperwork, registration. Because of the address, it had to be a good catholic school. The travelling. I had come from Ireland, the questions, The forms she had had to fill in.

She stopped a moment, the white door slightly ajar. Her brown hair fell by her ear, her hard face giving no comfort. 'It'll be okay... You have to go to school and learn... Get an early night. I want you ready for the morning.'

She came in and kissed my forehead. A quick thing more with necessity than with love. 'In the morning, now.'

She had left.

I lay on the bed, my eyes fixed on the artexed grey/white ceiling and the cracks. The feeling of being in a strange place was heavy around me. There were still muffled sounds of people's activity somewhere outside. The room filled with the shadow of late evening as the sun dipped behind the flats… I was wide awake. I yearned for the comfort of sleep. I followed the screeching sound of the kids outside playing as they moved further from our vicinity… A 10-year-old, terribly thin, scared boy, I lay on my bed, eyes wide and considered what my life would have been like in Ireland, where I knew I was loved and wanted.

Foster home, London, Age 11

I had been introduced to the family by the social worker. At eleven, settling in England was still a hard road for me. It had been eighteen months since my arrival from Belfast, and I remained an anxious child. One who had energy to burn and was always in mischief. The house was a normal two-story with a tiny garden in front and a slightly bigger, longer one out the back.

Another new family, I thought.

My new foster family, the young dark-haired parents of a little boy and girl, a little younger than me, huddled with the social worker, a middle-aged man with a soft voice, brown wavy hair and round spectacles. They were out of earshot in the little dated but clean kitchen. I watched them from the front room. I strained to listen across the green carpet through the open white door.

'Your name, Stephen'? She sat with her brother, who was smaller and younger, on the settee on the opposite side of the room. Her smile was contagious, trusting, with the brightness of her blue eyes and long fair hair.

I was on the chair by the TV. I felt alone with my bags, alone again in my future. 'Yes, I'm Stephen'. I had been unsure, but I found myself matching her smile.

'Great'. The little boy in short trousers and a diamond jumper had jumped up a glint in his eye. 'I'm Arthur, this is Ann. So, do you like cars? Racing?' He was already pulling out a toy box full of toys... I felt good about them. They had a real trueness in their smiles and voices that indicated easy trust. Ann gave another engaging smile. She was on the floor with her brother, beckoning me to get involved. I moved to join them.

He smiled. The social worker was in the middle of the room. Beside him, my new surrogate parents smiled as one. They had soft features, round faces and a calmness that matched their projected happiness. It had been agreed. They were to be my foster parents, while my mother and Michael had my new brother or sister. As soon as she'd realised she was pregnant, Kathleen had sent me off to be fostered. I didn't understand, it was just another reminder that I was not wanted and I was not 'their child'. Everything would be Okay, I was reassured again; my new foster parents had fostered more than 30 other children. They were very experienced. Arthur and Ann were great children who kept me company. I would settle in quickly. It would be a good break for me, good fun. I would have a great time. It would not be for long, maybe 6 to 9 months. I was not to worry.

The faces smiled. I stood there in my little jeans and black coat, and I had questions. It was voluntary... Yes, I would be going home again. Yes, it was only temporary... They were gathering around me, and there was talk about dinner and what I liked eating. Arthur was next to me, and I could smell sweets. It was happening fast, and I had no control of the situation. My bags were being moved. I was to be shown my room. It was ok. If I needed anything, I was just to say...

I watched the social worker out the window go down the path to the car. There were other questions... I was to treat it as my own home. Ann was behind me now as I was guided up the stairs... It was another house, another family. Why was I passed about like a book to be signed in, I wondered? Ann was beaming. We could play lots of things. There was a special camp in the garden, hidden... I realised my little life was one of instability, I was very unsure of what the future would bring... Ann's excitement was building. We were due to go see her cousin in Wimbledon. He was a footballer and played for Crystal Palace... Arriving at my room, I had my bed in a shared room with Arthur.

Ann twirled in her white and blue striped dress. It's great she continued. I would love the travelling over to south London. Sometimes, we go down the common. There were lots to do there...

I smiled my best smile at her. A soft, mirroring, engaging sign that curbed my unease. My bags were at my feet. I started to unpack, uncertainty niggling at my thoughts and body. I would not know it then, but it was the beginning of a pattern in my life that would nearly destroy me and would destroy others. A life of possessions in bags, moves, strange places and faces. A surreal reality that presented a future without shape or destination, a half-life of extremes and wandering and adversity, where great danger was a central theme and uncertainty a constant. Arthur had joined her, and together they grinned. I turned my head from them as I put my clothes in the drawers.

School, Age 13

The schoolteacher, a young, mousy-haired man with a thin, spotty face, slammed the book on his desk.

'Enough! Now you will listen. Class, again, the square route of twenty-five?'

The class was small. Six wooden desks sat on a white tiled floor; to the right, filtered light streamed through a large bank of metal framed windows. A selection of coloured drawings was pinned to the wall, and there was a small globe of the world on the table near a tiny sink in the corner. A wide wooden desk, stacked with blue exercise books, in front of the oblong blackboard, was where our teacher would sit.

Not today, though. Our teacher turned from the blackboard, frustrated eyes, chalk poised.

'Three hundred past six, Sir!' She had tight, fair pigtails, laughter in her eyes and rebellion in her face. She was one of two girls in this class of six. A special class. For special children. Ones who had been so unruly that every school had deemed them rotten eggs, and they'd been placed in one heavy basket.

'A thousand over twelve'. The boy to my left. A friend, annoying with short ginger hair and freckly cheeks.

Sniggers rose, erupting quickly.

The teacher stamped now. Up and down in front of us. 'Bloody well enjoying this aren't you?' The chalk was tight in his swinging hand. 'No one? Not one wants a sensible guess at the square route of twenty-five...?'

I looked around me. My cohort's pissed themselves laughing. My stomach ached with it. I couldn't help myself.

The teacher paced. His large eyes blinked behind square glasses. He dipped his head to the side. A frown developed hard on his brow.

'Not one for...?'

It was a rubber, thrown with great speed and accuracy. It had stopped him in mid-sentence, hit him on the head and bounced from the side of the blackboard.

His anger flared.

The laughing erupted, giggling shattering the space. A contagious spillage of noise that rippled.

He sat at the chair in front of his desk. He was used to the torment. Trained in the specialist manner of managing delinquents. Overcoming the frustration and anger was vital.

A slow voice, soft but commanding, 'You lot are well aware of the line. There is a line here, now. It is in front of this desk, and the repercussions for crossing it are dire.'

The rubber moved between his fingers. 'This is assault'.

'That algebra we're learning on the board is assault, Mr Denning.' I pulled a funny face. Leaned back in my chair. I had to let the sentence out, I hadn't been able to resist the rhythm of it.

They fell about their desks beside me, laughing.

I felt alive in these moments. There was a loose freedom that I couldn't explain. I had always felt different. Here in the class, we were different together, special.

It was a comfort to me that others were different, too, and in being different together, being different could be accepted. The laughing continued. Hands were covering stomachs that quivered and turned and rolled. A boy held his ears back, twisted his face, stuck out his tongue and rolled his eyes to the back of his head.

The teacher shifted around and narrowed his eyes. A piercing look that could shatter concrete but had no effect.

'Five,' He spat. 'Five is the square route of twenty-five...'

'But of course.' One of the boys said. Just managing to get it out, monosyllabic-like, between his giggling.

I felt it then. That amid trouble and pain, laughter could be found. That is the shame of being branded bad and different and not worthy, a light could be found and held onto. That the terrible feelings that settled in me could be transmuted to fun. I smiled with them. Together, we were one. We had twisted shame, turned trouble, upset bad feelings and found better times. I settled in my chair. Elation was circulating inside me. My anxiety had been diluted by excitement. Fear was further away, and the great anger that had started to grow deep inside me was stable.

I sat there, the laughing had subsided. Excitement was with me again, overpowering my thoughts. My lips tightened. It was inside me these movements, I lowered my head, my hands were in my lap, and I looked at them. The teacher rose to the board.

My face moved, tiny unseen nuances of hope, anguish, rage, love, insecurity... fear... I fidgeted.

I was a long way from the diligent child who might have been terrified of the nuns but had a keen mind and an eagerness to learn. I'd slipped out of mainstream education due to my temper; I was learning different things now, and I was already gaining a reputation, slightly crazy, the one that would always go too far. I was a magnet for trouble and enjoyed the thrill of pushing boundaries.

Foster home, London Age 11

She stood by the doorway in a red patterned dress and her face was a picture. Ann had dreaded this moment and her downcast features and the twist in her mouth showed it.

'Ann's in love.' teased her brother, Arthur. He danced around her. 'Why the long face?' He stopped now and smiled at her.

She was in from the kitchen doorway screaming inside and had wanted to kick out at him. She softened, a half grin playing at her lips.

I watched and looked at them, saw Ann's eyes and felt sick inside. My bags were packed beside me and waited on the grey carpet. I had enjoyed it here. I had loved the brightness they brought, the love. I enjoyed belonging and having my own brother and sister. I had found joy inside me as their natural warmth and innocence had pulled me out of my anxiousness. We had laughed and played and fought and sometimes sulked.

But we had remained together, looked out for each other, and been kind.

'They'll be here in a minute, Stephen OK. Are you alright?' It was Tracy, the children's mother. Black short hair, a round face, soft brown eyes, and a caring demeanour. She had been wonderful. With her husband, Kevin, they had always been kind and warm, giving in their time and focus to my care. They had listened, and they had smiled their understanding and love. They had seen the great joy of me with Ann and Arthur and they had looked on knowingly. In the last seven months I stayed with them, I felt safe and would miss them all.

I looked out the window and saw the social worker walk up the path. The pensive feeling tightened in my stomach. The door was opened and he stood there. His eyes smiled through his round spectacles and he had not changed.

'Stephen, make sure to come and see us.' Ann was beside me. She held me by the elbow the sadness etched in her eyes.

'I will, I promise, you know I will.' I had a heavy heart; my shoulders were weighty and my stomach turned.

'You better. Do promise.'

'Of course, Arthur. As soon as I can.'

Tracy was there with Kevin. Together, they smiled. 'Come back now, Stephen and see us you hear!' They had understanding mixed with concern in their faces. By the front door they watched us go down the path. Ann and Arthur joined beside them, and I questioned how they could keep going through this with the children they cared for. I had wanted to stay but knew I had to go. They were waving a last goodbye as I put my bags in the back of the car and got in. I smiled as hard as I could as we pulled away. Then, the picture of them was gone.

'Stephen, you'll be happy to know everything is OK. You have a brother. I'll let your mother tell you about it.' The car weaved in traffic.

I had heard him, understood. My mind was with the picture of them standing at the door. Of Ann, the softness of her touch, the brightness of her face. Arthur and his laughing. Tracy, Kevin…

'This will be good at home. Oh, your new brother's name is Brendan. A happy, strong little thing. What do you think about that?' He glanced from the road in front, just a moment to gauge my expression.

I looked ahead into the moving traffic. 'That's great news.' It sounded good, but I felt the grip of things in my heart. It felt like worry, insecurity, uncertainty. The usual anxiousness was under the surface, fear there, and rejection. Since coming from Ireland years ago it had found a place inside me where it lurked and taunted, poked and haunted. I had carried it, walked with it, slept with it and it had turned into resilience.

The car found the motorway. I would soon be home to my mother, Michael and their new baby, Brendan.

I would see her; she would be sweet, and some of her friends would be there. Rose and her family Joyce and Michael would be there. Everyone would be smiling and quietly excited in the front room. My new little brother would be wrapped in warm, brilliant white woollen blankets. He would be fed a bottle in my mother's arms and we would be introduced. I would look at the little figure swaddled and closeted, the tiny fingers and toes and feel amazement and love simultaneously. Everyone would sit and stand in the front room with the daylight streaming through the big bay windows of my mother's friend's house. There would be no mention of where I had been for seven months, how things had been there. There would be no honest discussion of what, why or when. The time would be erased and the matter would be buried.

The social worker drove carefully. We were in the middle of a good summer. His voice continued about the strain on the care system; things were better, and foster care was great in some areas.

I had left him to talk.

Words rattled monotonously over my head; my mind was on my future. Its uncertainty. My inability to settle within myself, my hardship at living with my family... at school and outside the wider world.

The traffic lights changed. I wound down the window and looked above the passing buildings into a clear sky. The air was warm, and pastel clouds hung in calm clusters as the sun dipped behind the clear horizon. I closed my eyes as the car accelerated beneath me. In the distance the voice of the social worker continued. I centred my feelings, I felt the well of anxiousness circle, and I felt anger growing from deep fear inside me.

London, Age 12

The move had been easy and the new house was much larger. A three-bedroom with a tiny postage stamp of a crazy-paved garden at the front. Behind a tiny little wall, it was a new start. It was unremarkable on an ordinary, similarly house-lined street on a typical estate in London. Brendan was a baby just beginning to walk, and my mother was pregnant again with what would be my brother, Shaun.

It was a calm place where I could ride my BMX bike and wander the estates. Down the road was my mother's sister, Ann and her husband, Gerry. He was a fighting man, a big, tough character from Dublin who had been to prison and hated the law. They had a busy house where we all congregated. Together with our friends from the estate and my cousins Margret, Gerard, Damain and Tony, we would be in and out of the house and sneaking cigarettes when we could get our hands on them.

Ann was a happy, soft, but feisty woman with dark black hair who would drink endless coffee, work from home and chase us for fighting, arguing and not being respectful. My Uncle Gerry worked on building sites and was at home in the evenings. He was banned from the Workingman's Club for fighting and wrecking it while drunk. He would take a good lot of drink and then go to bed. When we played at their house, he'd bang the ceiling with a stick on the floor upstairs and tell us to quiet our noise. We would fight, my cousins and I. Long, bitter, sharp fights where hair was dragged, eyes gouged and bodies punched and kicked. It was rough and tumble; I wasn't quite one of them, but they would have my back should I need it.

The good Catholic School, St Michaels, was over in Hoxton. Every morning, I would walk there with my cousins and friends down the busy street, cutting through the estate and up the lane. We would laugh and play. I was still only twelve, but we would fight over my funny accent. I had only been in the school a short while and had had three fights already. Two in classrooms over desks with metal chairs scattering. One was on the main field at lunchtime while a circle formed around us, and a great crowd watched. We had grappled and tore, punched and kicked. I tripped and pulled the bigger lad to the grass and bit into his cheek as hard as I could. It had been broken up as teachers approached, and I had stood outside the headmaster's office, being blamed for the lot and suspended for two weeks. I may have been small, but I was scrappy. No one was going to get the better of me; I fought hard and dirty; after all, I had so much experience with violence by now; there was little one of these boys at school could do to hurt me, and that gave me an edge. I knew viciousness didn't scare me, which made me different and quite dangerous; even the other kids could see it.

The house door was open, my brother Brendan played on the floor, and Kathleen screamed, 'You will eat it. Open your mouth!'

We were in the small kitchen at the back of the house. There was a small brown breakfast bar by the sink and cooker, a brown-patterned lino on the floor that split the room, and a wooden round table and chairs at the far side.

I gagged, the mincemeat, onions and cooked tomatoes sliding down the side of my mouth and face.

She was at her wit's end. 'The fuckin' mess. I cook this good food, and you don't eat.'

She had another handful of food from the white bowl on the table and rammed it over my mouth. Tried to push it down. I coughed, gasping for breath, spraying food on the pale cream walls. It dropped around me, over my jumper and jeans. She stood there screaming, eyes wide, dark hair jumping in anger. 'You fuckin little shit. You will eat it! You're lucky to have a dinner!'

'Ma…' I spluttered. 'I can't…'

'You fuckin can. We work hard for this food.'

I was choking, twisting, turning from her grip. I turned my head and slipped away from the weight of her hands and body cornering me at the table. The bowl of minced meat and potatoes smashed on the floor. The silver fork spun on the table.

'Get back here!'

My side hit the corner of the breakfast bar as I flew into the front hallway.

'You little bastard!' She screeched now. It had built in her, this rage for many months as I had struggled to eat the food she cooked and hid it in strange places like behind the bin in the kitchen or the chair in the lounge. I don't know why I thought that was the best place for it, I don't know; I just knew it wouldn't stay in my stomach if I ate it, and I'd get a beating if I didn't.

She was behind me as I flew through the open front door and out outside into the daylight. I could feel her and the fury inside her. Knew her flashing eyes trailed me. My brother Brendan bawled. He started when the bowl crashed as my mother's voice rose, and the chair scraped and fell at my escape.

'You wait till you come back here! You will fuckin' eat...
You're nothing but trouble!'

I was out and running over the little stretch of grass past
my bike in front of the house. Her voice died behind me. I ran.
I wanted my place of safety by the side of the shops, which was
a fenced area that housed a small iron electric transformer for
the council. There was a gap in the fence where a panel had
been removed, shrouded in bushes and tall trees. I wiped the
old food my mother had tried to force down my throat from
my face and my cheeks. I gasped for air. I would go there, crawl
through the opening, and, shielded from the road by the canopy
of the high trees and the green of the shrubs and bushes, I would
have peace. I would have quiet, I would have safety, and I would
make myself calm and gather my thoughts.

Woodside Children's Home Aged 13

The children's home was shrouded in gathering darkness
when the police car turned into the concrete car park at the top
of the hill. The two buildings, the main and the annexe were
close together, split only by a small patch of grass and a slim
winding path of block paving. Anxiety was inside me, twisting
in the pit of my stomach. My heart was beating fast, and I
frowned in hatred at being back there. It had been two days
since we had wrapped the stolen Escort around the fence post.
We had tried our best to stay free, taking bread from the back
of bakers in the early hours and stealing little things to eat, like
chocolate, to stave off the hunger pains. We had wandered the
streets of London, passing time and looking for opportunities.

We had searched for hope. The evenings had brought their lonely, icy cold conditions and we had struggled, getting into any place we could to shelter our young bodies from the unforgiving nightly freeze, causing shivering limbs, numbed brains and chattering teeth.

Tony had his head down, laden with dark thoughts, as we exited the back of the police car. There were lights on in some windows, small bulbs over the building, illuminating the pathway into the middle of the yard between the houses towards the main entrance doors. I remained silent, thinking as we walked. We had tried to stay away, to keep the freedom we had taken. It had been hard; we had had another adventure together in excitement and adversity. We had felt joy at our independence from this place. We had laughed because of it, even when we had nearly killed ourselves in the car crash when we had felt the icy night wind torture our bodies when the hunger had gnawed at us as we searched for shelter from the early hours; we had felt joy.

The brightly lit main doors loomed forebodingly as the two police officers motioned us forward. We felt the warmth hit us in the main reception as we stood on the grey carpet. Mr Windmill was with the police officers. He glared at us as he talked to them. Two other staff members, old Miss Clark and young Mr Burrous, were with them. They glanced sidewards as the police officers left.

…The man who was well known and thought about and was from the west part of Belfast had received the address of the children's home from a trusted contact in the old country. Far back, hidden by the covering bushes and tight tree line, his week of daily

vigils was paying off. He had done research and reconnaissance on the children's home and the staff who ran it. He had come from his digs close by every day for hours at different times, painting a picture in his mind and watching closely for signs of the boy. For days, at the different vantage points he had chosen, he had sat, waited, and searched for signs of the boy.

From his hide, he had watched through the trees as the police car had parked, the officer had opened the doors for the children and escorted them to the main entrance, and he had seen at last the face of the boy he had trailed from Ireland. With his three-fingered hand, he dipped into the deep pocket of his jacket and looked at the white paper with the written words, addresses and descriptions. It was there, written in a scrawled hand that needed to rush. He looked at the top line. It was the name of the boy, Stephen Gillen.

I saw Windmill; he approached with two others behind him. Windmill's eyes flashed anger. The tight lips surrounded by a black beard said words dripping with sarcasm.

'Well, glad to have you back, I'm sure you are happy to have returned safely. You've caused more trouble, of course…'

He pushed us, me first, then Tony. A forceful movement on the centre of the back reinstated his supreme authority.

'Move. Get upstairs to your rooms!'

It was 2am. Through the silent corridors on the first floor, by the games and pool rooms and the TV room to the left next door, past the main staff room. The dimmed lights along the hall added to our subdued silence. The staff were behind us as we were marched. I was aware of their heavy silence and tight faces, of Windmill's eagerness to lash out at any slight misdemeanour. Up the blue carpeted steps to the second-floor dorms, round the white-walled corner corridor through a fire door and onto our main landing.

Tony was pushed into his room, and the door slammed.

They walked me further down. I opened the white glossed wooden door to my room, into its blackness and violently, a hand pushed me in.

'Get in, Gillen. The fun's just starting. You try to leave here tonight, and you will see what will happen to you.'

I turned in the shadowed space of my room towards the light. Towards the voice that growled, the faces that showed malice in the crack of the door. It was Windmill again, and he spat it out,

'You'll be seen in the morning, both of you… for your little outing. You'll be watched and lose everything for a month!'

A psychopathic grin broke on his face, 'As I was saying, it's great that you're back safe, although you're nothing but trouble, Gillen. But whether you like it or not, you were sent here by the local authority, and this is where you'll stay… This is your home!'

The door slammed, and I was left in silence. I stood there momentarily, checking for the sound of the floorboards squeaking to confirm they had indeed left the landing. It was a habit. Listening and checking the noises of the hallway and the movements of the building at night to be aware of staff footfall. I sat on my bed, a little low single with starched sheets and blankets. I had a window behind me that looked out into the woods at the back of the building, a little cupboard, a side locker with a chair and some books and comics. I looked at the book spines; my eyes had adjusted in the darkness to the light outside that streamed in my closed window. One of the volumes was a geography book from the classroom in the back of the Children's Home annexe, where we were taught. I opened it, flicked the pages and felt the sharp edges of the pages as they turned. There was an index, and my finger moved down the glossy paper as I tracked the words.

'Countries of the world.' I whispered.

I was searching quicker, passing a map of the globe until I arrived at it. Ireland. The pictures showed me green pastures, fields, blue/grey mountain rocks and high hills, loughs and deep rivers painted in riveting colours. I flicked the pages. Dublin, it said. It had the picture of a long winding river, the Liffey. The low, dull buildings of a tight city bordered and collected around it, and there were small boats and a longing for scenes set in older times.

I listened. Silence. Only in the background was the faint hum of the generator that fed the kitchens. I moved back on the bed, I had kicked off my trainers and, cross legged, using the shadowy light from the small window, searched the pictures in the book eagerly with my eyes. I flicked the page; it talked about the free state, the Republic. Then there was the Union Jack and the end of gabled walls, I remember it said Northern Ireland & The Troubles. I could not understand all the words, but I knew the pictures. The grey, cold, drab streets with the armoured vans, the checkpoints, and the police, in the distance, rolling hills wound through with grey roads that had flaming, lit skies.

Compelled, I looked hard at the photos in the book. Buses and cars were being used as barricades, groups of people throwing petrol bombs. There were graphic pictures of the soldiers, their guns, coffins carried to Milltown's cemetery, balaclavas and painted murals. I searched closer the details in the images as a twisting feeling gripped my stomach; memories that stirred deep inside me were translated into a picture show inside my head. I held the book and felt an icy chill skitter down my back. There was residual panic in me as I saw the face of the boy, was transported in time back to the scene of the bullets and the night fires and the calling for a mother who was not there.

Sweat began to appear along my hairline. 'Please, Mother. God, Mother, please.'

I felt it, my little hands clawing in the cold, damp mud as a distraction from what I witnessed. The lids of my eyes tightened, the smell of cordite and fuel and burning in the air as petrol bombs spread fire and the tracer rounds riddled the evening… I was on the bed, my breathing constricted by fear… I had dropped the book to the floor. I put my arm across my eyes to hide from images that danced in my head. The sorrow was a wave over and through me, and tears were in my eyes. The feelings, hard to control, washed over me, and I was in the corner of the bed, coiled in a protective ring, screaming for escape…

And I heard it in my mind, a soft, loving voice with a hint of mystery.

'…And the great Monkey Puzzle Tree stood tall, strong, and resilient in the light of the fine morning. It was said they were magical and came from a faraway land that no one had ever visited or found. In their great wisdom, the Gods knew a place that was in dire need of their magic, strength, and courageous ways, so they were brought to us here to help, watch, and add their magic to the land's soil. It is said they can live to be a thousand years old and still be strong, that they are a beacon of hope wherever they live and that they can see and hear all people, places and things. But even more extraordinary is their unique way of knowing special people with special gifts like themselves…'

My thundering emotions had calmed. The pictures and the face of the boy were lost. The dampness of my tears was drying, Uncle Gerard, how I missed his strength.

'Stephen,' I heard a girl's quiet voice in my room. I returned to the reality of the darkness, the window that spilt soft light from outside. My body was clammy. My nose had sniffles, and I wiped the tears in my eyes.

'Stephen…?'

I focussed on the space by the door, and she stood there.

A short figure in a light pink dressing gown tied with a belt at the waist, fair hair falling and tangled haphazardly at her shoulders, eyes that blinked in the darkness and a little voice that had enquired.

'Debbie?'

'Yes, Stephen, it's me.' She was in from the shadows at my bed, and I saw her cheeky, curved, wide smile. She had smashed again the little round glass of the fire door that separated the girl's rooms from the boys.

'Are you okay? God, I missed you; we were all worried. Where did you go?' On the bed, she sat, and her face had the brightness of longing and the beginning of questions. 'We thought you were really in trouble. You and Tony were not coming back. Windmill said the police were all out looking for you, and you were going to prison. I said you were too young to go to prison. He laughed and said we were all going to prison here; he...'

I had my arm around her shoulder. My voice calmed her.

'We're fine. We're back, right. I'm here.'

'But you have to go to court, you...?'

'It will be fine.' My heart was recovering, but it hitched a little as I saw her face crumble. Debbie, the head girl in the home, was protective of the other kids even though she was only fourteen. I had watched her fight injustice in this place like me biting, scratching, and pulling, and she would try to give as good as she got. The silence of the night was around us. We listened for a moment, checking for noise disturbance.

Whispering, she continued, 'I don't want you to go, Stephen. We are all a family now. Little Anabelle was so thankful for what you done for her in the dining hall. But you must not get in trouble, she says.'

I felt her little body close by. I could smell the shampoo in her hair and see the light in her eyes and the concern in her mouth. I looked into her face for a moment. I didn't know what to say; I didn't want to leave the family I had made here. It was terrible; it was violent and cold. It was all these things, but there was a togetherness at such moments.

I thought of my upcoming court case. It was just after my fourteenth birthday. The juvenile court had been adamant in its decision last time I was there. There had been a difference in their manner, in how they looked at me and how efficiently things had been shuffled back. I had a premonition of trouble then. It returned a deep stab in my solar plexus and the centre of my forehead. We sat in the shadows. She had my hand in hers, and I was glad of the warmth that we were together for a moment.

I thought of Debbie. I thought of Annabelle, the little girl who had problems, and the other children who had emotional baggage and behavioural issues. I thought about my overwhelming anger. I thought of Windmill and the people who were controlling my life, and I wondered if when I went to court just after my fourteenth birthday in two weeks, they would send me to prison for the first time.

Woodside Children's Home Aged 14

'It's good that you have your accompanying adult and guardian from the Woodside Children's Home, representing the Local Authority, Master Gillen, for what we are about to say to you...'

There were three of them; a man with horn-rimmed glasses and two stern-looking women magistrates on either side of him. They had heard the charges against me and wore expressions of shock, sternness, anger, and business-like professionalism. They huddled together, whispering, deliberating, and stopped to focus on me with cold-eyed precision while tidying the papers before them.

I sat in a chair in the small room, surrounded by two long tables on either side. It was an old courtroom in Hertfordshire, with dark-stained wood on the walls, floors, and parts of the ceiling. The air was dusty from the unkempt, heavy, blue curtains at the stained windows. The smell of disinfectant filled my nostrils, and an impending sense of dread tightened in my chest.

They were seated at the long table at the bottom, stretched along the two others on either side of me. 'Stand up, Master Gillen,' the man with the paper in his hand commanded. 'We have looked in-depth at these charges...'

The paper rustled in his hand as he gazed down at it. 'Taking and Driving Away without consent. Theft, criminal damage. There are many counts which we have taken into consideration. At this point, we must say we feel much has been tried with you. Everything in the way of correcting your behaviour thus far has failed. You have consistently shown a disregard for the law, the public, and the Local Authority, which has guardianship of you. You are already under a care order...'

I stood there, shoulders drooping and bowed, weighed down by expectation, my hands fiddling behind my back in anxiousness. I had just turned fourteen a week earlier, a small boy for my age, now adrift without a paddle or a guiding star, for I had no home. I wore a brave mask, trying desperately to hold back tears as I continued to listen.

'Under these conditions, we are clearly responsible for protecting the public and the rule of law. You are now fourteen and, therefore, can be sent to a young offender Detention Centre and held in custody. In this case, we feel that a detention order is justified. We will proceed on the other charges for which you will be sentenced today...'

My hands clenched into fists, my breathing slowed, and my stomach churned with suspense and apprehension. Fear coursed through me. I felt a lightness in my limbs, a dryness in my throat, and my brain raced forward pre-empting my internal panic.

'We have tried, Master Gillen. All of the people charged with your care have tried. Us included...' He paused, leaving a menacing silence hanging in the room, stretching too long and too high. '...It is, therefore, our collective decision, and the decision of this court, that it has to be a custodial sentence at this point. We sentence you to eight weeks in a Detention Centre. You will now be taken from this court to your place of custody, where you will serve your sentence. We hope this will be the last time we see you here, Master Gillen.'

The burly jailers in short-sleeved white shirts stood at my sides, holding my elbows, turning me, and handcuffing me. I was ushered towards the doors and headed for the cells.

Behind me, their voices continued in a raised, sharp, final tone, 'We also very much hope that this may serve as the needed deterrent to prevent you from committing further offences...'

The accompanying social worker from Woodside, who had taken me to court, a kind man with a bushy brown beard and casual clothes, walked beside me as I was escorted. His demeanour tried to bring comfort to a terrible time.

'Sorry to hear about this, Stephen. Don't worry; it'll soon be over.'

I passed through the door, catching a glimpse of him, but I was unable to channel my fractured emotions into anything meaningful. His face disappeared behind the closing heavy wooden doors.

'I'll handle everything, Stephen...'

Dread consumed me. I had entered a state of meltdown due to my current level of anxiety. Around the corner, I entered a place with filthy, silky cream walls that echoed. Through two sets of old, worn, iron-barred gates, they marched me forward, their faces impassive, our footsteps resounding in my head, panic and fear gripping my stomach, and tears welling in my eyes.

The cell door closed behind me, and a reverberating silence enveloped me. I stared at the green, closed cell door. It was a milestone, and I knew it. I was going where I had never gone before, and all I could see, feel, experience, smell, and hear was the overwhelming fear.

Everything in my life so far had led me to this place. Looking back, it was inevitable. The options were that the abuse would have either broken me and I'd have become a weak shell of a person or rebelled and chosen the path I had. There was little choice really, it was never in my nature to be broken.

Huntercombe Youth Custody aged 15

When the day of freedom arrived, the sun was a high disc radiating warmth in a clear azure morning. The prison officer opened the small green Judas gate, and I entered. My first time in prison had been tough and frightening, a rite of passage, I reflected. Overwhelmed, I was relieved it was behind me. The prison staff waited until the social worker who was to pick me up arrived and waited outside. He approached me with enthusiasm. A short, chubby man in casual jeans and a checked shirt, his shoulder-length, straggly mousey hair, a beard, and thick round spectacles framing his face.

'Stephen, you're out. How do you feel?' He was one of the good ones, always trouble-free. He was fair, considerate, and caring, but sadly, he was outranked and outnumbered by the less pleasant colleagues he worked with.

As we reached the car, he offered me a cigarette, which I lit gratefully, inhaling the gently wafting smoke. We drove off, navigating the pitted and cratered old tarmac up the narrow country lane, veering left, then right through the twisting, turning roads surrounding the prison. I coughed, and the social worker chuckled.

'So, how was it? Your first time away?' he inquired.

My head spun slightly, the first cigarette in months taking effect. Through the windscreen, I observed the greenery and the winding black road stretching before us. 'So,' he repeated, 'how was it, Stephen? Did you learn your lesson?'

His questions, both intrusive and leading, made me hesitate.

'Yes, I've learned my lesson,' I responded. 'Going in there for the first time was terrifying, akin to joining the army. We marched everywhere, no cigarettes. It felt like eight years, not eight months.'

He listened as he drove, offering a slight smile.

I turned on the radio, increasing the volume of the pop music, and leaned back, taking another drag of the cigarette. The lightheadedness persisted, but the question and my reaction to it lingered in my mind. A trick question, open-ended, demanding an answer. Returning would be unthinkable - the loss of freedom, the constant hardships, the violence, the strict discipline, and the uncertainty of the outside world. The daily grind of menial tasks was daunting. My firm resolve was to avoid returning at all costs.

Deep down, a new realisation dawned on me: having survived my first stint behind bars, I had crossed a long bridge of fear. The idea of prison, a place of locked doors and lost freedoms, had haunted my thoughts for too long. Inside, I had faced my fears head-on and emerged unscathed. Thoughts of my mother, her life, and whether I crossed her mind surfaced. She had her new family and had tossed me aside; I would make my own family, one of my choosing and no one would take that from me.

The social worker drove on, leaving the rural roads near the Detention Centre behind, entering busier, more expansive streets leading to the motorway.

As he accelerated, the conversation turned to Woodside, the home still much the same, albeit calmer than the tumultuous period before my detention. Incidents of unrest and personal crises were now past. The thought of seeing familiar faces, especially the girl who had become close to me, brought a mix of anticipation and reflection.

With the window down, the morning traffic rush sounds and the sun's warmth filled the car. The noise of the Detention Centre faded into the distance, along with the smells, fears, and oppressive atmosphere. Shielding my eyes from the sun's glare, I recognised the deeper aspect of the lesson learned: hope. The comprehension that my future could be different, clear, and secure filled me with determination. While hoping never to return to prison, I acknowledged the strength and readiness within me to face whatever came my way. I didn't want to be imprisoned, but if it happened again, I would be ready for it, and I could cope.

I was returning to Woodside, a very different boy; they would not find me so easy to beat this time. Whilst I had people here I cared about, I knew inside I'd not be staying there very long.

Woodside Children's Home aged 14

The children's home had been filled with a heightened sense of alarm that day. A turbulence that stretched and released uneven emotions amongst the children. A twelve-year-old girl, scarred by memories long past and unable to erase them, had self-harmed again, adding more deep cuts to her already damaged forearms. The conjured images of an abusive father had become overwhelming once more. One of the boys had flung a pool ball through the window, shattering the glass. The staff moved with heightened vigilance. I searched for the boy, striving to contain the burgeoning anger within me. I traversed the home - from the front by the swinging main doors, through the desolate dining-hall being mopped, upstairs with my footsteps hammering the creaking carpeted floor, round to the back by the education building. My eyes scoured the area, but he was nowhere to be seen.

I thrust open the doors to the games room, the action slamming the wooden frame against the wall with a resounding slap. I knew he was there; I had glimpsed his silhouette from outside, drifting across the floor tiles, a snooker cue in hand. My thoughts turned to the girl. Petite and fragile, she struggled valiantly to play with dolls and ward off terrible memories. He had grabbed her hair in the hallway and swung her around without provocation. I remembered seeing her doll, broken with strands of blond hair flowing, and rage had finally seized me.

'What do you want?' he challenged, towering over me by a good foot, broad-shouldered with a mocking sneer on his face and closely shaven brown hair. In his hand, he brandished the pool cue, which he angrily slammed against the side of the table.

My smile disarmed him, a soft expression paired with calm eyes and a head tilted in feigned submission. I gripped a table tennis bat, small and compact. Confusion flickered in his eyes as he lowered the snooker cue. With assured, stealthy steps, my trainers squeaked across the shiny grey tiles. The memory of his bullying ignited my resolve. My grin twisted as I swung the bat with pinpoint accuracy, striking him squarely on the forehead. His cue was raised, but my proximity allowed for another swift hit, draining his resistance. We grappled on the floor, a tangle of limbs and fury.

'You won't bully me anymore. Not me, not Anabella. No one,' I whispered fiercely between breaths, as his finger clawed at my eye, but he was listening quietly to the words. It was the come back, I thought. For his sneaky kicks, mental and emotional torture. I had him locked with a hand at his throat and another pulling his ears. He was beat now. I could feel it in his subsiding movements, his waning defence. I could see it in his bewildered eyes, his flushed, pimpled cheeks.

The commotion had drawn an audience - the other children had gathered.

Strong hands pulled me up; the staff had intervened. Three of them, effortlessly separating us, their grips firm on my neck and arms, one fist yanking my hair. Dragged up and back, my ability to resist was stifled by their forceful handling. Windmill, Brownson, and a lackey - it was their hissed words and the fear in their eyes that conveyed the real violence to come. I was locked in a crushing headlock, gasping for breath. They yanked and jostled me along the hallways towards the rear of the building, a swift and scraping violence that strangled, clawed, crushed, and pounded. The bully's face, the girl, the others, all had vanished from my mind. I fought against their vice-like grip, but consciousness was slipping from me, ebbing in and out.

With the morning light filtering through the clutching arms, I knew my destination, and my insides recoiled. They were determined to beat the resistance out of me, along with my spirit. I heard the keys jangle and screech in the rusty metal lock of the boiler room door. The room was shrouded in darkness, only specks of light piercing through. The dank odour of copper, cobwebs, and the scurrying of rats in the shadows filled the space. They hurled me in, a small frame with grazes, collapsing onto the hard concrete floor, longing for the morning brightness I'd just been torn from. The slab's cold bit into me, and I could feel the grime and dust coating my fingers.

They slammed the boiler room door shut with a rattling cry, the neglected hinges screaming for oil. Darkness enveloped me, save for the slivers of light that snuck through the cracks. Their grunts and a snide snigger filtered through as they gathered their breath outside. Windmill's panting voice reached me through the door. 'You'll stay here with the rats until we decide otherwise. Plead later, and maybe you'll get out sooner.'

I retreated to a corner, shivering, as the staff's laughter and banter faded outside. Alone, I hugged my knees, familiar with this punishment. I closed my eyes, seeking solace in my imagination - a place of comfort away from the scratching noises and the looming fear.

There were memories of joy, racing a bright yellow Tonka Truck, mountain goats defying capture, the girl's smile on a better day, her doll intact. And then a voice, a soothing narrative it came in above the steaming water that travelled through the boiler pipes, comforting and taking away the pain.

'...*It was way back at the time of the first kings, and all the heroes of the land had a special knowledge of the monkey puzzle tree. It was said on cold misty nights they would even act as a beacon to help the travellers who were lost find their way back home. Tall in the worst of weather they would stand and keep the secrets of their magic against the dawn of the morning. Through the ages, standing proud against the events of the day they would keep the secrets of all the conversations they had heard and listened too. Eternally they listened and watched. Through the cold damaging evenings and the soothing morning mist. The fine tall, strong, courageous and immortal monkey puzzle trees. Solitary, strong and unmoving the grip of the moving seasons would pass them. It was said the monkey puzzle trees were each a miracle with a gift of real treasure inside and that their spikiness was a protection so that it would never be found...'*

Gerard's voice had gone, waned into the blackness. Its comfort, in the little garden with a step. Through the garden window was a woman who washed dishes and wore a tied headscarf. I waited for our eyes to meet, for her to look up. But the image had moved before she did, before I could see and remember her face.

The tears were silently running down, they were in streams on my cheeks and flowing freely. It was increasing, the pain in me at not being able to remember and see her face. I sat, for comfort and hugged tighter on my legs.

I sat, curled in on myself, as the scratching grew louder. Edging further into my corner, the cool darkness enveloped me, a cloak against the harshness of my reality.

Woodside Children's Home aged 14

It was late evening, around six, when they finally released me from the tight, damp darkness of the boiler room. I first heard the footsteps outside, worn shoes scraping the narrow path towards the door, then the jingle of keys. The door squeaked open, and the night streamed in. It was one of the tall men, Windmill's close associate, the one who favoured corduroys and square glasses. He hoped I had learned to behave, he said; fighting was not tolerated. My limbs were yearning for freedom, yet I emerged gingerly. Our pace back to the main building was brisk.

I noticed the strain on his face as we rounded to the front of the building. In the half-shadows, just before we turned towards the main door, he paused - a brief, peculiar moment. In the fresh evening air, where we were hidden from view, he confessed in a hushed tone that he disapproved of some of their methods. Being locked in the boiler room, he felt, was wrong, yet he was powerless to change it.

I remained silent, my mind weaving the final threads of the plan I was concocting. I trailed him, allowing him to wrestle with his guilt, as we entered the main doors into the light and headed left towards the kitchen for a late supper.

Through the empty dining hall, we entered the kitchen, with its dim fluorescent lights, brown floor tiles, industrial units, and humming fridges. 'It wasn't always like this, you know,' he murmured, subdued as he opened the tall silver fridge. 'There used to be staff here with better temperaments, who found other ways to discipline.' He handed me a plate covered in clingfilm - cold ham, pasta, potato salad, mixed carrots and sweetcorn. A pack of crisps, an orange drink, a straw accompanied it.

As he continued, I sensed his sincerity, yet caution nagged at me. His watery eyes blinked heavily behind the glasses. 'Sometimes, Stephen, a few bad apples really can spoil what's promising. Just keep away from the bad ones. Some here do try to help discreetly.'

He watched as I ate quietly in the dining hall. 'After this, I must take you to your room. Windmill insists you shouldn't mix with the others tonight.' I devoured the food, the semblance of normality returning. I longed to be in my sanctuary at the far end of the second floor, away from the darkness and the haunting memory of the boiler room with its scratching rats and unseen insects.

'I'm sorry, Stephen. There's nothing I or the other staff can do,' he lamented.

I was fixated on escape. Once confined to my room, as the building quietened, I planned to pack a few essentials, shimmy down from the window, and disappear into the night. A ten-pound note stashed in a book for emergencies would cover my train fare to London. I was resolute; I would not face another dawn here, nor return to the stifling fear of the boiler room. I would go to my mother.

London Age 15

The dream unfolded in the soft glow of dawn, the figure of a woman I could not see but who I knew loved and wanted me, I tried to reach her, but she was always too far away, I called, and she turned to me, just as I was about to see her face…

'Stephen! Stephen!' The voice pierced through the dreamscape.

I was jolted awake by my two-year-old half-brother, Shaun. His plump, sturdy frame and mischievous green eyes animated with life. His blonde hair askew, he stood in just a t-shirt, giggling with the unbridled joy of childhood. His antics were infectious, and I played along, feigning sleep before springing into a bout of tickling, our laughter echoing. The quilt lay discarded on the floor, a casualty of our playful scuffle.

But the game had to end. 'Out now. That's enough... Out!' I managed between laughs as his mirth reached a crescendo, mirroring my efforts to usher him out of the room.

As he scampered off, I reflected on the situation. The authorities would be aware of my escape by now, and my status updated to another runaway in the world of the missing. The journey had been smooth so far: a steady train ride, a bus, and a final walk to my mother's home.

After a refreshing shower, I wondered how Kathleen, my mother, would face the day. Dressed in fresh clothes, I joined her in the kitchen, where she stood ironing, her brunette hair framing her face with an expression mixed with surprise and concern.

'Well, see you made a run for it again, Stephen. They'll come here for you. You know you can't stay...' she remarked.

I sat on the wooden chair by the round table facing the main kitchen sink. Shaun thundered down the stairs, five-year-old Brendan with him. They flew in chasing each other, giggling, laughing, then went next door and played in the sitting room.

STEPHEN GILLEN

I said, 'I know, Ma. I couldn't stay there. They do bad stuff there. I'm always fighting.'

The room was a comfortable temperature. The sun was filtering in from the garden, spreading the walls and floor around us with warmth and soft, glinting light. But her mood was shifting. She rested the iron upright on the ironing board.

'Stephen, you're always fighting. That's your problem, you will never listen.'

'Ma, some of us are forced into this hardness.'

She was moving the iron. Its steam was in the middle of our silences.

'Stephen, you don't know hardness. It was hard for me, too. I came to this country I had nothing.'

I continued, 'I have to survive, Ma. They beat the shit out of us there.

Kathleen returned, 'You put yourself there.'

It was what she did. Deflected and twisted things to fit the narrative that was more palatable for her.

I could feel it. The frustration that rattled around inside me. Sarcastically, I said, 'Mind you, things weren't any better here…'

She turned then. The iron was lifted but still in her hand. Her eyes flashed, a look I knew well combined with her sharp tongue. 'Now, Stephen, he might not be a saint, but Michael was good to you. We had to work hard for everything we ever got. No one ever gave us anything.'

I was silent. It was another strategy she used, moving the furniture of her life around in her head to suit the circumstances of her feelings. A patchwork tapestry where things could be hidden, buried, shifted and remodelled to dovetail with the season or the moment.

I had made a coffee, and its strength would keep me wired for hours. Kathleen was still my mother. I had missed the smell of her, the Palmolive soap that was freshness and a quality face cream and shampooed hair. The rare times we had achieved a special and bankable moment as mother and son. Fleeting seconds that would arrive and dissipate like unplanned fog.

Forcefully, she said, 'You'll have to go, Stephen. We can't have you here. You got yourself into this again, you'll have to get yourself out of it.'

'But I can't see them coming here, Ma'

'I don't care, Stephen. Michael and I have the kids now. We can't be having no more trouble. This is the way you learn.'

She had always taken this role. A person who was there but not there, who would arrive but would always be gone again.

My mother stood there now, a figure that blocked the inviting light behind her. The iron hissed, steam scattered as it was pushed forward. The children were around, a cluster of noise that rose and fell with their play fighting. They appeared, withdrew again, ran out of the kitchen along the hallway and crashed up the stairs towards the bedrooms and new pastures.

'Ma?' I asked softly, hoping for a sliver of empathy.

'Yes?'

'Did you ever think of me? I just wondered if I ever crossed your mind?'

Her eyes clouded; I saw it, but the barrier she had positioned for that part of her life would never be allowed to be removed. I knew it hurt her.

'Things are different, I'm sorry, Stephen. I always wished the best for you and did what I could, you are with good people. We took you when you needed a home. Your Aunt Margorie and your uncles gave you the best of care… you were lucky, you could have been without a home.'

I saw the iron moving faster, fanning movements with more focus and force.

I said, 'I need to know the past; I want to know why? What did I do that meant you couldn't love me as you do Brendan?'

'Stephen, sometimes it's better to leave the past alone and let sleeping dogs lie. You're here now, aren't you? Jesus! We do try our best with you.'

I got up and stood from the chair, seeking more of the light and warmth of the morning sun from the window. An uncomfortable knowledge was niggling and gnawing at my insides.

'But how will I truly know my future if I do not understand and unravel my past…?'

The iron stopped abruptly. Kathleen had her head up, eyes boring into me and through me. I had missed the little times we had had alone in the dark, cold nights when we had snuggled on the sofa watching an old film.

She said, 'Stephen. People, all of us, sometimes have to make choices we do not want to, sometimes we want circumstances, sometimes we don't. To survive is the job of most people.

Kathleen was back to the ironing. All knowing but keeping the past close to her like a padlocked closed book.

I moved to the door to the hallway. My back was to her silence, but I turned and said, 'Ma, I'm going to go now. In case they come. I agree the kids are here now. But I feel isolated, Ma. Lost. Like I don't know what to do or where to go. All I feel is loneliness; the anger is all over me. I can't go back, Ma…?'

The iron resumed its steady rhythm across the fabric, a metaphor for how she ironed out the wrinkles of her past to maintain her present. I yearned to understand, to reconcile the disparate threads of my history. Still, I was met with a wall of stoic practicality.

Kathleen gave one parting comment, 'Stephen, catch on quickly, or you will never learn. You've made your bed now you must lie in it.'

Belfast Age 14 (released for a funeral)

The freshness of the clear morning, as light broke, saw squawking birds hovering and traversing, holding and cruising on the lifting winds in their diligent search for food. At fourteen and a half, leaving my mother's house and England behind had been difficult, but still under the care of the Local Authority, the prospect of returning to a children's home was unbearable.

The great ship sliced through the blue and green waves. From the safety of the top deck, gripping the white metal railings, I watched the gulls. The morning light dominated the dawn; a sky streaked and striking, flecked with spidery yellow, orange, and blue-grey, stretched far out over the vast expanse of water ahead.

My feelings, though my consciousness attempted to maintain a semblance of calm, ebbed and flowed with an unexpected intensity. Within this quietude, memories began to emerge, casting vivid light into the corners of my present thoughts. Margaret sat on the settee, laughing, her black wavy hair free of her headscarf, and with her hands clasped in her lap, happiness and contentment were stamped on her face. She roared with laughter, a contagious moment, gripping. The embers of the fire in the front room crackled. The fire guard surrounded the hearth, and Gerard rushed as soot and smoke dislodged from the chimney, powdering the light brown tiles of the clean hearth.

The soft, awakening winds rushed along the contours of the ship, caressing my face and brushing through my short black hair. It had been only five and a half years since I had left Belfast, yet it felt like an age. I watched a large white seagull from across me, on the open water, effortlessly aligning with the ship's movement, matching its speed. In my mind, I saw the younger me, a vulnerable boy on a ship, clutching a small suitcase tightly, with a strange land beckoning.

The moment's intensity overwhelmed me, reviving the acute pain and profound loss I had endured, alongside a glimmer of hope for the affection of a mother and a brighter future that might lie ahead. A a tiny child, clutching nothing more than a suitcase, cast adrift into an abyss, oblivious to what the future might hold or how to navigate it.

I walked a little to the front of the great ship. Here, the wind and the vastness of the morning were fiercer, open, and stretching out in a wide, coloured tapestry. I stared into the beautiful sky, my hands gripping the white iron railings tightly against the strength of the blowing wind. As I felt the freedom of being at one with everything around me, tears overwhelmed the defences I had steadfastly built around my heart. Memories returned, grasping like an icy claw.

Going Home, Belfast Age 14

With birdsong in my ears and the scent of freshly cut grass and turned earth filling my nostrils, I observed the shadow of a red kite hovering against the sun's glare. The majestic bird of prey, once nearly extinct in Ireland, dipped and veered eastwards, riding the shifting winds in search of its quarry.

The ferry from Birkenhead had swiftly navigated the choppy, wave-littered Irish Sea, leaving England and the children's home a distant memory. As I watched the waves during the crossing, thoughts of a less remembered childhood filled my mind. Disembarking, I took a train directly to Milltown Cemetery on the Falls Road. Amid the stone angels, Gaelic crosses, and headstones of paramilitary volunteers, I walked the curving paths in the growing sunshine, paying respects to long-passed relatives. Then, I took a bus to Greencastle Cemetery. Along the way, I dreamed of Madge, remembering her washing dishes and preparing an evening meal.

Before me lay two modest graves with simple marble headstones, the grass slightly overgrown and faded flowers drooping against the black marble. They were unremarkable graves for two of the most significant people I had ever known.

I tidied the graves, removing the detritus that marred the grass. It was a peaceful haven on a respectable street, bordered by a low stone wall and black iron gates, it felt like a resting place for royalty.

Reading the epitaph, a lump formed in my throat: 'Gone, but never forgotten. A beloved Sister, mother, and friend to all. An Angel taken to her place in heaven most high…' I placed the white chrysanthemums I had brought on my Aunt Margaret's grave. The gentle breeze brushed my face, stirring the deep, hidden currents of emotion within me. Tears welled as I stood by Uncle Jack's grave, the warmth of the sun bathing my skin, the pain across my chest almost tangible.

I lingered for hours, haunted by images and words unspoken. I spoke questions to the silent graves, offered prayers for peace, and as the sun merged with the encroaching darkness over the mountains, I felt a lifting of my past's weight.

At the gate, with one last glance at the tidy graves and the newly arranged white flowers, I noticed the clouds gaining definition above the Mourne Mountains. The red kite was nowhere to be seen. I walked down the hill, around the road by the quaint houses, up the lane to the bustling main road. Passing the mirrored, fortified RUC barracks on Whitewell Road, I hastened up the steep hill, eager to reach Uncle Gerard's house in Serpentine Parade before nightfall. The houses, closely packed and two-storied, trailed off as the road veered left into the backstreets towards Antrim Road.

Their anger was palpable, the scowls etched deep into their faces. Three youths, in old jeans and jackets with black Doc

Martens, turned on a boy as I crossed the road by the concrete-fenced secondary school playground at Stella Maris.

'Fancy you can outrun us, wee man?' The boy had long brown hair, a sandy complexion, and a fire in his eyes. They crowded over him, raining down kicks as he tried to shield himself on the uneven pavement.

I passed, my head down, their warning glares following me. The boy's pleas echoed as I walked on, then a spit behind me: 'Hey, you! Wee man.'

My heart compelled me to stop, to intervene.

'Yeah, you. Where you from, wee man? Don't remember you around here. What's your name?'

'Why don't you leave him be? What's he done to you?'

They paused, my accent throwing them. They encircled me, the boy now a moaning heap on the ground between us.

'Wee English man, is it?' one sneered.

'You gave us a funny look as you passed, wee English man,' another accused, shoving me back into the hedge as I instinctively swung a hard fist, hoping to take him by surprise.

We grappled in the hedge, the others joining in. 'Get away from the house! The RUC are coming now to fix ye!' It was the old man from the house behind us who owned the now broken and ripped hedgerow. The boy who was on the floor had risen and swung a stick at our assailants, but all I could do was grapple, my back bouncing and breaking the hedge behind me as I was pinned down and tried to switch round my body weight. Crackling twigs filled my ears as the fine interior of the hedgerow fractured further.

'The police are on their way ye wee fuckers!'

I had the better of them now. The older, bigger boy clung to me. Our arms were locked on each other's shoulders as we circled and stumbled. I elbowed him hard a quick crack flush on the jaw. He yelped, and I swung him to the ground ready to give him a kick.

He moaned as I knocked the wind from him. He had serious wounds now, blood flowed from his mouth and nose.

The police arrived.

I saw them too late and was too tired to run as their grey armoured jeeps accelerated around the corner. They appeared in a second, big black uniforms that swamped the pavement. Peaked caps and bulging bullet proof vests, imposing side arms and shiny buttons on black uniforms.

… 'They fecked my beautiful hedge they did. A bloody state it is look at it.' The redness travelled his features and his finger pointed.

'Bloody, ruffians!'

I felt the cold metal of handcuffs clasping around my wrists, even as I protested the innocence of the other boy. They released the three instigators without a second thought. Sitting in the back of the jeep, I looked up the road to where I had come from. At the hill's crest lay the street of my childhood. Uncle Gerard would be there, likely smoking an Embassy Red and prodding the fire with a poker, blissfully unaware that I was being taken to the police station and that I was just a stone's throw away.

London, 1989, Age 18

As I ran to save myself with a river of fresh blood that ran down the side of my clothes and body, I kept to the darkness and shadows of the street. Camden was a strange manor, I considered. Of the four corners of London, there were differences in trends about it that set it apart in my mind. Unlike the harsh and cold council estates of East, North, and South London I knew so well, the busy and glitzy affluent parts of West London - I didn't know. I thought of the police passing. I must not be caught on the road like this.

I stumbled forward. It was a cold evening but a busy street. Shop lights bathed the footway in luminous half-light. People saw me and jolted as I passed; a couple crossed the road in front of me. I must have projected a grisly sight, as I had left my shirt somewhere in the fight at Camden Palace, and the blood poured fast from a deep, slice wound at the side of my head. My body ran red with blood, the top of my jeans was saturated by the moisture and dampness of it.

'My God!' Another woman moved away from me with a hand to her mouth. No one stopped.

I pushed forward into the unknown, my body hugging and seeking the seclusion of hidden darkness. My eyes had to keep adjusting to the road in front of me as the blood ran freely. No one helped. I was someone to stay away from. A spectre of trouble had appeared from the shadows with the madness around him and a quickening step. The gushing blood was a clear sign to keep walking. My head spun like the final cycle of a washing machine.

I could not believe they had done me…We had been in a gang war with other similar factions who were fighting for control to run the serious crime in certain areas.

They would pay dearly. There was madness in me, anger; I was not of sound mind. I had been released not three months previously from Portland Borstal. I had returned to the streets with no fear and learnt the streets had not changed since I had been away. The East End was as busy as ever, with everyone trying to make a pound note, and there were no options or opportunities for me but crime. You had to eat or be eaten everywhere you went. You had to be careful. I had travelled on the train from Portland to Bethnal Green in East London. My thoughts on the way back had been positive and hopeful. I would get a decent job; things would be different. I would be able to turn away from my criminality, the gangs, the trouble and the drugs.

I wiped the blood from my eyes. The bottle that one of them had smashed over my head had cut cleanly, a deep slice about two inches on the side of my head. I had left youth custody and thought the East End would be different; nostalgia had clouded my reality. The poverty surrounded me again, like the old streets and acquaintances. I had been pulled quickly into the same haunts and patterns of thinking and serious problems, and I had been wrong about my hopes to create a positive future.

Where had the girl gone, I wondered? She was pretty and we had gone out for the evening together. We had laughed and were having a great time. We had chosen Camden Palace for the dancing, I had said hello to Lenny McLean, who was head of the door, and we had got in much quicker than the people who stretched away down the road. My head rushed; it was still full of the ecstasy tablet I had taken earlier. My eyes were wide in my head, and my body felt light and jumpy… The girl would be back in the club…

It was the roaring eighties and the age of dance music. The age of crack cocaine, paranoia, people killing each other and standing with their backs against the wall had not yet arrived. It was the time of E's and the dancing love drug ecstasy. A time of getting secret directions out to somewhere in the sticks where there would be thousands of people in a field. All of them were out of their nut on varying cocktails of drugs and dancing. The main events of the time were 'Sunrise' and 'Biology'. In those times, we were out for days, sometimes seven days at a time, lost in the dance, club and rave scene. We loved it. But with the lifestyle came the drugs and money, and with the drugs and need for cash came the wars over territory, the enemies, and the violence. We were slick dressers. Always in top designer wear like Armani, Gucci, Aquascutum or Burberry, both casual and smart. Always with the best of trainers, expensive boots and three-quarter length jackets.

I remember entering the interior of the club. A massive open space that was the main dance floor, swarms of dancing bodies writhing on the dance floor, on the balconies, by the many bars on the different levels. The dance music thundered. The smiling, dancing, jumping bodies moved in dimly coloured light in unison. Whistles, luminous strips of light, headbands, clothing, and makeup moved and shook.

It had started raining slightly from the dark, moonlit sky. I moved along the road, still looking for a way out, back from the main lights of the street and shops.

'They fuckin done me! 'I barked into the phone. 'I can't believe they had the bollocks to do me!'

'Where are you?' I had known Del since we were kids. There was a gang of us. We were at war with other gangs like us in London. For this reason, we were usually always together.

'Camden Palace. It happened in the pally. It was that mob from last week, D… I went into the Champaign bar with some soppy bird, and the whole lot of them was there…'

'Shit, Stephen. I told you when we go out, we should always rave with the firm.'

'I know. I stuck it on them. All of them. I was lucky to get out of there; I can't believe they had the front to do me…!'

I kept my voice down as the blood continued to flow from my head, and I quickened my pace on the darkened street. My head was low. I told them to come to bring the tools, the guns. I was going to make an example of them and catch them all together when they came out of the club. I touched the cut on my head, the blood. I had seen them when I entered the blinding light of the Champaign Lounge. The leading players were there, five or six of them, five white guys and one black well-dressed. They had girls with them. The main one was John.

John and I went back years….

Our eyes had locked across the crowded carpet, and my mind was filled with how we had left them… We had blocked them in the car. There had been four of them. We had struck quick and hard, scarves around our faces and guns in our hands. They had been warned with the guns stuck in their ears; they had been robbed and stripped of the money they had. The keys to their car were taken, and they had been left stranded in the cold back streets in a part of our manor, frightened, mugged off and broken.

They glared over their drinks. One was fat, another had blond hair and a brown suede jacket, and he held a beer bottle. The two with darker hair lurked beside them. John, an oversized fit-looking man with sandy hair and flashing blue eyes, stood forward.

'You won't leave here tonight without a scar down your face. You watch!' he hissed. He wanted to come forward as he said the words, but he was wary.

'Fuck off. You see what I do to you lot of mugs!' I thanked God for the knife down the side of my sock on my right calf. I always carried one. I had put it down the front of my trousers for the bouncer's search on the way in. I had gone to the toilet and transferred it for easy access to be held by the sock on my right foot. Tonight, this action would save my life.

He slunk away from me, a brooding look of menace in his eyes. I felt no fear. I stood my ground. The music thumped around me. The tablet I had taken earlier was kicking in, and the acid that had been mixed with the MDMNA spun the room in my mind. My heartbeat was alive with the adrenaline that coursed through me. The girl had noticed something was wrong. She had seen the change in my mood and the look on my face. The six of them, at the far side of the lounge some eight feet back, like a pride of lions, watched me. I needed to move. I shifted from the blinding brightness of the place we were into the sanctuary of the dim lights and heavy crowds of the main interior.

I knew they would make their move as soon as I approached the doorway.

The fat one had manoeuvred himself in front of me. I headbutted him hard on the nose. His face collapsed, but a bottle had been swung over the top of people's heads from the side somewhere, smashing completely on my head. Colours scattered in my mind. I saw blues, reds, and yellows. The force of it had caught me unawares and threw me down towards the floor, but somewhere in the haze, my body knew that to go down was to die. To this day, I don't know where I found the strength as my body dipped, bloodied with the force, and in one motion, got the knife from my sock firmly in my hand. I rose to face my attackers. They stood there, one with the broken bottle. The blood ran immediately down my face and neck from the cut on my head. The music was jarring, almost tribal. I jumped towards them, cut and slashed and thrust. I fought for my life, and all I could remember was people had tried to protect me as they had closed in for the kill, and I had pushed them away to fight and defend myself.

I had lost my shirt somewhere in the fight. I had fought my way down the packed stairs, ran through dancing people on the main dance floor, made my way to a side fire door by an ally, kicked it open and escaped into the night...

A man was in front of me, suddenly shielded against the cold by a heavy green tweed jacket and matching tweed cap that shadowed his face. He slightly bumped into me, and I turned.

'You ok, son,' It was the harsh accent of the north of Ireland.

I stumbled on, 'Yes, I am.'

Into the night, I forged forward. In my head, lingering a moment was the sound of the accent. The damp smell of the man's tweed jacket, mixed with blood, was in my nostrils.

The man watched the figure that dripped blood move forward along the road. He thought it was appropriate that he bumped into him at that time. For a second, a flashing moment, he felt to make his move. He smoothed his tweed jacket and put his three-fingered hand into his front jeans pocket, protecting it from the night. The young man's shadow was waning now, the blood that fell from a wound by his head hidden. A silhouette that stretched into nothingness. He bit his lip. He had missed his chance to act. He had waited a long time for his chance.

Long months that had grown into longer years as the little boy he had watched and studied had grown into a young man.

He turned into the night, taking the anger and bitterness that drove him most days. The man known as the Gardener would pick another time. There would be another moment, another dark night of safety and seclusion. Head down, he walked, crossed the road and was lost in the London traffic.

The rain was damp and cool on my face. My head throbbed. Unbelievably, it still bled profusely. I had to escape the lights of the busy street and the people. I saw the bright light and wide-open window of an Indian restaurant. Inside, I saw the waiters. One of them locked eyes with me. He saw the blood as I went to come into the shop.

'No. No...Not in here,' his hands were up to shield himself, barring my way forward. People were eating. A woman on a table beside me with her husband looked at me. Her eyes widened at the state of me. I was drenched in blood. Her mouth was open in shock.

'You can't come in here,' the waiter was desperate to get me out the door. The shock of the people dining had become apparent. Maybe I had not thought this through. I backed out the door, telling the waiter I had wanted to use the washroom to get cleaned up and that I needed help.

He still panicked. It was annoying, my head spinning, the blood running, no shirt and the anger of revenge upon me. I had looked at him angrily, disappeared into the rising night rain and down the street. I found a cab station. They took me into the back so I could wash my face, eyes and the blood from the side of my face, body and hair and stem the bleeding.

Reflection

Reflecting on my past, there's a part of me that wishes things could have been different - a different family, a different starting point, different chances. Yet, this life, with all its trials, has been unequivocally mine. The lessons learned are deeply personal. It's not about destruction; it's about creation, about striving towards a better existence, not just for oneself but for the greater good. We're woven into the fabric of life, not isolated strands but integral threads.

The issues I've faced, the lessons learned through hardships and trauma, they once made me feel like an outsider. Now, that sense of alienation has faded. I see health in being part of something larger. It's vital to perceive the world as an ally, a place ripe with endless potential. To believe in a universe filled with infinite possibilities is to step into a realm where anything is attainable, where experiences, both joyous and challenging, are invaluable.

This perspective shifts the focus away from a world filled with suspicion and malice, where trust is a rare commodity and life is a grim struggle for survival. While these shadows exist, we're not just passive inhabitants; we're the architects of our lives, the sculptors of our destinies. We hold the power to shape our journey and carve out our own future.

CHAPTER 3

Bethnal Green And A New Family

"I am what you designed me to be. I am your blade.
You cannot now complain if you also feel the hurt."

— Charles Dickens, Great Expectations

St Patrick's Approved School For Boys, Belfast Age 15

As the fresh mist rolled down from the Mourne mountains, Belfast was recovering from the turbulence and civil unrest of the previous night. I had been transported by the RUC to St Patrick's Approved School, a home for troubled and disruptive children, while the streets were being cleared of debris and the British Army set up new checkpoints.

Following the long black robes of the tall Christian Brother in front, he led me down the quiet, echoing corridor. In my little room within the juvenile section, I had spent a restless night as the comforting blackness turned into a suffocating darkness, filled with a deep longing and a tumult of igniting, worrying emotions that brought back old fears. Seated on my small chair in a spartan, colourless room, I watched the early hours tick by, peering out of the third-floor window of the old Victorian building.

'In here,' he said, his stern face and hook-like nose concealed behind round glasses.

I entered the office, already knowing some of the De La Salle brothers for what they were: faces stern as stone, hiding the reality of abuse and harsh discipline. Three weeks I had been at St Patrick's, which had moved in 1957 to a new site on the Glen Road, West Belfast, becoming an approved school to replace the old system of Reformatories and Industrial Schools.

The door shut behind me, sealing me in a wide, study-like office, the shelves filled with books and the air tinged with the sweet, musty scent of incense.

'Stephen…'

There he was, my Uncle Gerard, slight and fragile like a bird with a broken wing, sitting quietly in the corner.

He rose. 'Stephen.'

I was in his arms before I knew it, the warmth of his embrace dissolving the coldness I'd felt for so long.

'How are you?' he asked. 'Have you been alright, Stephen?'

His soft eyes held the weight of past hurts and days filled with worry.

'I'm okay, Uncle Gerard. God, I'm glad to see you…'

'Sit down, please,' instructed the Christian Brother from behind the desk, his smile not quite reaching his eyes.

'So, Stephen was brought here a few weeks ago. He's due in Crumlin Road court tomorrow. They should release him into your care. Whether they'll let him return to England is uncertain.'

Gerard was beside me, the newspaper still rolled in his hand.

'It'd be good to have him out of here. It's been a worry. He hasn't lived here in years. You can hear the strong English accent now,' he said.

The Christian Brother's eyes narrowed. 'Ah, the wee man's doing fine here. We've got juniors and seniors, and he's fitting in well with the other boys. He's under the same watch as all of them…'

I glanced at the rolled newspaper in Gerard's hand, and it sparked a memory. Suddenly, I was a child again, playing in the forest near Cave Hill, oblivious to the world's cares.

'You're okay, wee man, aren't you?'

'Yes, no bother…' I replied. It was a half-truth. The other children were a diverse yet solid group. It had been tough at first, but they had come to see that the strange boy with the English accent was one of their own. Despite this, I despised being here.

As the moment to part ways arrived, everyone stood in a cluster at the centre of the room. The long black robes of the Christian Brother, a peculiar sight, fluttered near the open door.

'Stephen, take care now,' Gerard said, his loving arms enveloping me, drawing me close. The embrace was heavy with yearning, a tangible reminder of lost years and time gone by.

'I'll be fine...' My voice was hesitant; I didn't want him to leave. An internal force was urging me to grab his hand as I did in childhood and let him lead me away from this place.

We began to walk down the corridor.

'Reflect on your past missteps, Stephen. Consider the series of events that led you here. Pray to God for His mercy tomorrow at the Crumlin Road Courts. Seek forgiveness, and perhaps you'll be granted release...'

The Brother's back faced us, his figure an ebbing shadow amidst the narrow corridor, his robe a flowing veil of black. Gerard's gaze met mine, the newspaper still rolled tightly in his grasp.

'Stephen, take care. I'm going to get you out of here,' he affirmed.

As the Christian Brother unlocked the main doors, Gerard leaned in close, his words a soft whisper meant for my ears alone – words to remember.

I watched him depart, his sentiments echoing in my mind. The door clicked shut behind him, sealing me back into the cold embrace of the institution. I clung to his parting words, letting them reverberate through my thoughts: 'Stephen, remember, son. Sometimes you have to walk with the Devil until you cross the bridge. Hold onto that if times get tough...'

These words, straight, clear, and true, became a mantra in my head, a potential beacon through the looming darkness.

London, East End, Age 16

The judge at Crumlin Road Court, Belfast was even more benevolent, releasing me into my Uncle Gerard's care and permitting my return to England.

The Irish Sea crossing had been gentle, with soft waves and a cool breeze. At Birkenhead Central, I paused for a moment, my bags resting on the floor beside me, coffee cup pressed to my lips, observing the hustle of busy commuters. My thoughts drifted back to the judge at Crumlin Road – an intimidating figure with a white curled wig and piercing eyes. Standing in that grand wooden-panelled courtroom with its lofty ceilings and the stifling air was an overwhelming ordeal.

'He's a tough little man,' the judge had remarked, peering over his spectacles with an extended gaze. It struck me as an odd comment for a judge to make to a young boy barely tall enough to peer over the dock.

The station was a hive of activity, with people bustling and darting about like busy bees.

Fortune had smiled on me. Finally, I was allowing myself to dream. Away from Ireland, the oppressive atmosphere of St Patrick's, and now beyond the reach of the Local Authority Care as I had turned sixteen, I tasted freedom for the first time.

I took another sip of my coffee, relishing the warmth of the drink. My thoughts turned to London, to my good friend with his flat in Bethnal Green. We were tight-knit and had sworn an oath to each other. We had plans and aspirations for a grand future. Making my way across the concourse, I noted the train's departure was imminent, and anticipation for my life in the East End buoyed my spirits. Passing through the turnstiles, I thought of my soon-to-be housemate. Callum Slaney was a true character – a great laugh, a nutter, and I was eager to reunite with him and meet his sister Lily.

Bethnal Green, 1987, 10am

We all crashed in a two-bedroom flat on the second floor just off Whitecross Street Market, near the Old Street roundabout. The flat was drab, with tired wallpaper, carpets crying out for a clean, and a sink too often filled with unwashed dishes.

Struggling out of bed at sixteen, I grasped the morning, feeling a sense of freedom for the first time. The previous night had been the usual late one, with the four of us who shared the flat drinking, chatting, and smoking cannabis. It had been a good laugh, teetering on the edge of hilarity and violence, as we brainstormed ways to make money.

Callum appeared at the door in blue boxer shorts. 'Have I got news for you, son. We've got a proper bit of work; Stevie, I'm telling you...'

'Callum, the shorts, mate. You're hanging.' I couldn't help but smile.

'Don't worry about it, son. Wait till you hear what I've got for us.' He slumped into one of the worn armchairs that desperately needed a clean, crossed his bare legs, and began, 'Had a great meet with this bloke this morning...'

'What, in them shorts?' I joked.

'No, for Christ's sake. Stop mucking about. I was down the market earlier, grabbing breakfast. There he was. A bloke from back in the day. Proper stuff. Old school...'

He talked while I finished dressing, brushed my teeth, splashed water on my face and hair. He rattled on about some guy, a nearby building, and a job involving safes brimming with jewellery just up by Farringdon.

I listened while stepping past old John, our alcoholic housemate sprawled on the sofa, and young Peter, a good lad and a runner for the gang, scoffing a bacon sandwich in the cluttered kitchen.

'Stevie, this is the one,' Callum said, suddenly breaking into a mock Irish dance that resembled a Cossack routine. 'We'll make a tidy sum. I've sorted our way in. Nice and easy. We need a serious chat about this, Stevie... I've got a good feeling!'

His gaze snapped to Peter, mouth full of sandwich. 'What you staring at? Like what you see, do ya? Fancy a go with me in these shorts, you dirty little sod? I know what's on your mind, Pete, you filthy bugger!'

Peter, nearly choking on his bacon, managed a grin. 'Do one, Callum. You're not my type, mate.'

Callum feigned offence. 'The cheek of it!'

Laughter seized us, leaving us doubled over, struggling for breath. With the toilet window ajar, I headed across the small hall to the front door, seeking respite from the giggles.

'Right, I'm off to get changed, then we can get down to business with this little earner.'

Stepping onto the landing, the midday sun cast North London in silhouette. A sense of joy and belonging, unfamiliar to me, welled up inside. It was the bond with these like-minded rogues that truly resonated - a band of outlaws with no rules or codes. Free as birds, the world was ours for the taking. I closed my eyes for a moment, letting the sunlight warm my face.

I could picture the great waves of the Ferry crossing the Irish sea a few weeks past and the freedom stretched out now in front of me.

'You Okay mate, not disturbing a daydream am I...?

I jumped. It was a short, sweet female cockney accent that pierced and sliced. It continued, 'I mean, penny for them and all that, but any man worth his salt at this time of day would be out grafting and getting the shillings in...I mean, unless of course you're someone who's already had it off. Judging by the clobber you're wearing and the fact you're hanging round this shit hole with my nuisance of a brother I'd say that highly unlikely...You are by the way?'

I starred at her.

A slender figure stood before me, dressed in a coordinated blue dress and bag, her knowing, light blue eyes set in a finely sculpted face, with red lips poised in a questioning half-smile.

'Well, I'm flattered by your robust vote of confidence,' I replied with a hint of sarcasm.

Her eyes sparkled, her smile broadening. 'You must be Stephen?'

She stood taller in her blue heels, eyes looking me up and down and I returned the gesture. In a closed voice, I said, 'I may be, depends who's asking, love. Been a few dodgy birds round these parts lately.'

Her hand went to her hip. A mouth that was well formed turned up at the side. 'Joker too are you mate. Listen... I know you're, Stephen. I'm Lily, Callum's sister. There's something you better know. I know my brother Callum's a mental case and a nut-job and a nuisance. But he's my nuisance, and now it seems your nuisance. He's my brother and comes from a good family. What I'm trying to say is he's my brother and we love him dearly, so you look after him when you're out and about the pair of you and that kid in there doing whatever'.

Her blue eyes examined me intently. The ascending sun and a gentle breeze rustled the browning leaves at the entrance to the flats, casting a dance of light and shadow around her, highlighting her figure. Her steely demeanour, combined with her slender elegance and sharp wit, was compelling.

'I promise I will, Lily. On my life, we stand and fall together.'

We looked at each other a moment. In the background, through the slightly open window, in the flat's bathroom amongst the sound of moving water we both heard, 'Oh…my old man said follow the van and don't dilly dally on the way…!'

She turned away, her smile stretching further, and strutted back the way she had come, hips swaying. I watched her go, her heels echoing on the floor. I watched the contours of her body move. She shouted behind her as she walked, heels clicking. 'Remember what I said…Okay. I suppose I shall have to take your word for it. I'm late. Got to go. Tell him I turned up, I'll phone him later…'

She pivoted on her heels. I watched her. She was at the end of the landing ready to descend the concrete stairs and turned with a softer smile.

'Only joking about the clothes, Stephen. Don't be a wanker all your life. You've got a good sense of style. Word of advice though, change the red shirt, it's too loud. Use pastel colours that go with your skin and match your hair. Bye…!

She was gone. Her words were in my ears. Behind me Callum's voice echoed in the untidy flat and my nose was filled with the compelling scent of the perfume she had left behind.

Bethnal Green 1987 Age 16

From the moment I set foot in Bethnal Green, it felt like my fate was already sealed. My life up to that point was a series of events that shaped me into someone who could survive in this world, but at a cost. I often reflect on how it all started, the roots of my journey into crime, and it's clear to me that it was almost inevitable.

I was born into chaos, into a life where everything I loved was ripped away from me before I even had a chance to understand it. Growing up in Belfast, I was taught to be cautious of everything and everyone around me. 'Be careful what you say, where you go, who you talk to,' were not just words of advice; they were a means of survival. Violence wasn't just something you saw; it was something you lived, breathed, and somehow managed to avoid, if you were lucky. But that luck didn't last long for me. My family tried to shield me from the worst of it, cocooning me in love and protection. Yet, the violence and suspicion outside our door permeated every aspect of our lives. It was the air we breathed, thick with the scent of imminent danger and loss. This environment, this constant state of alert, it forged something within me - a resilience, yes, but also a deep-seated anger and a readiness to fight at a moment's notice.

When I lost my aunt, my mother figure, everything changed. I was just nine, suddenly uprooted and transported to England, an alien world with unfamiliar faces and customs. The loss was a gaping wound, and the isolation only deepened it. My real mother and stepfather provided no solace; instead, they introduced me to a harsh reality where vulnerability was a liability. I had to harden, to build walls around my heart to survive. And with that survival came the violence within me, a companion that seemed to grow stronger with each challenge.

The transition to life in children's homes was swift, but the conditioning was swifter. I was young, yes, but the need for a family, for belonging, drove me into the arms of those who could only offer a semblance of it through the adrenaline of chaos and crime. I gravitated towards the bad crowd, not out of choice, but necessity. In that world, I wasn't just the abandoned child from a children's home; I was someone with potential to rise, to make a name. But it was a distorted sort of fame, one built on the shaky grounds of illegal activities and fleeting loyalties.

By the time I was sent to the detention centre at 14, the die was cast. I thrived in that environment, not because it nurtured any good within me, but because it affirmed the harsh lessons life had already taught me: trust was a luxury, strength was paramount, and fear was your worst enemy. Success in prison wasn't a badge of honour; it was a sign that I had fully embraced the world I was thrust into. There were no lions or tigers here, just the realisation that I could survive - and perhaps even excel - in this jungle of concrete and barbed wire.

The streets and gangs provided a path, albeit a treacherous one, a path I knew as my only option. With every fibre of my being, I committed to this life, resolved to excel in anything I turned my hands to, no matter the stakes.

Dover Borstal 1988 Age 17

Dover was different, yet the same - another institution filled with London and East End lads like myself, each with a point to prove. The air here was charged with the energy of youth and the unspoken challenges that hung between us. I recognized the look in their eyes; it mirrored the one in my own.

It was in Dover that I learned the hard truth: violence was a language that could only take you so far. When an argument over a stolen cigarette turned bloody, I saw the line I had crossed the moment my knuckles connected with the other lad's jaw. The fight was overkill, a brutal ballet that ended with him on the floor, and me, the victor of a hollow victory. After enduring several months of intolerable behaviour from myself and the tight-knit group that ruled the roost, the authorities decided they wanted me out.

The consequences were swift. As I was dragged away, my hands slick with another's blood, I knew that Dover could no longer hold me. I was too much of a liability, too volatile for their walls.

The doors of Portland Borstal opened to welcome me with a cold embrace. It was a place that whispered promises of reform but shouted the reality of hardened criminality. If Huntercombe and Dover were the minor leagues, Portland was the majors, no one ever left there, despite how disruptive they could be, and I had just been called up to the big games.

As the van carrying me away from Dover faded into the distance, I caught a glimpse of the chalky cliffs through the barred window. They stood impassive, indifferent to the turmoil of the souls that ebbed and flowed like the tides below. I was leaving behind one version of myself, but I wondered what new form I would take in the crucible that awaited me.

Portland wasn't just a Borstal; it was the anvil upon which I would be struck, shaped, and, if I wasn't careful, shattered. A place full of Welsh lads with other strange, foreign accents and ways of being I hadn't encountered before.

Bethnal Green 1987 Age 16

The silence of Bethnal Green's streets was deceptive, a veil that barely concealed the thrum of power from the old guard who ruled its corners, with the business of the many layers of' up-and-comings' that were always out on the hunt to be more and get more. It wasn't the restless youths that I needed to impress but the seasoned veterans, the architects of the underground empire that had their fingers in every illicit pie, the money getters who had dominated cleverly and, with brute force got what they wanted.

Callum had laid the groundwork, talking me up as more than just a fresh face - a potential asset with a mind for strategy and a stomach for the gritty work. His family name carried weight in these parts, a legacy etched into the very fabric of East London's underworld. We had carved a path between us on a rocky road, becoming prominent for our ages and known in the right circles already.

I was led through a nondescript door and down into the belly of a pub that smelled of stale beer and secrets. The basement was dimly lit, the air thick with smoke and the murmurs of men whose faces were etched with the tales of their exploits. These were Callum's people, the old school and their enforcers, who pulled the strings and to whom everyone else looked for nods of approval.

'Gents, this is Stephen,' Callum announced, his arm draped over my shoulder with a brotherly grip that belied the seriousness of the introduction.

A man detached himself from the shadows, his presence commanding the room without a word. His eyes, sharp and calculating, fixed on me. I met his gaze, unflinching. His name was Donovan, and he was a legend, a whisper on the lips of every wayward youth aspiring to a life of notoriety.

'City life treat you well, then?' Donovan's voice was smooth, a stark contrast to the lines of his weathered face.

'City life's what you make it,' I replied, my voice showing no cracks. 'And I'm here to build, not just survive.'

Donovan chuckled, the sound like gravel rolling down a hill. 'Callum says you're hard as the cobblestones son, game and twice as sharp. We need lads with gameness and brains, not just muscle.'

'Guts, brains, and loyalty,' I said, each word a quiet promise. 'That's what I bring.'

He nodded slowly, eyes never leaving mine. 'We'll see, won't we? The street's a forge; it'll either shape you or melt you down. If you're going to be wrapped around us,, you'll need to be forged from steel son, bright as a pin, staunch all the way to the end.'

Callum's grip tightened, a silent message of support. '

He's steel, Don,' Callum vouched, his confidence in me as unwavering as the Tower of London itself. 'Give him a chance to prove it.'

Donovan considered this, his gaze shifting between us as if weighing my fate against the scales of his vast experience. Then he stepped aside, gesturing to a table where a map of the city lay sprawled beneath the tendrils of smoke that wafted through the room. It was more than just paper and ink; it was a canvas of opportunity, a depiction of the territory we operated in.

'Sit down, Stephen,' Donovan said, a test in his tone. 'Let's give it a go. We're just discussing potential opportunities, it may be that we can use you.'

I took the chair, feeling the weight of the room's attention. The conversation resumed and I swiftly saw the untapped markets, ripe for the taking, if you had the right teams.

The older men leaned in, interest in their eyes as he outlined a plan that was audacious, yet tinged with the street smarts they valued.

When he finished, the room was silent, save for the soft drip of a leaky pipe. Donovan's eyes glinted as he looked at me.

'You got the minerals to do a job like that?' he asked quietly, the others watched intently.

It was more than I had hoped for. Opportunities from these men wasn't a given; they were earned, one word, one deed at a time. And I had just made my first deposit.

As I emerged from the pub into the crisp London air, the city felt different beneath my feet. It wasn't just streets and buildings anymore; it was a chessboard, and I had just made my opening move. With Callum at my side and Don's wary endorsement, I was poised on the edge of becoming 'City' - not just a boy from Belfast but a name that would echo through the alleys and avenues of London's underworld.

The game was on, and I was ready to play. Staunch to the end, no turning back.

Bethnal Green, 1987 Age 16

A slight drizzle swept in from Holborn, shrouding Barbican and Farringdon in a damp haze. Behind us, the barrow boys divided, stacked, and transported goods for Smithfield Meat Market. Callum, Peter, and I clung to the shadows of a building near Cowcross Street, tucked away in a side street that receded from the main thoroughfare. Although it was 3 a.m., some windows on the higher floors of the adjacent building still betrayed signs of life with their luminescence.

We gazed upward. The building, a repurposed warehouse, rose four stories high, its facade punctuated with wide windows. Jutting from the roof was a red metal hook, a remnant of an old loading pulley once used for hoisting sacks of flour and grain. Above, set into the roof, were the diminutive windows we had been briefed about.

Testing the black metal drainpipe, slick under my fingers from the rain, I gauged its sturdiness. It stretched upward to the roof, reaching the guttering hidden beneath the awnings. Callum, beside me, nodded in agreement, it would support our weight. The drizzle washed over our faces, tracing rivulets down the black balaclavas we had rolled up to resemble hats. We listened intently, tuning into the night's symphony, our senses as keen as a nocturnal predator scouting a path in the darkness. Rainwater from a clogged drain nearby splashed in a steady, irritating rhythm. The hum of traffic from the main road murmured in the distance, mingled with the faint strains of music and the murmur of voices carried by the wind.

'Peter, head back to the corner,' we instructed. 'Keep a sharp lookout and stay hidden. Send a text if you spot anything.'

I scaled the drainpipe first, with Callum following. My feet found purchase on the wall's features and the clasps securing the pipe. Ascending to the third floor, I peered through a window and caught sight of two tall, grey metal safes anchored against the interior wall.

'Hey, Callum. I see it!'

'What, what can you see?'

'Two safes. It's magnificent. All the tools are there - benches for the jewellery makers and diamond cutters...'

'Come on, shift it. You're blocking the way up here,' Callum pressed, implying I should climb higher.

'Callum, this isn't about pride, it's about being in the right place, and on top.' I shot back with a hint of amusement in the tension of the moment. I can see everything, the files, beading pliers, sizing gauges, magnifiers, anvils... There's even a pen for testing the stones. Your contact was spot on.'

Reaching the roof, I swung my legs around to peer through a small, stained window set back from the street view.

A floor below, Callum glanced into the jewellery workshop and beamed upward.

'Come on,' I urged.

As he reached the top, I leaned against the window, feeling the cool touch of the small .22 calibre pistol pressed against my bare skin, tucked into my waistband. On the ledge, with the rain sweeping the city's darkened skyline, we exchanged knowing grins. Callum patted the gun in his pocket.

'Right, Stevie. We'll smash this glass behind us and hole up in the toilet until morning. They'll disarm the alarms when they open up. This place is like Fort Knox - sensors everywhere. We can't risk a move until they deactivate everything.'

The rain and the climb had soaked our jeans and buttoned jackets. I nodded. In the slight light of the rooftop, with the night rain soaking through us, I saw the excited craziness in Cullum's eyes. Forcefully, he said, 'When they come in the morning, when we hear them, and the bells are off we'll get the combinations, and get them to open the safes and clean them out...'

Family, Bethnal Green, 1988

The evening air was thick with the promise of adventure as we returned to our flat, as we stepped inside, the pulsating rhythm of the city outside seemed to fade into the background, replaced by the electric buzz of anticipation that filled the room.

We gathered around the makeshift coffee table, our improvised altar of celebration. Lines of cocaine and joints were meticulously arranged, the white powder shimmering under the dim glow of side table lamp. I was only sixteen but already cultivating a serious addiction that would one day cause my mind to fracture.

The job was done, and we'd gotten away clean, a testament to our skill and nerve. Callum, Peter, and I exchanged triumphant grins, a silent acknowledgment of our success.

Inside the flat, the atmosphere crackled with energy, the air thick with the scent of victory and adrenaline. We passed around bottles of beer as we toasted to our prowess. Amidst the celebration, I felt a sense of belonging I hadn't experienced before. For the first time in my life, I was part of a family - a band of brothers bound by more than blood.

As laughter filled the room, Lilly, Callum's sister, sauntered in, her presence commanding attention. With a playful smirk, she caught my eye, a subtle invitation in her gaze. The corner of my mouth lifted in response, a silent acknowledgment of the unspoken connection between us.

The night wore on, drugs flowing freely as we shared stories and memories, our laughter mingling with the faint strains of music. Cocaine lines were meticulously laid out on a mirrored surface, the sharp scent mingling with the sweet smoke of cannabis. We indulged, the drugs heightening our senses and intensifying the bond between us.

In that moment, surrounded by my newfound family, I felt alive in a way I never had before. The world outside faded away, replaced by a sense of euphoria and camaraderie that enveloped us like a warm embrace. As the night stretched on, I knew that this was where I belonged, among these fearless souls who dared to defy the odds and seize their own destiny.

Huntercombe Borstal 1987 Age 16

The stark reality of Huntercombe loomed over me as I sat in the holding cell, the echoes of the officer's words mingling with the steady drip of a leak somewhere in the corridor. At just 16, I was facing 15 months, but it wasn't the time that weighed on me - it was the silence, the absence of the street's chaotic symphony that I had grown to rely on.

Huntercombe was a cauldron of tempers and testosterone, where fights were as common as the morning roll call. I was just another ingredient in the mix, but I wasn't about to be simmered down. Every punch thrown and every altercation was a mark of not just survival but defiance. My reputation as a fighter cemented my status, but it also painted a target on my back. It wasn't long before my fists wrote a check that Huntercombe couldn't cash, and Dover Borstal became my new home.

London 1987, Age 16

Whilst my earliest memories were a mixture of green hills and the sound of Aunt Madge's soft lullabies, Brendan's were of big hands, tenement blocks, anger and sudden violence.

I had begun my life with bombs and guns, life with Kathleen and Michael was a different kind of battlefield, one where every meal was a minefield and love was a word wrapped in the sting of a belt. Initially my lanky frame and anxious eyes were the target of Michael's anger, the man's hands more familiar with the hardness of construction than the delicate task of nurturing a troubled child. Once I was gone though, Brendan became the focus of his frustration.

As I spiralled into a world of fights and vandalism, Brendan watched with a mix of awe and confusion. Until I was no longer a part of their everyday life. Simply gone one day without anyone telling them why. They overheard snippets of conversations from their parents but no one told them anything.

To young Brendan, Theresa, and Shaun, I was a figure larger than life - a spectre of rebellion who seemed to dance on the edges of their mundane existence.

When I did call to the house the children would be filled with excitement.

'Did you see Stephen's new jacket? It's like the ones in the movies.' Brendan half whispered

'Yeah, he looks like one of those popstars on telly.' Said Theresa with a hint of jealousy in her voice.

'Is Stephen a baddie then?' Shaun was hardly old enough to comprehend what he was saying but like most small children, he heard things he wasn't supposed to.

Brendan shook his head, a mix of hero-worship and confusion in his voice 'No, he's not a baddie. He's... Stephen. He gets things, goes places. He's not stuck here like us.'

Theresa looked confused, 'Mum says he's troubled. That he's been to bad places.'

'But he always comes back for us, doesn't he? He's got stories. And he doesn't have to eat Mum's awful dinners or... you know.' Brendan glanced to where Michael was stood glowering at Stephen.

As it was clear another argument was brewing, I turned to go, ruffling Shaun's hair as I passed, kissing Theresa on the top of her head and mock fighting with Brendan.

'I wish he'd take us with him.' Brendan sighed quietly.

Despite Brendan's admiration, the children were only privy to the glamour of my life - the allure that comes with money and the illusion of freedom. They remained unaware of the children's home that had hardened my heart, the borstals that had become my school of hard knocks, and the nights I'd spent hungry and alone, stealing cars and food just to survive.

My visits were sporadic, each one a display of the life I'd carved out for myself - a life that Brendan, Theresa, and Shaun would perhaps dream of. To them, I had somehow escaped, while they remained in the grip of a home that was at times, more prison than sanctuary. They didn't see the cost of my 'flashy life', the shadows that clung to me, the history of abuse and neglect that mirrored their own.

Brendan, at the cusp of understanding, grappled with conflicting images: the brother who seemed to defy their grim reality, and the hidden scars he must bear. He couldn't know the full truth of Stephen's world, but in his young mind, Stephen was a hero, a survivor who promised a glimpse of something beyond their four walls.

In the innocence of their youth, Brendan and his siblings held onto the myth of Stephen, the brother who could do no wrong, who carried the torch of their hopes through the dark streets of London.

Bethnal Green 1987 Age 16

The East End's twilight cast long shadows over the cobblestones, a perfect shroud for the evening's work. The air was tinged with the anticipation of violence, the kind that had become as routine to me as breathing. There was a language spoken here that didn't need words - just fists, fear, and the occasional flash of steel.

It was a simple job: persuade the local pub landlords to pay their dues for 'protection'. Protection from lads like us. It was extortion with a polite mask, but no one was fooled. The money was a tribute to fear, and fear was our stock-in-trade.

Callum and I entered the pub with the swagger of the untouchable. The landlord, a portly man with a face red from either drink or anger, likely both, glanced up. His eyes narrowed, not in fear, but in defiance. He had decided to stand his ground tonight, a decision as foolish as it was brave.

'Evening, Jim,' I said, my voice calm, betraying none of the tension that I felt tightening in my gut. 'Time to settle accounts, don't you think?'

Jim's response was a spit in my direction, the glob of disdain landing at my feet. The pub fell silent, the only sound the crackle of pork scratchings being chewed at the bar.

The fight was inevitable. Fists flew, chairs broke, and glass shattered. Callum and I, we were a whirlwind of rage and bone-crunching blows. It was over as quickly as it began, with Jim crumpled on the floor, his bloody testament to our 'negotiation' skills.

But this time, the fight had an audience that mattered. The blue sirens painted the walls, and before I could wipe the blood from my knuckles, we were cuffed and shoved into the back of a police van. The charge was Actual Bodily Harm, a name too clean for the mess we left behind.

In the sterile glow of the police station, reality set in. The walls were close, the air too still. The clang of the cell door echoed, a stark reminder that my freedom was no longer mine to claim.

'Stephen,' the officer read from his clipboard, a litany of my sins laid bare. 'Charged with Actual Bodily Harm, demanding money with menaces, and extortion. Quite the evening's work.'

Portland Borstal, 1987, Aged 16

'Gillen, hurry up!' The prison officer growled. A big, barrel-chested man with a thick, black beard. He was ex-naval and took pride in the blue uniform he wore.

I was strong and lithe, the anger I felt inside me burned bright and could be focused easily. I had been incarcerated for nine months already on an eighteen-month sentence handed down by the court in Bow Road for affray charges. A fight had broken out outside a club, people had fought, bottles and knives had been used. There had been a lot of blood and someone had been stabbed twice. It had been a fight for survival that had spilt onto the street, and even the bouncers had struggled to contain it. Everyone had scattered, ran. Four people had been arrested; I was one of them.

Screws were my favourite target. I glared at him, the guards personifying all I felt threatened by, didn't trust, fought against. I passed him on the landing of the prison, a stale, long warehouse-shaped landscape painted in drab colours, with the crashing of gates and keys echoing. I pushed aside the annoyance I felt.

I carried my slop bucket, filled with urine, to one of the recesses. I was at the corner of the wing where the stale smell of old pee and faeces filled my nostrils. God, I hated this place. But they would not break me, could not break me. I emptied the contents of the bucket into the sluice and, as I rinsed it with water, looked out the barred window. It was a bright, clear day. I looked down the sheer cliff face below to the sea, felt the power of the sea, watched the big naval destroyers sailing from their base along the sea line, and my heart sank further.

I was on an island. During my life, I would end up on others, but this was the first. I knew how I'd ended up here, but the yearning to escape consumed me. As soon as I had arrived at the reception wing, with a special guarded escort from Dover Borstal for being uncontrollable, I had been hatching a plan. This sentence of youth custody had started the pattern, one that would be my life for a very long time, a violent battle of wills against authority. Those in charge, well-versed in solutions for characters like me, were throwing everything at changing who and what I was. It was mental, emotional, physical, even spiritual torture, aimed to help me see things differently; it only served to harden my resolve. Right now, both sides were only warming up.

I paused for a moment to feel the beauty of the day on my pale face through the window. A glimmer of hope, of freedom, was dangerous to a man's mind in here.

I considered my dilemma...

Portland Borstal was seen as the end of the road. Opened in 1848 as an adult prison for convicts of the day, they had used prisoner hard labour in the construction of the breakwaters of Portland Harbour. Before that, it had served as a prison during the Napoleonic period. It stood at the highest point of Portland, on Portland Bill. There was one road on and off the island, and in bad weather, the sea would rise so that it was unpassable. The prison had high, menacing grey walls that formed the first level of security. Inside, there was a high fence topped with coiled razor wire, 24-hour cameras, and guards. But beyond the fence was a no-man's land with a grassy moat.

It had been chosen especially for me. Already classed as a highly disruptive prisoner, I had been moved from Huntercombe in Henley-on-Thames to Dover, situated on the white cliffs, and now to Portland. I was trouble, a nuisance, a serious problem like the others I associated with, and they were upping the pressure.

The screw was still on the landing, craning his neck to track my progress. There was hatred and confidence in his gaze. As I strolled past him again on my way back to the cell, swinging my bucket, I imagined wiping that smug look off his face with a good hard uppercut to the belly that protruded from his blue jumper. I entertained the thought with a smile.

His eyes followed me, a silent challenge.

'Move yourself, Gillen!' he barked. 'Get in your cell. You know it's one trip here. On the double!'

They had jumped me not two weeks prior, six heavy-set bodies twisting my arms into submission, punching, kicking, and dragging me along the segregation unit floor to a strip cell, where the struggle continued, and they burnt my leg against a scalding water pipe as they held me down.

They had laughed, enjoying their chance to restrain the flash Londoner, reminding me that I was in Portland now. Here, no one left for another prison; it was the last stop, and they boasted of having broken those much tougher than me. 'One trip here, on the double,' was their rule, and I was to obey or suffer more of the same.

I passed him on the landing, feeling the coarse heat of his contempt, and in my mind, I smashed his head across the iron bannisters. 'No worries, governor,' I said. Their penchant for quick, reactive violence here had made me rethink my strategy. I'd play the long game; show one face, hide the others. However, I would plan and scheme for escape and retribution. The cell door slammed behind me, and I was alone again with the torture of my thoughts, enveloped in silence.

Incarceration is a profound thing for the mind. It can educate, punish, torture, destabilise, or even liberate. It all depends on one's core, the strength of their convictions, the resilience that runs through them like the lettering in a stick of rock. The conditions within these walls test and stretch even the strongest men, demanding the summoning of strength they never knew they had. In my cell, with its simple wooden table and cupboard, the solitary chair, and the blue metal bed bolted to the floor, I found solace. The walls, painted in depressive blues, showcased the old brickwork. Now, as the sun dipped and shadows crept in, this space became my sanctuary.

My world here was ten by eight feet. Each day, I readied myself for the unknown, training rigorously before the doors opened. The natural chemicals released by my body during those intense workouts momentarily freed me. As the sun rose and faded, I'd sit drenched in sweat, my thoughts clearer than ever.

The prison housed around 800 inmates, mostly Welsh and from nearby areas. There was a rugby field by the quarries just outside, which we seldom used. The prison, divided into halls named after admirals like Nelson, Benbow, and Raleigh, maintained stringent security and an unbending regime. On the sports field, where grudges often surfaced, I played with a weapon secreted away, prepared for anything.

Freedom was a constant yearning. The streets of East London, the bustle of Bethnal Green Road, the familiar comfort of Kelly's pie and mash, and the 24-hour bagel shop in Brick Lane - all were far from me now. The lively evenings of Shoreditch, Hoxton, Bow, and Limehouse seemed a world away.

The cries of the seagulls, harsh as they swept past my window, were a reminder of the life beyond these walls. I stood on the chair, gazing past the prison walkway to the open sky, feeling like an alien in this place. My one ally was Connie, a sharp-minded Londoner from Islington. Together, in solidarity and brotherhood, we maintained our sanity amidst the chaos. We'd already been in fights - one in the TV room, another in the steamy tension of the communal showers, where we'd faced off against those who thought to intimidate us.

The screws ran this place, treating Connie and me like exotic nuisances to be closely monitored. They nicknamed us Ronnie and Reggie, and their watchful eyes were ever-present.

As night fell, I surveyed the prison's formidable defences, calculating distances, heights, weaknesses, and possibilities. I examined the iron bars of my window, noting a weakness I'd been exploiting for weeks.

The evening settled into its rhythm, and I steeled myself for the night ahead, contemplating an escape attempt that simmered in my thoughts...

Portland Borstal, 1988, Aged 17

I walked the tight length of the reception holding cell. It was less used and had a different feel and energy than those on the main prison wing. The red floor, shined by the orderly, squeaked as I paced. A wooden bench and pale blue wall with a grey, white ceiling. I could hear the keys pulled on a key chain to open a cell door further along to the right. I listened. My heart was full of excitement, of the unknown, of embracing a new-found freedom.

Freedom.

I went to a small lightly barred window at the end of the room. The side windows were screwed and wouldn't open. I could see the sun of a fair day. I could sense a soft breeze out there, and I could feel it massage my face already as I walked away from this place. I waited for the reception officer to bring the rattle of his keys towards me. That would be freedom to me. The spark of it, the start of claiming my life back. One of them whistled out there as they signed a prisoner out, completed the paperwork, issued his discharge grant and travel warrant.

The orderly whistled, another scrubbed the corridor with the industrial cleaner. It was a good job, I thought to myself, reception orderly in a prison. Specially picked by security as a goody two-shoes, no trouble, and not a security risk. Trusted. I paced, I felt elation at finally having completed this sentence, this test, this torture. Within the hour I would leave this place, I would be in London three hours later. A smile spread across my face, and I felt it through my body, now chiselled from relentless training, from an unnatural but stable thirteen months away from drink, parties and late nights wandering. I was ready for the streets. I was ready to execute my dreams of wealth and remaining forever with friends. I would keep my liberty. No one would ever take it again. I would be clever, I would stay away from crime, gangs, police and trouble. I would leave these walls where pain, loss, depression dwelt. I would learn the needed lessons and make a life that lasted.

Standing at the window, squinting into the brightness of the sun, bright rays transmitted downwards infused with the calming lightness of a soft wind. I could feel it. More crashing doors.

Jesus, I considered… and my mind thought of the nearly falling out cell window back on the house block. How I swerved that was beyond me. I considered the desperation of this place. That it had impelled me to fight and scratch. To dream, to dig, to push and pull at people, places and brickwork to end the torture of my mind and escape.

It had been a miscalculation.

I sat on the wooden bench a moment. The memory filled me. The silence of the night as the prison had slept and a changing wind whistled. It is a strange landscape, the inside of a prison at night. Darkness hung, lingered. Silence floated timidly. Always, in the distance or close, splitting the peace, jingling keys. The padded feet of the night guard as he checked the landings the other side of the door and his check-in key turning somewhere on the wing every hour. The changing wind was a cover. I had fixed my eyes on the escape route in front of me. Sweat rolled down into my eyes. I was on the second floor, I knew that if I was successful, the whole window would drop with a thud below into the quietness. I listened for alarms from outside the window and the other side of the light green metal cell door. I dug, I scratched, I pushed and braced. I hissed and swore and ruined my hands, trying to get the window out. I had looked out at the green of the moat, and I had seen a bit to climb. I had makeshift spikes made from pieces of metal worked into a pair of boots to scale the fence. I had fashioned a rope from shredded sheets tied around my waist. I would have the green wool sheets to cushion the piercing razor wire, and I had plotted the section I would climb next to the side of the gatehouse that would help me scale the wall. I had pushed and leveraged the barred window. It was the way out for escape, I had realised. I had braced it, dug with a piece of metal with my ears as my guide, a long and sharp piece of metal from the bedframe and a length of wood as my tools, I pushed and scratched the wall and the concrete that fixed the frame of the bars.

I had felt so close, but it would not move as I had hoped and expected… I'd had a bolt of clarity of what would happen to me if I failed but worse if I was discovered attempting to escape.

The reception orderly hit the outside of my cell with the spinning plate of industrial cleaner. My mind jolted to the realisation of imminent freedom.

'Thank Fuck,' I reasoned. I remembered the worry of that night. I had made papier-mâché from toilet roll. The window frame although solid was hanging off on one corner. I had plugged the hole and had dressed-up my nights work. I had put toothpaste along it as if laying filler in an office refurbishment, and I had even sprinkled dust and dirt on it to add age. I had not slept a wink for two nights for fear of capture and then had been shrewd and got a move from the cell to another part of the wing. I felt a momentary pang of guilt for whoever was in that cell when they discovered my work and hoped that someone wouldn't get beaten for it.

'Gillen…' He stood there blocking the light, the key in the cell door was fixed to a belt on his waist. He weighed me up, glanced quickly at the blue file in his hand.

'Stephen Anthony Gillen?'

'Yes.'

'This way'.

I followed, across the shining red tiles, with closed green metal cell doors with peepholes either side. The whistling had stopped. The humming of the floor cleaner. White crashing closing gates.

…It would soon be over. I was happy the escape had failed. I had got away with it, and the bad ending it would have brought on me. I had done my time and paid my dues.

'Sign here,' he pointed to the line on the other side of the counter. There were three of them now. 'And here…here.'

'Your address?'

'No fixed abode.'

My stored property was presented in the see-through plastic bag it had waited in. A good quality watch, few coins. A little worn address book. Keys. There were some trainers, a few pieces of clothes… not much to show for a life. Apart from jewellery a friend kept diligently for me, I had nothing. He counted the money out in front of me on the hatch.

'One hundred and seven pounds… and thirty pence. Sign here… Travel warrant'.

It was in a white envelope. Two weeks social security money.

The screw looked at me knowingly. He reckoned I would be back. Along the way we had come, faster across the same route.

My body felt lighter. Excitement knotted my stomach.

London, 1989 Aged 18

I stood in the small kitchen at the back of the house, its ceiling adorned with wooden beams. At eighteen, I was young, fit, and agile. Bare-chested and clad in jeans, I fried eggs on the hob, my thoughts back to the night before. It was the era of hip-hop, drum and bass, and house music, and the previous evening, after embarking on a secretive journey and heeding cryptic directions, we had found ourselves at the illegal rave, Sundance. As the eggs hissed and popped in the pan, memories of the pulsating beats, the field alive with dancing figures, the entrancing rhythm, the beaming faces, and the scantily clad women gyrating in gilded cages consumed me. The memory of the ecstasy that had surged through me and the reckless drive down narrow country lanes dominated my mind.

My step-father, Michael, emerged from the shadows cast by the dimly lit staircase, just up from sleep. Caught and surprised at finding me there with strange eyes that were uncommonly wide.

His broad shoulders and muscular arms were as imposing as ever as he leaned in, his face close to mine.

'...Go on then, do it!'

I turned away. My infrequent visits to the house in recent years were the result of striking out on my own, especially after Callum and I had fortuitously acquired £400,000 worth of gold, watches, and diamonds two years prior. I had transformed into a robust and self-reliant young man, with a spark in my eye and the world at my feet. Since then, we had never looked back. An unyielding fervour burned within me, confidence permeated my actions, and a steadfast gleam settled in my gaze.

'...All those years, Stephen. If you're going to do it, do it now!'

His bare cheek and the profile of his face were exposed. He had been a decent man but also a tormentor who had intimidated and bullied us throughout the years.

'Finish it, Stephen...' he urged again.

My gaze sharpened. The image before me was jarring. He loomed large, yet his granite-like shoulders belied the vulnerable, remorseful figure that stood before me.

I observed him closely. He seemed earnest, bracing for the blow he expected to come. With the spatula still in my hand, I found myself rooted to the spot, unwilling to act.

A wave of revulsion and rekindled anger surged within me, then receded just as quickly. The kitchen, pristine and home to a corner cupboard filled with delicate china and ornamental vases, became the backdrop for our confrontation under the soft morning light.

As the impulse for retribution faded, so too did my long-held desires. I had never spoken the words. Through the years he had never heard me call him by this name, had never heard me utter the words.

I said, 'Dad, leave it. It's OK, don't worry about it…'

Armed Robbery 1992 Age 20

We had taken every anti-surveillance precaution we knew. We removed the batteries from our throw-away phones in our pockets to avoid tracking. Coming from our separate places in London, one from Bermondsey, the other from Bethnal Green, we took the tube, making a couple of swift train changes each, blending into the crowds. Meeting at Tower Bridge, we reached the car and then drove to the decaying Bonamy Estate in South Bermondsey. Near the paper factory, beneath the estate in the desolate underground car park, we made our first car change and transferred into a white Volkswagen.

We were travelling through the heart of Bermondsey, keeping a watchful eye on the banks, the jewellery shops, and the security vans. In the passenger seat, my gaze sweeping over the pavements and the people outside, I said, 'We need to be doubly careful today, Connie. If it's not right, we pull out, agreed?'

He was broader, taller, but the grey-white streak still marked his jet-black hair, and his demeanour remained unchanged. Watching the road, his serious and trained eyes were focused just like mine. He replied, steady and soft, 'Of course, Steve, we don't want to get nicked. I'm feeling what you are. If we get caught, they'll throw away the key.'

Then he smiled. 'You never know, maybe someone else will do the prison time for us.' His eyes sparkled with mischief as he glanced sideways. He hadn't changed one bit over the years, I thought. Even in the most chaotic and darkest moments, he could turn on his humour like a switch. Outside, the afternoon threatened rain. It was a busy late December, and the fading evening light would soon give way to brisk inky darkness.

I remained vigilant. We turned the car, heading back to East London, passing Connie's mother's house on Southwark Park Road, and over to the place where firearms and ammunition were stored.

A sense of desperation had closed in around our world in recent weeks. My universe had folded inward like a collapsing building, each level being destroyed at an alarming rate. Like a general atop a hill, observing the landscape below, I felt the ground shifting against me, the shadows of my impending isolation creeping closer. I would be consumed. I pushed the swell of negative emotions down, to a place of inner strength. The cocaine I'd taken earlier was still coursing through me, trapping the cold clarity I needed to push forward. We circled the roundabout near the Rotherhithe Tunnel three times to check for tailing cars.

Connie Slaney floored the accelerator. The car sped up, his face set in a stony mask. I reclined in my seat as we plunged deep under the River Thames, into the concrete claustrophobia of the tunnel. My thoughts were a whirlwind, honed and focused solely on the heist ahead. Glancing in the rear-view mirror, we had been vigilant, constantly observing, feeling, and testing throughout the day. I was determined to turn defeat into victory, to transform a fate of lost liberty into triumph. I could sense the hum of the car beneath me, the echo of the tunnel. I steeled myself internally. The car continued on, the tunnel lights flickering at the periphery of my vision. I stared ahead, numb, oblivious to all but the cage of my personal thoughts. Mentally, I prepared.

Reflection

Reflecting on the essence of our existence, it's clear that we're woven into the tapestry of life, part of a greater collective, not solitary entities. Our core objective is to grow in understanding, to expand our consciousness. Life's challenge isn't solely in seeking the truth but in peeling back the layers of deception that often cloud our path.

In the orchestration of the universe, nothing is random. There's a design to the good that unfolds, a pattern that we're a part of. Our voyage through life, with its trials and triumphs, is paramount, eclipsing any destination we aim to reach. If we harness our potential with precision and purpose, the seemingly impossible becomes attainable.

To ascend to our fullest potential, to touch the greatness within us, we must transcend our own limitations, step beyond the ego that often hinders us. Each small, deliberate action can set the foundation for leaps of progress. History has shown us that those who've made an impact, who've altered the course of events, have done so not without cost. They faced mockery, exclusion, betrayal, and adversity.

Our pursuit of higher understanding, of enlightenment, comes with the expectation of discomfort. It's in embracing this journey, with its inherent hardships, that we exhibit the utmost humility. It is through enduring, through overcoming, that we fulfil our purpose and contribute to the collective elevation of humanity.

*Aunt Madge with a friend
in her younger days*

Uncle Jack

Uncle Gerard with his dogs

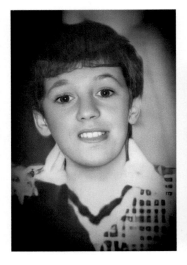

Age 6 in Belfast

My grandmother who died when my mother was 16

Uncle Tom with Aunt Madge

With my sister Teresa and cousins, aged 11

In Hull Special Unit 1997

Wedding Day,
Whitemoor Prison 1998

Where I almost died in 1988

With Michael, Shaun and Brendan 2015

On stage with Kul Mahay -
Two Extremes 2018

With my pal from the old
days in the Est End, Jack
Ramadan 2019

With Oscar winner Tim Cavaign & CEO Twickenham Film Studio
Andrew Boswell at the private screening of Bohemian Rhapsody 2018

Receiving ny nominees award for the Sunak Peace Prize in 2019

Speaking to dignatories on International Peace Day 2019

On BBC Prime Time _What The Paper's Say_ 2019

Fiming in my old manor -
Bethnall Green 2019

With BBC Presenter Sally Burdock after
filming _What the Papers's Say_ 2019

A moment of contemplation by the Thames 2020

161

Filming for Sky's _The Essex Murderers_ 2021

With Lucia & Stevie 2020

Flying to Zurich 2020

Enjoying a coffee at the Oxo Tower 2021

CHAPTER 4

A Life Of Crime

"When a man is denied the right to live the life he believes in, he has no choice but to become an outlaw."

— Nelson Mandela

Organised Crime 1989, Age 18

The start of criminality was for most, due to the adversity of circumstances and environment. For me I had had a great deal of upheaval and abuse before I even contemplated a life of crime. The stories could be different but in these streets were poverty, pain, emotional baggage, a lack of appropriate role models, inadequate knowledge or resources, necessary social support systems and meaningful opportunities. History shows us, true long-lasting peace unfortunately is forged by war, not by trusting others to do the right things and abide by the rules. As we have become more advanced at converting our environments into populated cities from the ancient feudal systems of the past the 'haves' had become less, and the 'have nots' vastly more.

'I haven't got no money here, honestly,' said the wiry man with flecked greying hair in a blue tracksuit bottom and a grubby white tee-shirt. I could see the panic running through him. It was the afternoon, the pub had been closed, but the three of us had walked straight in an open-door way.

We had a knife somewhere, but my partner Paul had found a rounders bat behind the bar.

'Expecting trouble? 'He was a big lump Paul. He looked at me and winked.

'We just have it there,' the publican said. 'we get trouble some nights, drunks.'

'Are you taking the fuckin' piss?' I was behind him, quick. On purpose so he could feel me near him.

'No, I...'

My eyes flashed, 'You stuck my pals name up. The old bill are there now... Do you know what they found...'

'I didn't... they just asked a few questions. I told em' I didn't know anything,' he pleaded. His hands moved around, and he didn't know where to settle them.

Paul said, 'Cut him!'

The publican folded. Paul had the bat in his hand.

I stepped in. 'Leave him... now I'm not in the mood for your moody bollocks.'

'Fuck this, cut him.' Paul repeated.

'I'm only a publican, I'm not involved in none of this.'

Paul glowered at him. My other pal Zak narrowed his eyes, 'The money' he demanded. 'where is it?'

I had stepped between them. We were behind the bar, rows of bottles with every drink at the side of us.

'Just leave him a minute,' the publicans' eyes were wide. I made them stand back a little more.

'Now I'm telling you,' I had him by the elbow, guiding him into the centre of the pub, 'We lost all sorts... the money. We want five grands for our losses...' I looked at Paul, Zak was beside him swinging the knife. 'They'll cut you to ribbons. If I can promise you one thing I can promise you that. Shall...'

A young boy had appeared from the cellar steps. He was about thirteen and looked frozen to the spot. I ignored him.

'Okay...Okay, Okay... in the cellar.' The fear dripped from him. A hand rose slightly, shaking, 'I can sort it, I can sort it.'

Zak had locked the front pub doors and watched the boy. We walked, the publican, Paul and I down the cellar steps and under the pub. The concrete floor held a wide-open space stacked with crates, beer barrels, pipes, and tubes to feed the bar. I could smell the dank dust, beer, sense the cobwebs and creepy-crawlies.

The publican opened a safe. There was money counted. It was short. Eighteen hundred pound short.

Paul snarled 'This is bollocks. I'm sick of being treated like a mug. You've brought this on yourself, you should keep out of other people's business, keep your mouth shut. I'll be back for the rest next week.'

He was not to think he was getting away with it. The publican, a slippery character, was used to playing Peter against Paul, at playing two ends against the middle. He had taken the piss and he knew it.

He followed us up the stairs, round the side of the pool table. 'I'll see you next week.' He said.. We blanked him on the way out.

Zak was laughing. Paul moaned, said it was a liberty. There were too many people thinking they could have everyone over. I agreed. If you let one person get away with it. There would be lists of people lining up. Sure, clean strict boundaries. That's what it was going to be all of em'. We got in the car; the evening was drawing in slightly as we drove through Hackney and Dalston.

The streets were littered with people. The traffic, always fierce around this area thinned a little as we moved closer to Hackney Road and Bethnal Green. I watched, rows of flats, streets, a concrete jungle flitted past. Every street had a memory here, I thought. The darkness changed these neighbourhoods.

When the last remnants of light were gone, all would change and metamorphose.

Busy walkways for school children, mothers and professionals, would transform into a warren of cops chasing criminals, drug dealers and junkies. The nightmare, hidden in the brightness of daylight, would then descend with night's arrival into no go areas, closed doors, prostitutes, gangsters, racing police cars and crack houses amongst the slums. It was a cold, hard place London. East London could be one of the darkest parts of it.

We had planned many an operation and graft there, out of the way upstairs. We met Johnny, a good friend and grafting partner, Dicki, his father a short, serious man who owned it. We were stuck around the half bar and I sipped a coke. There was music on, people laughed, watched the TV, held drinks and talked. There was another room with a private bar upstairs. We would use it sometimes for parties, meet ups, planning jobs and discussions.

I left them, we had split the money, they had laughed and replayed the incident. I had listened, I had a leadership position amongst the group and I kept myself measured as always, held my power.

I had said I had to go, left them in a happy mood, drinking and reminded them of things that had still to be done, people who had to be seen and things that had to be seen to.

I had a last look at them, huddled, smiling and laughing at the bar as I left. The evening was still young. The cars passing me on the road beside me had their lights on as the even light of the day waned. I had my head down into the collar of my three-quarter length black mac as I walked forward along the busy road into the fresh evening. The homeless man sat by the off-licence in tattered dirty clothes and a beard. His hand was out and his head down.

I took a hundred quid from the money in my pocket.

'You got to look after yourself my friend,' I said softly.

He looked at the notes I had pushed in his hands. 'God bless you. Really, sir. God bless you!'

I stood and I listened to him. I had seen him before and knew his sad story. In the shop doorway shielding from the drizzling rain, by the entrance to the flats avoiding the cutting wind. I saw him, and I always took the time to stop, talk and give him some food money. I instructed him to get some food, to make sure to at least find a bed for the night. These streets, hard for all, open to a few, were unforgiving to most.

I took the next right and into the back streets and flats by Colombia road. My mind was filled with the events of the day, the problems of the week. The people, places and things to watch out for. The night two weeks previously outside Camden Palace crept back into my thoughts. The anger coursed through me, a sudden, uncontrolled and gripping thunder and lightning movement that tingled my body, put a churning in my stomach and pounding in my head. I saw my route from the club, no shirt on and blood that wouldn't stop, the cold escape into the night with rising fear and panic. Then the seizing unaltered anger. My friends had come with the guns and weapons to the meeting point. I had cleaned myself of blood in the cab station toilet filling the bin with bloodied green paper napkins, and then looked at the weapons in the opened car boot on the corner. They had given me a jumper to cover my nakedness and shivers. A pump action, baseball bats, golf clubs, a pistol with a full clip and a flair gun. My three friends had stood and listened with concerned, angry faces.

In the background, far across the main roads above the sound of the traffic, dance music coming from the Palace thumped with the movements of bouncers and people at the front of the club. My mind was crazy, my rage a torrent. I had the flare gun; I was going to wait for them to come out and use it to burn a hole in the night. We would use the guns; the bats were a back-up. They would pay tonight for nearly taking my life and the revenge of it would be good enough. My crew had listened, they knew me well, but my best friend Del stepped up, he had said I wasn't of sound mind, the blood was dripping again heavily from my head. We would all be nicked if we persisted, I needed to go to the hospital, get stitches. They put their arms around my shoulders. The boot was closed firmly, the weapons transported in one car. I was guided to another that would take me to A & E. They wouldn't get away with it, I had been promised. We knew where they were. They were easy to get.

I walked at a steady pace in the evening air as I remembered. I was aware of the five stitches in the side of my head from the swung bottle two weeks previously. It ached, itched. I had reached the Birdcage pub on the corner of Colombia Road. A busy place of known villains and family friends, where we would spend many a private night drinking and dancing. I took the road round and swung into old Bethnal Green Road. My mind still wandered.

I thought of them in the pub back in Hackney Road. News was, that Gary Hutton and another close friend of mine, had been arrested by National Crime Squad with three hundred thousand pounds worth of counterfeit fifty-pound notes in a hotel room four days ago. It had been a setup by a News of the World investigative reporter and it had been all over the papers. The paper had called them an 'East London crime family in Italian suits.' When they had told me about the meeting, I had said it sounded hooky and not to go. I shook my head as I thought back to the conversation, sometimes you just 'knew' when something wasn't right, well at least I did, and I wished they'd listened.

The road grew darker, small, dirty cream bricked flats were either side of me. The streetlights had dipped and the shadows lengthened, a kid on a bike passed me. I walked, hands deep in my pockets, alone in the night with my thoughts. The sound of my shoes broke the night steadily. My breath was appearing now in front of me, darkness was here, threatening with a coldness that forced through my coat and into my bones.

I considered my life. The paper, the article in the News Of The World - Crime families, gangsters, organised crime... The Underworld. My eyes narrowed with annoyance; they wrote this stuff but the reality was much different. It was more bleak, cold, cruel, emotional and present, deceptive and painful.

I walked, glancing at my watch made me hurry my pace. On old Bethnal Green Road, and the tall grey flats of Charles Dickens House rose high in front of me. Lights from people's flats littered it clustered in the darkness. I kept going, up towards Shoreditch and The Boundary estate.

People were naturally territorial. They had a problem fully trusting the unknown and stuck with people and places they knew. The unknown meant uncertainty and change was always uncomfortable. They called it the underworld. Mafia, Organised Crime but actually it was a kind of dysfunctional family. Tightknit firms and groups that vied for position, money, dominance with the power and leverage notoriety would bring.

I walked, kicked a stone in front of me.

I knew the criminal families of East London and beyond, of the wider city and beyond were made, not born. They congregated together in their actions and thinking. In this loosely connected labyrinth some were more prominent than others, more resourceful and skilled. Some would have worked together; others would know each other. They may have heard of each other, but many would be close to people and family members in the same circles. Many prominent criminal families in the East End would have gone to school together, forging the relationships and circumstances that would stretch out like the branches of a tree, into other boroughs where these wider relationships and alliances would repeat themselves.

I had heard it said that there were approximately eleven hundred criminal gangs in London. Some of them had a hierarchy, internal rules, structures, and were highly organised. Like a corporation with different divisions, a pecking order and levels of leadership and skill, the criminal fraternity would stretch out across London. Across the country, city to city and gang to gang. Then from nation to nation like stock and bonds and commodities. Money was the name of the game -

reputation, power and violence the tools that carved and maintained a fast direction forward.

Organised Crime, 1989, Age 18

We met to look at the guns at a pub in Watney Street, near Limehouse and the East End Docklands; a friend who I'd known for a long time and someone else who was close to him and who knew who I was. A normal-looking meeting in a busy pub notorious for the inhabitants who frequented it between three men who were not there to discuss everyday things. The Thomas Neale pub in Watney Market was a place I knew well, it was one of the collection of pubs in that historic area, like the Hungerford Arms or the Dean Swift that were frequented by the Watney Street mob.

I was nineteen and although from Bethnal Green, I knew this area well and had many friends here. We stood at the bar talking in hushed tones over our drinks; it was a well-used open-plan pub with a separate area at the back near the toilets and pool tables. It was busy, a street office to a few, with eyes that would watch when a stranger was present. Laughter filled the air, sideways glances looked up from drinks, banter that weaved with the red carpet, wooden floor, and the stale smell of alcohol and tobacco.

It was great to catch up; we spoke of a few local known names and the issues around them. There was a quarter of a tonne of hash that had been hidden in a scrapyard and had gone missing. Talk of the people who were known to us, who were looking for it, kicking down doors, and threatening local 'faces' to find it. We spoke of the fallout between two friends of ours who were well-known East End villains and their wish to kill each other on sight. There was talk of stolen goods that had been hijacked from lorries and were going cheap. There was a discussion about counterfeiters and a mention of problems being caused locally.

We left the bar as quickly as we had met there, the fresh night air hitting our senses as the alcohol rose in our minds. We were in great form. We felt in good company; we were so busy in our own problems and affairs that we only met now when there was real business to attend to. Walking through the busy narrow shop-filled main walkway of the market, our conversation from the bar carried on, speaking of the police, who had been nicked, who was suspected of being under observation. Who was a wrong 'un, who to stay away from. Who was flying and doing well with their operations and making the most money. We took a left towards Limehouse, the overhead bridge for the train was in front of us, and one of the exits into Shadwell Station. We hurried our pace, focused our minds together as we spoke in the fresh darkness of the late calm evening.

We travelled through tight back roads that we knew well. Rows of cold grey, faceless similar streets. Limehouse had got its name from the lime kilns in the area. The potters that crafted products for shipping companies in the East End Docks and the sailors who disembarked from their ships in the old days. The night air was filled with the vibrant sounds of the main roads of Commercial Road and the Highway. The overhead tube clattered on the track somewhere close. Police sirens raged close by. Shouting, laughter, activity from the shops floated in the air. We shuffled more as a tight unit now sought the darkness of the shadows the street doorways offered. Our voices had dropped an octave. A left, then a right with a smooth quick pace, we passed near Whitehorse Road aiming for my friend's container near Ropemakers Fields, a quiet private place on the second floor, where no one would disturb us.

'It's a great tool,' my friend offered.

'A good nine-mil, Steve. I've had no problems with it. There are a few longs. One is a side-by-side twelve bore. The other an Uzi. I can give you the Uzi for twenty-two hundred quid, the handgun thirteen hundred and fifty, the shotgun six hundred – but it's full length; you'll have to saw it off yourself. Plenty of ammunition for both, bro, and cartridges.' He had turned to me then, winking, his face calmed by the alcohol in his blood and happy. 'You wanted a short one, Steve? The nine?'

Matter-of-fact, measured, I said, 'Yeah, sounds good. Let me see them all, though. But if the nine mil is what I think it is, I definitely want it.'

We were close to the 'slaughter,' the private place where things could be hidden and clandestine work be done. I wondered why getting this gun had become a sudden priority in my life. A loose association of serious villains, one of them had come to me with a load of money and asked for an introduction to buy something heavy in the underworld of my connections. I had facilitated a meeting, and unbeknownst to me, that meeting had gone very badly. I was now highly sought after, with stories circulating of people armed and ready to shoot me on sight.

'Stevie, your lot had that lorry down in the city. Nice bit of work,' he said, his plain features blending into the crowd. His hands were buried in the pockets of his blue bomber jacket. 'Had it right off, didn't you!' His laughter was genuine.

'Yeah, nice bit of work. The information was spot-on,' I replied in a low, guarded tone.

'Any more of that parcel left? I could shift a bit of it for you.'

'Nah, all done, only bits left, and they're already spoken for,' I sidestepped, cautious. People talked too much and didn't think. To say more was to talk out of turn. 'We' had done well out of it, but the reality of what had actually happened was far different from what they imagined.

The 'jump-up' in the city was a lorry in transit, loaded with six hundred thousand pounds worth of Gucci gear. We'd received clear, targeted information. We knew the summer collection was in there, along with bags and accessories. We'd followed in two cars, the route for the hijack meticulously planned.

When the lorry reached the quiet stretch of road we'd chosen, our car overtook it, forcing it to a grinding halt. The driver, amazed and panicked, was quickly relieved of his duties at gunpoint and secured in the boot of our car. One of us drove the lorry to a predetermined location where the tracker was swiftly disabled, and the merchandise was transferred to another empty lorry waiting nearby.

'Ok, we're here, it's just inside.' The night seemed to close in around us, heavy clouds thickening with the late hour. We ascended the stairs, manoeuvring through heavy metal doors secured with latches and padlocks, guided by the sounds ahead. The door slammed shut behind us, sealing us in a room with windows overlooking a desolate yard, an unused expanse of wasteland by the train tracks. The dim light from the windows, combined with some light from the next room, allowed us to see. He retrieved it from behind the plumbing pipes, wrapped in a dirty green cloth - a nine mil. Taking the gun from his hands, I noted the black stains on the cloth and the unmistakable scent of oil. The weight of the black handgun felt right in my grasp as I ejected the magazine.

'Fifteen in the magazine, one in the chamber,' he announced, bringing out a long gun case containing the shotgun and an Uzi wrapped in a brown towel.

The clip snapped back into place with a satisfying click. I checked the safety with my thumb.

'This is heavy... beautiful, isn't it?' he said, cradling the black metallic Uzi with its unfolded stock resting on his shoulder.

'That wasn't a bloody question,' he quipped, his grin etched in the half-darkness. He aimed the Uzi out of the window, into the night blanketing the unused ground by the derelict building.

'Beautiful, eh. This could take out an army. But watch it, if you leave it on fully automatic, you'll empty the thirty-two-round clip in seconds.'

I examined the nine mil, the Uzi, and the shotgun removed from its case. I'd held and checked each one, appreciating their form and potential. I already owned other weapons, including a shotgun, but the handgun appealed to me - it was a perfect fit for my hand, the weight reassuring. Concealment was key, and a test was in order. We positioned ourselves at the window, peering into the darkness of the wasteland, the arches supporting the overhead train tracks barely visible. The roll of money in my pocket was a tangible reminder of the night's business.

'Only thing with automatics, they're dodgy. Prone to jamming. I've always preferred revolvers, .38s, got any of those?' I asked.

He shook his head. 'The Smith & Wesson Special I had is gone. But this nine mil is reliable. It's been tested. Never let me down.'

I chambered a round, flicked off the safety, and readied myself.

'They're behind me in the shadows as I listen.

'When the next train comes, I'm going to let one fly.'

'Aim down by the derelict buildings,' Panic in his voice.

I aimed into the shadows of the broken brickwork of the collapsed building, checked it was desolate. 'Well, I'm not going to aim at the bloody train, am I!' I retorted with a tight smile as the others snickered at the absurdity of it.

The distance rumbled with the oncoming train, a thundering noise growing closer. I steadied my aim at a piece of old wood propped against the derelict building's shadowed wall. The silhouette of overgrown grass, trees, and bushes stood stark against the darkness. The train's movements reverberated through the night, the vibrations resonating against the window's metal frame.

Holding the weapon firmly with both hands, I waited for the right moment. As the train approached, my finger tensed on the trigger. Two shots cracked through the night - CRACK! CRACK! The recoil nudged my grip upward, but I quickly adjusted, aiming more precisely with each subsequent shot. The train, now my auditory shield, continued its journey, blending its mechanical roars with the echoes of my gunfire.

I observed the aftermath for a moment, feeling the weight of the gun in my hands. The cold seclusion of my reality settled in, a stark contrast to the fleeting power of the fired rounds.

As an enforcer now, it was my job to intimidate, to retrieve money owed, by any means, and nothing said you were serious like a handgun to the head. I usually gave them to the count of ten and I rarely got past five before they were offering me some payment or a deal. There was good money to be had in collecting debts, and I was excellent at what I did.

Back in the urban sprawl, three men sat in a car, surveying a club entrance with keen interest. They were well-acquainted with the venue, having frequented it on numerous occasions. Located just off Kingsland Road in Shoreditch, the club boasted a beer garden fenced off to the side - a detail not lost on the men as they watched partygoers enjoy their drinks.

The train's intrusive clatter above them disrupted the night, a stark reminder of the city's never-ending pulse. The road thrummed with life; people bustled by as bouncers, large and imposing in their suits, guarded the club's entrance.

The man in the back, his presence made larger by his dark attire and cap, leaned forward, his gloved hand gripping a pistol.

'What do you reckon?' he asked, his voice barely rising above the din.

'Looks busy,' replied his companion, a thin-faced man whose voice carried the rasp of experience.

'We don't care. Gillen's done for, along with anyone keeping him company,' declared the man in the blue coat, his sharp features set in determination.

With their intent clear, they exited the car and briskly crossed the street, their hands never straying far from the weapons concealed in their pockets. The bouncers stepped aside, the thumping beat of CeCe Peniston's 'Finally' spilling out from within.

The trio navigated through the throng, searching for Stephen Gillen. They moved with a hunter's precision, scanning each face, checking each corner. After an exhaustive search, they confronted a familiar face.

'You seen Stevie Gillen in here?'

'Nah, he was here,' the man replied, casually patting the handgun in his jacket.

'Where is he now? It's important - we've got something for him.'

'He left about half an hour ago. Headed towards Roman Road, I think.'

As the music shifted to Alison Limerick, the men huddled, cursing their timing. Stephen Gillen had slipped through their grasp, leaving them to stew in the night's frustration.

Under Observation, 1989 Age 18

I had crossed the little green in the middle of the high flats. Past the wooden benches where people hung out drinking and smoking, by the tall wire and fencing of the small football pitch, over the grass and stood at the little wooden gate at the ground floor flat on the Boundary Estate.

'Look who it is,' she grinned, 'long time no see,' and her steady laugh filled the night air.

I smiled. We had always been the deepest of friends and she had always looked out for me.

There were three of them.

They sat just in the concreted garden, by the short wall on two deck chairs. Lily, brown eyes shining, well-kept mousey brown hair hanging at her shoulders and a cup of tea being nursed in her hands. Harry was beside her, a big man with a presence, he was always immaculate, the light above them bounced off his sliver, grey hair and highlighted the smoke in the air from the cigarette he smoked.

'Alright, Stephen.' He smiled, a cheeky smile that showed mischief. Harry Draper was well known in London. A half traveller from South London, him and his brother Alfie had fought through life the hard way. They were fierce fighting men. They had had many businesses and were now in the furniture and welding trade with outlets all over London. I stood there, it was a safe place, protected. They were like family, Harry had always treated me just like one of his own kids, and I respected him very much for it.

The door was ajar.

Callum appeared, in an expensive, dark blue suit, a white shirt opened at the neck, his dark brown hair gelled back. He pushed through them at the door and his dark eyes glared at me.

'Alright, Steve. I was waiting for you. We need to talk.' He was up the path and his hand squeezed the side of my arm slightly. 'How you been, OK?'

'Where you going Callum?' It was Lily, an engaging grin on her mouth, enquiring eyes.

We were at the black Mercedes and looked back towards them. 'Got to go somewhere. Just down the road'.

'Bye Stephen, look after yourself now,' she was at the other side of the gate in jeans, hands pulling a red coat tight against the chill of the night. She smiled widely. Bright red and her eyes searched mine with a knowing look.

'I will, Lily…'

The car flew forward. I saw a last look at her behind me, the night swallowing her as we raced forward.

There was incredulity in Callum. A laugh at his lips, anger in his voice.

'They're on to us!' he roared.

'What?'

'The other people. I'm telling ya… I was in the flat with the Tandy, listening to Bethnal Green police station.' He spat the words out. We joined the flowing traffic. 'We're under observation, I'm telling you I can feel it.' He continued.

'Callum, strange things have been happening. You reckon they're there?'

'Steve, I know they fuckin are. I was down with that fuckin Robert at the club the other day… Flash sod, there's going to be a lot of trouble. I'm not sure I want to be part of a few things out here.' He turned from the steering wheel, an unsettled look on his face.

I answered, 'Is he for fuckin' real'.

'Stephen, there were terrible rows.' He added, 'I said I have something better, diamonds and bullion in Hatton Garden…'

He put his foot down and overtook a car in the fast-moving traffic. He was angry. His face in the half light of the car painted a worried picture.

'I bet they're bugging, Callum.' I offered. 'We'd better sweep everything. Got to stop meeting that mob down there.' My head was in overdrive. I was watching the cars all around us. A feeling of being closed in settled over me.

Callum raged, he talked about the boys from Whitecross Market, Old Street, 'I told 'em you have another one of them and we're going to be nicked!'

My watch said 10pm. I felt open, vulnerable. I needed to seek sanctuary. 'Callum, we're going to have to watch the meetings. Be careful. Watch the other mob, stay away from them.'

We were near Spitalfields and I tightened the button on my mac. 'Callum, drop me off in Kingsland.'

'Where you going?'

'I'm going to pop into the 'Weigh IN' club a minute.'

'The Weigh IN…? Fuck that! I'm staying away from that gaff.'

We had pulled into the side of the road. A train thundered along the overhead above me. The cold night air was in my lungs, the main door of the club with its bouncers across the road. At the wound down car window, over the deafening screech of the train, I said 'Callum be careful. Get everything swept. Watch talking anywhere. I'll phone you.'

He was there, a moment, a wide smile splitting his face, serious eyes and hands that made ready the car. 'Don't be in there too long.' he said.

It had been a quick visit to the club. I wanted to see Bob, the owner, as a friend of his, Dickie had asked me to pass on a message and ask him to do something. I had wanted to break the day, have one or two drinks as I assessed everything. I was on the manor, I knew people, it suited. I had got chatting to someone I knew from North London for a moment outside. We had navigated the crowd and with a drink, found a place to sit and talk. The music was belting my ears, I couldn't hear properly and was thinking of what Callum had said in the car. Then the trouble came, a man staggering with his drink had barged into us, stood on my boots and peppered the bottom of my jacked with spilt alcohol.

I had pushed him back and told him to 'Fuckin' mind', and because of it I had left the club early. The busy street was the same outside. There was a crowd at the kebab shop across the road. I had moved quickly, along Kingsland Road, hands in my pockets watching the people who paraded past me and were out for the night.

As I swung into Hackney Road I was unaware of the car with three men that came from Hoxton. Unaware that it was pulling into a side street on the opposite side of the road to the club. I was unaware that they searched for me and had firearms to shoot me on sight.

I felt the coldness of the evening wrap around me now. I should have brought a scarf. I thought of the conversation with the publican, the money he owed. There was the dull pain of the wound on the side of my head from Camden Palace. I thought of Lily, Harry and his engaging smile. The police, the observation. I walked on into Hackney Road by the bingo hall.

I was oblivious to the car that waited. The nature of the men in it, of their intent. They were parked by the shadow of the bridge, and they watched for me with eagle eyes. I could not hear the men who mentioned my name, could not see the guns they concealed, that they searched for me and were ready to use them.

On the road ahead of me, along the dirty street pavement an old woman in a headscarf walked, I watched her back as she moved away in front of me, the headscarf that was knotted tight at her face to shield her from the weather. There had been another time, another woman. She had walked with a headscarf, and she had been taken from me when I had needed her the most. There was a sadness in my eyes, a tugging at my heart and a longing in my mind.

Head down, I walked. I don't know how the men in the car missed me. Maybe I had a lucky guardian angel with me that night.

Kill or Be Killed, London 1989, Age 18

I wasn't even aware of the reprieve until a message was delivered a few days later. I'd facilitated a deal between a local Scottish gang based in the East End, and Travis who was looking for a large amount of E's and other drugs, unbeknown to me, it'd gone south. A shady set up had been organised at a local squat and when the deal had gone down, a member of the Scottish family had been robbed. They'd taken the money and the drugs, the family now needed a 'body' to pin it on and I was on the hook for a lot of money and or pain unless I could arrange for them to meet my original contact. Travis's crew wasn't one I knew well, they were a new gang, black guys that had started hitting the club scene. I was pretty annoyed as I hadn't made a shilling out of the deal, just done the introductions.

I'd spoken to Travis and he'd told me he hadn't been the one to stitch them up, he was full of himself, thought he was a big time dealer, I'd smoothed it with him and said he just needed to come along and explain that to the family. Honestly, I didn't think he'd have the balls to show up and I needed to arrange the meet somewhere I knew well and could potentially have back-up.

I'd arranged for us to meet at Willesden Lane, West London, an area close to where I had a flat and I knew the roads and had arranged a quick getaway should things get dicey. I sat with Callum waiting for Travis to arrive, it was getting tense as he was late and I thought I would have to make a move, when he showed up. I couldn't believe what I was seeing, he strode up wearing a flowing, white silk shirt half tucked in his trousers with a woman on his arm, looking for all the world like he was off to a club and not to explain a drug deal gone bad to one of the hardest families in the East End. I thought he must be having a laugh; everyone was trying to kill each other and he brought a date!

I quickly said my goodbyes and Callum & I took off. As we walked past a seating area a few guys that had pinged my antenna as being just slightly 'off', folded up the newspapers they'd been reading and stood up, I knew it was definitely time to get out of there.

Wrong Place Wrong Time, 1990, Age 19

The square mile of the City of London had pulled tighter the leash of its safety. The IRA had been stepping up its mainland bombing campaign and the security forces up and down the country were on high alert.

In the passenger seat of the XR3I my eyes scanned the traffic around us. My senses were heightened and I took in everything. People, places and things. The afternoon was bright, the day busy. There were three of us in the moving car as it moved sleekly through the winding East End traffic, but I knew I was more aware to the dangers than the others. There were weapons in the car. On my lap my blue/green jumper covered the sawn-off shotgun held there. The shops, moving people, cars and the cracking light and shadow of the hovering sun behind the buildings filtered past me. I kept watch and controlled my mind.

There were people gathered outside shops. I looked in the rear-view mirror, the black BMW had not long slotted in behind us. The red Volvo, soft top Audi, each car following far behind us was checked and recognised, remembered. I watched the smooth movements of the cars and their occupants a moment longer in the mirrors. A sign of nervousness, of haste and edging forward out of the line of traffic unnecessarily, of not belonging and going about normal business. A feeling. An instinct of eyes that stared too hard or for too long. My existence was a life of encoding signs. Signs I knew if you looked hard enough would teach you everything. Reading them well and correctly was keeping me alive.

I searched for the sign of a trap. Observation that worked in the background, constrained by what the eye could see.

There was something wrong, the car jolted forward as the driver changed gear. Silence. Strange things were happening round me. The cars that pulled out when I did, the noise of walky-talkies in the air, weird vans parked everywhere I went. It was in the air, a difference that dictated caution. My senses spiked now, it was in the churning in my gut, the light paranoia always in my thoughts, the shiftiness of my movements, the darting way my eyes travelled. I always felt like this when they watched me, when I was under observation. We had driven around the roundabouts a few times to draw them out, darted through the traffic lanes, changed vehicles under the flats in the underground carpark and pulled back slowly from suspect cars. Anti-surveillance techniques always needed to be used consistently.

We were planning the job, watching the route and preparing.

'Over there.' From John sitting in the back seat. His head turned, a hard face with a chiselled chin and a thin scar near his ear.

The blue Securicor van had just made its drop. The helmeted guard slid the black box through the hatch at the back of the van, thumped the back of it with an open hand.

I studied the scene.

'I see it,' I said. 'Looks like his first run. Bet it's a dummy. This is not BrinksMatt they're not carrying fifty k. This crowd are only insured to take twenty-five grand across the pavement'.

I imagined the guard behind the armoured interior. Inside, with the money cages.

The guard outside at the back was joined by another and together they waited, preparing to receive the boxes that were to come back to them produced from inside the van.

Ian had slowed the car as much as he could in the traffic. He stopped, made a 'u' turn so we could be close to the bank.

I studied the movement of the guards, the confidence of their walk, how synchronised their movements were. In front of the blue Securicor vehicle, a box van unloaded crates from its elevator at the back. Behind it cars looked parked badly. The shops either side of the bank, a baker's, a supermarket had a sporadic flow of moving customers.

'One Box... Two... Three...' I counted aloud. I watched the guards turn for the bank. What was wrong with this picture?

We had to position ourselves better. The next run would be the best. The trick was to be on them with force before they knew it, drag them both with guns to their heads quickly to the side of the van where the guard inside could see them. John would hold back the public at gun point. Holding one guard I would bang hard on the side of the van by the hatch. The guards would be pushed to the floor. We would shout to the crew inside that we had their colleagues.

They were to throw out all the money bags at the back of the van. They would execute our instructions or we would shoot.

Our car was turning in the road, quickly seeking the right spot for the ambush. There was traffic in front of us and behind, stationary. They awaited our final manoeuvre. The feeling of high fear mixed with propelling excitement thundered through my body. Like electricity it sparked and frizzled in my mind. Adrenaline hammered behind my eyes. Our car stopped, reversed. I looked at the front of the bank, the open glass doors…

I was imagining it in my head. The picture of it replayed clearly in my mind. They would soon appear, walking holding the long black boxes. Inside would be a tagged hard plastic pouch that held the separate denominations of notes and sometimes cheques. We would catch them quickly on the pavement. People would scream and gasp, guns would be pointed and orders given. Cars would stop. It would pass in slow motion. Primitive feelings would be evoked deep inside me, panic, fear, survival, anger and excitement. There would be a moment, like the flicking of a light switch and there would be no way back. Only forward to the end.

Ian moved away, we had seen all that we needed to and were ready for the job. All of the planning done, we just had to wait for the day it would come together.

'That's us. Let's get out of here Ian before we draw attention. We don't want to take out a dummy run, ain't worth the hassle.' I said. I felt the metal weight of the sawn-off shotgun in my hand comforting somehow, steadying me.

We drove away, each of us in our own heads, finalising our parts.

Suddenly Ian swore, he was from South London originally and didn't really know the roads, he'd taken a wrong turn and driven into Bishopsgate and then driven the wrong way into Liverpool Street, right into the middle of the City. We were trapped and couldn't turn around.

The sound of a siren behind us, 'Fuck!' swore Ian, but he acted quickly and pulled the car over to the side of the road. We were stuck, we had nowhere to go, it wasn't like we could tear off, we weren't going anywhere, so we had to try and style it out.

I moved the gun slowly down between my legs, not drawing any attention to my movements.

'Steady now, don't do anything stupid.' I said calmly, my brain was going one hundred miles an hour trying to process everything and mentally reviewing all of the incriminating evidence we had on us. John in the back of the car had jiff ammonia and snooker balls in a sock on him and the boot contained ammunition. This wasn't looking good.

The security in this area was on high alert and Ian's car had an X-plate. This flagged as something worth checking out and the officer came over to speak to us. Obviously, weren't looking like law abiding citizens and he radioed in for back up.

Ian had gotten out of the car and was giving the old bill a load of waffle, trying to smooth it over, but his car was stitching us up, they couldn't trace the details and at this point decided they needed to take us in for further checks.

The officer motioned for me to get out of the car, the adrenaline was coursing through me and I had just one chance to get out of this. As I got out of the car I kept the jacket in my hand over my front, holding the shotgun behind it, in one fluid movement I kind of stumbled as if I'd tripped a little bit, and I dropped the gun on the floor kicking it under the car. I didn't expect to get away with it but my life was at stake and I knew I had one chance, I acted on instinct.

They sat us in the back of the police car, whilst other officers got ready to drive Ian's car to the station, as it moved off I could clearly see the gun on the road, bold as brass. For some reason the old bill didn't see it, I guess they weren't expecting it and so weren't looking for anything untoward.

I chatted away trying to keep their attention so they didn't see the gun and we started to pull out, I started to think we might have gotten away with this, when, a pedestrian came running up to the car shouting 'Stop! Stop! There's a gun in the middle of the road!'

At this point all hell broke loose and we tried to get away, there were too many of them and we were nicked.

Being Clever, 1989 Aged 19

I lay in the police cell surprised that I hadn't been stripped, I was still wearing my own clothes, including the jacket that had hidden the gun. My eyes travelled the spartan white walls and ceiling, the blue floor, the inside of the metal green painted cell door.

The metal hatch on the door clashed back.

'Gillen..?'

I didn't move from my place laid out on the thin blue cell mattress. I could see at least two of them outside, faces shielded by the door grate.

'We have the gun from under the car.' Outside the door they stood. They waited for a response. 'A 12 bore shotgun illegally sawn-off,' the gruff crackling voice continued. 'You were arrested at the scene and your two mates have been arrested. John Jefferies. Ian Thompson…'

I moved to the door. Someone banged the metal cell door further down the hall, shouted for attention through the side of it. I stood by the door frame, peered outside to see who was speaking.

'You're going to be charged, Gillen with *Possession of a firearm with intent to commit an indictable offence.*'

He stood in the plain clothes of a zipped wind cheater and trousers. Tall with brown greying hair, bushy eyebrows, green searching eyes and a grizzled worn face. He continued in a rasping hiss, 'You're going to prison for a long, long time, Gillen. This time you…'

I looked at him, at the tight forced lips he spoke with.

'We know what you were doing at the bank near the Securicor van.' Interrupted the other policeman. A tall man, with a large wide frame in a blue Barbour jacket, his fierce features zeroed in on me. Clear blue eyes, set in a hard-chiselled face stared at me. His bald head with trimmed fair hair hovered closer to the open hatch.

'My name is DI Finch. I'm with SO8, Gillen, Scotland Yard Flying Squad. We know what you're up to, who your friends are. We know what you were planning today.'

'You've lost me. I was out with some friends for the day, took a wrong turn, ended up in the back of police car, fucking liberty.' I stood back from the metal opening. They were trying to trap me. Engage me in conversation and trip me up.

'Anyway, I have no comment. My solicitor has advised me to answer no comment to all questions.' I moved to the back of the cell. Sat near the small toilet on the thin blue mattress.

The metal flap clunked with force as the policeman's face moved closer. It was the Detective Inspector, he pushed his clear blue narrowing eyes to the metal cell opening.

'You think you're a big man with a big gun... We're going to fix you, Gillen... You watch' The eyes lingered a moment as he looked in the cell. The open metal cell hatch was slammed closed with a finality. I heard them outside as they moved away from the cell door and walked up the shiny hall away from me.

I needed to ensure that there was nothing they could do to pin the gun on me. I thought back to the evidence they had and realised that I happened to have a key piece still in the cell with me and that my jacket needed to disappear. I was gutted as it was a lovely coat, a buttery suede, but it was damming evidence and could tie me to the gun. I made plans for the rest of the day and discreetly got busy.

Armed Robbery 1992 Age 21

At the bus stop, I scanned the scene in the cold freshness of the dark December early evening, as busy shoppers hurried past. The shop lights cast a dim glow onto the pavements, mingling with the glint of the Christmas street decorations. We had parked the car nearby. Wrapped tightly in clothes and gloves, with balaclavas rolled high under the peaks of our baseball caps, we blended in. Tucked into the front of my jeans and shielded by my dark green, silk bomber jacket was the loaded twelve-bore side-by-side shotgun. My movements were deliberate, structured to conceal the firearm's weight under my jacket, while my pockets bulged with cartridges.

Connie stood beside me. With sharp eyes, we assessed the scene. Shoppers bustling, teenage girls in groups laughing, a mother clutching her child's hand, the homeless man turning on the pavement, the shopkeeper retracting his awning in preparation to close - all observed with keen, dissecting attention. The crisp evening air nipped at my head and ears, our breath forming misty plumes. It all felt surreal, and I pondered the out-of-place elements in the picture before me.

The flow of cars on the busy Bethnal Green Road slowed as a red number eight bus pulled in. The passengers, a queue of routine life, boarded. For a moment, shielded from the glaring road, my mind wandered. I studied the faces at the bus stop: an elderly lady with a child, a young man engrossed in his headset, a schoolgirl in uniform.

A man with dark hair flecked with grey, clad in a square-patterned tweed jacket, stood out. His straight posture and solitary demeanour seemed to command his space. Our eyes met briefly, his green eyes deep and probing, like an unfathomable sea in turmoil. He rubbed his stubbled chin, revealing a hand with only three fingers, the smooth stumps bearing testimony to fingers long gone. He diverted his gaze and walked away, leaving a trail of evocative tweed scent in his wake, stirring a connection I couldn't place.

Lily's voice echoed in my mind.

Her call had come late that afternoon, her words rushed, tinged with panic and uncertainty. Callum had been arrested by the Flying Squad, caught up in a heist. A Securicor van had been hijacked in North London, and the team was now in custody. The police had stormed their homes, busting doors and brandishing weapons with a warrant as their banner. Callum was at Tottenham Police Station, and she was at a loss, her home trampled by searching boots. She'd fought back with words sharp as daggers but to no avail. The door remained off its hinges, a stark reminder of the intrusion... and she had asked me - was I safe? I needed to lay low; I had to stay away. They were still watching, they had said and were looking for other people.

The bus's doors closed with a hiss; its engine strained against the pull of evening traffic. Lily's desperate voice on the phone had rooted me to the spot, the chill of impending danger creeping over me. The network I relied on was being dismantled, my safety net torn apart.

I had envisioned Callum, alone in a police cell, and then thought of my new-born son, Syd My reaction was visceral - a fist through the wall, glass shattered, a table demolished in a burst of rage. That image of my child had been a week ago, and now the freedom I clung to was slipping through my fingers. Cornered and isolated, I felt the sting of vulnerability.

Across the road, Christmas lights twinkled atop a shop, pulling me back to the present. I surveyed the busy road, the people, the doorway we'd been monitoring - rumoured to be a counting house for a betting shop chain, ripe for the taking.

The evening's chill hinted at a later freeze, but inside, my senses sharpened to a near-breaking point. The familiar cocktail of adrenaline, apprehension, and excitement churned within me. Someone cracked open the door near the blurred light of the doorway, peering into the night.

We readied ourselves, watching intently...

Reflection

Throughout my life, I've encountered many who've served as beacons, teaching me the value of being perpetually open to learning. I've come to understand that within each of us lies an inherent potential for greatness. The key is to consciously choose to be in the company of those who embody excellence, those whose virtues and successes inspire and propel us forward.

I've learned to observe and emulate only the finest traits of those I respect, assimilating their most effective methods, insights, and strategies for rapid advancement. The mental blueprint of who I aspire to become is ever-present, shaped partly by the image of successful or renowned figures I hold in high regard. They serve not as templates but as touchstones for the qualities I admire: their achievements, their approach to life.

Central to this journey is the unrelenting commitment to hard work, the readiness to make sacrifices, and the unwavering belief in the destination. It is through navigating challenges and overcoming obstacles that our true selves are refined and strengthened. And there comes a moment when we pause to reflect on the distance travelled, only to realize that the person we once looked up to in others has been crafted within ourselves - often exceeding the very ideals that set us on our path.

CHAPTER 5

Organised Crime and Serious Offences

"The larger crimes are apt to be the simpler, for the bigger the crime, the more obvious, as a rule, is the motive."

— Sir Arthur Conan Doyle

Brixton Prison 1990

I'd pleaded guilty to Possession of a Firearm; I'd had no choice as one of the crew had grassed and they'd found more incriminating evidence at one of our homes Vallance Road, Bethnal Green including a sawn-off shotgun and cartridges. That would be dealt with when I got out, if not before. Without the key article that they had not logged into evidence they could not charge me with anything else and so my brief had done the deal, and I was sentenced to two and a half years.

I had thought I was prepared for incarceration having spent so many of my formative years in Borstal with Portland being the closest I'd come to adult prison, but nothing could compare to what was to come.

I was given a dark and immediate introduction to prison life, and I knew immediately it was kill or be killed. There were a few familiar faces in there with me, people I knew from the streets and so it didn't take long for my reputation as someone not to be messed with to get around. Of course, there were those looking to make a name for themselves inside and they'd always try to push it, but I was ready for them, and I was as ruthless in there as I was on the street.

However, there was something that I had not anticipated, and it knocked me for six..

I was going to be a father. I hadn't been in a relationship with Stacey, she was the sister of a good friend, Susan and we'd had a casual relationship. It wasn't until I was ten months into my sentence that Susan told me 'You're in trouble with my sister, Stephen.' I would take all the trouble she could dish at me if I got to see my son. It was a blessing and a light to see me through my sentence.

Scotland Yard Flying Squad 1991

Detective Inspector Donald Finch and Detective Sergeant David Truman strolled briskly down the corridor. The building, a dull and discreet four-storey grey-windowed monolith nestled in a busy back street in East London, housed twenty-five officers of Specialist Crime Directorate 7, S08 Scotland Yard Flying Squad. It was one of four similar units positioned to police East, North, South, and West London to combat armed robbery, organised crime, and the gangster problem.

The corridor was long and white, with windows stretching to the left, letting in the mid-morning light. DS Truman matched his Detective Inspector's quickening pace. He was a short man with a lazy eye, short black curly hair, a strong, jaw and pitted skin. He buttoned his blue Barbour as they pressed forward.

'We're hearing intelligence from Bethnal Green and Bow, Guv,' he said. 'It's been checked with a few of our informants. There's a new gang in town, flaunting their wealth. They're a troublesome bunch, well-known in the area, and everyone's afraid of them. They've suddenly come into money, driving top-of-the-range Mercs, buying businesses, and rising in the world. None of them seem to work a day in their lives. They originated from South London, with ages ranging from 20 to

30. Could this be related to the Security Van hijacking near the docklands last week?'

DI Finch grunted, a deep, imposing sound that conveyed both authority and boredom. He had been a wrestler in his younger years, and growing up in Glasgow, he had mastered the art of concealing his true feelings, always leading people astray and setting traps to extract more information.

'You're referring to the robbery last week, where they hijacked the van driver from his home, held him at gunpoint, and threatened him with pictures of his wife at work? The one where they used black tape to attach a bug to his ankle and ordered him to say nothing until the van was on the road?' he clarified.

'Yes, Sir, that's the one,' Truman confirmed. 'They had him follow a motorbike in traffic, leading to a quiet warehouse near the docklands, where four other gang members were waiting. They emptied a Securicor van of three hundred and eighty-five thousand pounds in cash. Quite a sophisticated operation, Gov. Do we have any additional information to corroborate this?'

DI Finch continued to stride forward; his determination evident. He took his job and his reputation very seriously. He considered it a compliment when the organised criminals he pursued considered him a formidable adversary. He was determined to hunt them down and fill their dreams with the nightmares they inflicted on others. 'An eye for an eye,' he muttered.

'Sorry, Sir,' Truman responded, staying close like a loyal dog. 'An eye for what?'

'You know exactly what I mean! Don't dwell on it. The ends justify the means, Truman. We're in a war here. They're on the defensive, and I intend to push them into a corner and then into the abyss,' Finch declared.

'Of course, Gov. Should I initiate surveillance on them?' Truman inquired.

Finch could see the swinging grey double doors at the end of the hall, as if they were trying to lead him into a trap. He considered his options.

The Flying Squad, initially formed experimentally by Detective Chief Inspector Frederick Wensley in 1919, had often been accused of foul play and corruption. As they reached the heavy chestnut doors at the end of the corridor, Finch knew his team awaited him, ready for the debrief on their next steps. He couldn't ignore the whispers he had been hearing about investigations into his squad's unconventional methods and the involvement of Scotland Yard's internal police investigative unit, the 'ghost squad,' in some cases.

He sighed, feeling the faint tremor of fear at the prospect of exposure. It hadn't been long since the 1977 bribery and corruption scandal that had resulted in Detective Chief Superintendent Kenneth Drury's imprisonment for eight years.

The noise in the corridor grew quieter as they approached the doors, drowning out the sounds of typewriters and office girls' laughter. Finch turned to DS Truman.

'Keep our records meticulous, and the surveillance logs concise, alright? We can't afford any gaps in our cases or our work. What do we know about this new group in East London? Do we have any names?'

DS Truman paused for a moment, his lazy eye giving his features a peculiar twist, and his mouth tightening. 'We have a few names, Gov. Some of them are brothers, and others seem to have connections from school and prison. One name that keeps coming up is Stephen something-G, and another goes by Con from South London. We've been receiving reports about them. Two rising stars, it seems, and they're associated with the South London crowd, especially the Bermondsey boys from the blue. That Bermondsey Triangle, you know.'

DI Finch's interest was piqued by the mention of the notorious Bermondsey Triangle, a term coined by the Flying Squad due to its reputation as a haven for London's elite armed robbers within that square mile.

He felt the thrill of the chase once again, the anticipation of setting a trap for the wolves, and the satisfaction of keeping them looking over their shoulders. He pushed open the doors, greeted by the bustling noise of his team.

'Alright then. Let's assemble a team to keep a close eye on them and find out what this lot is up to,' he commanded.

Blundestone C Cat Home Leave 1991

The morning of my release had arrived before I knew it, and all I could think of was my beautiful boy, Syd. As I had sat in my cell, I had grappled with the enormous responsibility of having a child. Throughout my travels to the Old Bailey and the Category A Suite for my court case, I had felt the change within me – the newfound responsibility and the underlying joy of being a new father. It marked a new season in my life.

I found myself in the airlock area between the two massive metal front gates of the prison. The gatehouse with bulletproof windows stood to my left. There was a metal drawer for escorts to leave and pick up their keys, along with a row of metal lockers. Above us, a large mirror on the high concrete ceiling served to check for any prisoners attempting to cling to the tops of vans or lorries. The area had a sterile atmosphere with a constant hum of a generator.

I had been in this situation too many times before, and as I watched the massive grey front gate slide open, the lightness of a fresh morning streamed in. The sounds of birds, traffic in the car park, and the hustle and bustle of the outside world filled the air. I clutched the transparent prison bag in my hand tighter, aware of the seven days I had ahead of me to see my beautiful six-month-old baby boy, born in the London Hospital Whitechapel. I

Walking into the morning light, I reminisced about the journey that had brought me to this point. Memories of the gun, the arrest, the grim cells and depression in the City of London. The prison gates had fully opened, and I breathed in deeply, feeling a sense of gratitude and hope rejuvenating my core.

Standing there alone, I contemplated the stark contrast of my current existence. No surly officers, no shouting or the banging pots on walls. Instead, I felt hope for a beautiful future, an energy that was freeing and joyful, a positive place of good people, places, and things, where I could build and create rather than tear down and destroy. Whilst I wasn't exactly clean from drugs, they were still accessible if you were clever, I was sharper than I had been when I went in, my mind was clearer and I was physically fit from the exercise I'd been putting myself through.

I cast my mind back over the last fourteen months. I had navigated the judicial system unsteadily as it rocked and kicked me through. I had orchestrated good fortune at my Old Bailey trial, beating a conspiracy to rob charge. My lighter punishment of two and a half years for possession of a firearm was still a shock. I had already served nine months on remand, and the low sentence had demanded they remove my high-security Category A status. B Category then C followed seamlessly. I had navigated fourteen months of this rollercoaster ride, and a significant difference had been the baby boy who waited outside.

'There he is! The man himself,' it was Callum Draper, a wide smile shining out to the world, eyes glinting. Dressed in grey trousers, a crisp white shirt, and a blue cashmere jumper. Immaculate, he had his arms stretched out, fingers beckoning. He shook the bottle of champagne, cracking its cork into the air.

'Great to see you, bruv. If I don't see you through the week, I'll see you through the window. Now I'll need to ask you a few security questions, make sure it's you?'

The bubbles shot from the bottle. He was in stitches, laughing at the joy of me being out, and the strength of it split his face in a wide-open brightness. He continued, 'It's fucking home time.'

We embraced. A brotherly feeling that was warm, all arms and shoulders and backs, comforting.

There was a genuine smile on his face that reached his eyes. 'Great to have you home, Steve.' He had the glasses from the back of the car and, on the concrete ground of the stone car park, poured us both one.

It was behind me. Blundestone Prison, with its long-stretching corridors, camp-like dorms, its strange people and energies and regime. With a final metal clunk, the prison gates closed far back behind me.

'God, it's good to be going home. Amazing. If I can't see you in the spring, I'll see you through the mattress.' It was one of our old sayings, and he loved it, and we were bent double together in laughter as we remembered.

'Can't wait to see my boy,' I added. 'Imagine the little thing.' We opened the door to the black Mercedes. We sat a moment with the drinks at our lips. We would have a few hours drive to London.

'...He's beautiful, a real beautiful boy. A blinder,' I said, the feel of his little fingers was in mine. He stood and jumped and bounced on unsteady legs and stood on my knees, tall in front of my face and his smile melted me. My firstborn. Syd.

Behind, his grandfather, Tony, who had brought him, and the social worker who had facilitated the meeting, smiled. Tony, a good man who was a black cab driver from Roman Road, was unsure and guarded but watched with no judgement, hopeful. The woman caseworker had her hands resting on her lap.

'Our wish is you can be a father to Sydney, Stephen, under supervised conditions at first.'

My focus was on the miracle that jumped in front of me. The soft new-born skin and the face that resembled mine. The chiselled chin, intense features. The same hazel, all-knowing eyes that danced and jumped and engaged and smiled and seduced. His little hands gripped my fingers, feet kicked and sprung and twisted. A mesmerising bonding smile linked us. It was love at first sight. I'd never felt anything like it and in that moment I completely understood why parents did stupid things for their children, equally a small part of my heart wondered why my mother hadn't felt this way about me.

The caseworker continued, 'We hope this can be relaxed as we go on, and more and easier visiting rights can be arranged.'

'I do hope so. I have great plans for a wonderful future ahead. I'm studying for an OU business degree in prison...'

She cut in, 'You have seven days home leave and are due for release in three months, is that right?'

'Yes.' Again measured tones, but inside I beamed.

'Okay then, we can hope to arrange something for then maybe.' She was up, and her movements indicated that the baby should be handed back to his grandfather, it had gone great, but the two hours were up. She was a stickler for time and her fingers were rattling the handle of the door. A reassuring tight smile streamed across the lines on her face.

'I'll see you soon, Syd, Okay! See you soon, boy.' Our eyes met then. A moment of knowing reserved for people of the same bloodline. Soft kisses on cotton wool skin, excited eyes, warm cuddles, a tight hug that lingered. It was terrible to go. The door was open, and the sign was to go through it. I left; my teeth clenched in frustration. A stab of longing in my heart and tears welled in my eyes. I didn't want to let him go.

The quietness of the grey street over the back of Vallance Road hit me. I stood outside the social service building in Underwood Road, Bethnal Green.

'Alright?'

My head turned to take me away from my thoughts.

Through the wound-down car passenger window, in the black Mercedes across the road, it was Callum who had been waiting for me. I buckled my seatbelt. The car pulled easily into the slow-moving traffic on Vallance Road. We went under the overhead past the old place where the Kray Twins were brought up, into Bethnal Green Road.

A right and, 'Glad that went okay, Steve. They're another load of spies, those people,' Callum spoke. He tipped the ash from his cig out the window, adding, 'Things are proper paranoid out here, Stephen, I'm telling ya. They're all over us. I know they're there, the other people. We'll go to my gaff. We bought all the police passwords for their frequencies. Bow Road is Hotel Tango Two. I've got the Tandy's receiver on indoors all the time. Been some interesting conversation between 'em, let me tell you...'

The car accelerated forward in the traffic. The busy shops of Bethnal Green Road slipping by us on either side. The market stall, pubs, Kelly's the pie and mash shop, a throng of people on the pavements that walked and jostled and weaved and pressed business.

'I've got your money at home, Steve. Sorry you have to come home to this madness.'

I lit a cigarette, inhaled, the smoke made me feel better. 'They still having that work? What's about? Callum... Even though I'm just out, I could do with a few quid. Got this baby now, Callum.'

He listened. Threw his cigarette out the window into the roadway. We were down in Bow at the back of Roman Road. He was getting ready to turn the car.

He told me to listen. There were bits about but to take it easy.

We were at the back of St Stephen's Road. The garages where a bike was hidden to be used and bullets were made, were pointed out to me. A small enclave of green doors that housed six small garages on either side of a concreted entrance.

There was too much activity. We would need to be doubly aware. Do anti-surveillance. There were strange things, no one could put a finger on it. Odd feelings and movements, and it was making everyone paranoid. I was not to worry. I was home, I was with family. Blood was thicker than water, right? I was not to think on it twice, everything was sorted. People couldn't wait to meet me. It would take a few days, but I needed to be vigilant to the people, places, and movements around me as there was something big coming up…

We parked the car by the small back street roundabout and took the concrete stairs to the third floor, where we stopped a while on the slim, tight passageway to the flat, looking at the surrounding street, the places of cover, vantage points of interest, and ways of entrance and exit for traffic.

'…whiskey tango, we have two IC ones at the end of Broadway tampering with a car. Other youths are attending the scene, copy.'

The radio receiver crackled in the corner. A walkie-talkie-looking device, it had two black buttons on the top for the fine-tuning of frequencies that the buttons on the front had pulled in from the air.

We were in Callum's front room. A clean, expensive spread of new pale grey carpets, crisp cream décor, and matching settee, chairs, and furniture. Classic, professionally taken pictures graced the walls. Callum with his daughter, May and son Mark. A family pose of him and his wife Dawn. Another of May in black and white. Colour photos of the wedding. Old photos of his much-missed Aunt Libby.

I sat in the chair and looked at the silent TV that played, and my mind was alive with pictures of the baby. My son with the vulnerable eyes, the jumping legs, and the wide grin. I couldn't get him out of my mind. I wanted to do right by him, give him a much better life that I'd had, make sure that he always knew he was loved and protected. Safe.

'Here, that's what I was keeping for you,' Callum threw it, the plastic bag with ten thousand pounds in used banknotes. 'This will keep you going, right?'

More of a question, but he was at the radio receiver, and he turned it up. His hand was up to quieten me, and he listened.

'Shhh… I just heard something?'

'…Over, over.'

Two voices, sharp, direct, drilling an exchange on a line that was meant to be secure but crackled with background noise.

'...Yes, over?'

'Target one and target four sighted. In flat. Target one with another suspect. Request hard stop for tango bravo Charlie. Known associate. Request execute warrant for questioning?'

Another voice barked.

'Denied! Charlie two, over? Denied. Repeat, Charlie Two... This is a sophisticated Divisional operation. Repeat, this is a separate Divisional operation involved in securing targets in Operation Nemesis. Not to be stopped. Declined for hard stop, Repeat.'

We stood there, our ears straining for more, incredulous. Breathing heavy, eyes wide. Our heads were close to the cabinet where the receiver rested. We listened closer. In the background of the police conversation, we could hear the clatter of a train as it passed, the passage of its journey covering tracks. We looked at each other, eyes questioning. We knew what we were hearing. We understood the seriousness of what was being discussed. We were aware that a hard stop was the barricading ambush of armed police on criminal suspected of being involved with, or carrying firearms, as they were mobile in their vehicles. We had the verified code word for Bow Road Police Station, Hotel Tango Two. We had the receiver to listen to police frequencies. Harder, we strained as the exchange continued.

'...Charlie two asking permission to close in further on targets.'

We listened intently. In the background, behind the voices, we could make out the noise of the train going on its journey.

We rushed to the balcony and looked out into East London, into the grey, smog-filled afternoon air. Our hands were on the black metal of the balcony. They tightened into the metal as we stood rooted to the spot.

We watched. We saw it, and we knew. Just across from us, not two hundred meters away, the train crossed, hammering over the tracks, the sound of it cut through our ears, matching the rattle it made on the Tandy receiver.

We looked at each other. We both knew we were thinking the same thoughts.

Unlawfully at Large 1991

It had been a typical Friday night in Bethnal Green. We'd stepped away from our plotting to socialise and savour the moment. The barrow boys had wound up their day's work, the throngs who'd browsed the shops and stalls were gone, and the din of pie-and-mash chatter had faded with the day. Now, the chill of the city's evening embraced us. We were upstairs in the White Hart pub, where a raucous dancefloor beat below. I snorted a thick line of cocaine with a fifty-pound note. The building vibrated to the rhythm of CeCe Peniston's 'Finally'.

Alfie, Ian, and George were with me. I moved with the music, my movements precise to the pulsating beats. The cocaine sent my mind rocketing, infusing me with a false sense of invulnerability.

Their laughter surrounded me, yet their eyes held a glazed seriousness as the drug tightened its grip. George rubbed his nose while my teeth ground together. I danced, feeling as if I soared amongst the clouds of my mind where no limits existed. The music throbbed, and I saw them, in various states of inebriation, against the backdrop of the pub room that doubled as an office but felt like a lounge. Keith, the new publican, had tried to create a relaxed vibe with red leather sofas and stained wooden desks, but the blue walls, needing paint, betrayed the room's true nature.

'Come on then... who's got the minerals?' Alfie stood by the leather-topped desk, brandishing a bag of white powder. He lined up the cocaine with swift, confident strokes, akin to an artist putting final touches to a canvas.

'Now look at these. Big, long lines... let's race with fifty-pound notes. First to finish takes the pot. Winner takes all.'

Madness flickered in his eyes, a disturbed intensity, like a surfer riding relentless waves without a shoreline in sight.

The walls thumped with the beat. I sipped my vodka and orange. 'I don't reckon you've got it in you, Alfie,' I baited him, and his reaction was instant.

'What d'you mean? Come on then. Show me what you've got, you lightweights. Fifty quid each!'

We lined up at the start of the glistening powder. The music vibrated through us as we stared each other down, gunslingers before a draw.

'Ready,' Alfie declared, our rolled banknotes poised.

'Go!'

I charged down the line, my sinuses packing with powder as I raced to claim victory. Cocaine dusted our faces, spilling onto the floor.

Robert flailed his arms. 'No way... you're the luckiest git.'

My head spun with the win's toll - a whirling sensation that unnerved me. I laughed, the secret of my pre-race nose-blow ensuring my edge.

Slumping into a chair, I felt the drugs' overwhelming rush. I needed a moment to stabilise, to maintain awareness amidst the day's excesses. The music shifted to Snap's 'Rhythm is a Dancer', and I settled into the chair, paranoia creeping in. I hadn't returned to prison after my home leave, swayed by promises of life-changing opportunities and the pressure to provide for my baby boy.

Inside, my thoughts spiralled, a maelstrom whirling through corridors of my mind. I was unlawfully at large, with one foot perpetually in prison. The drugs mingled with my elation and looming dread - a picture indelibly marked on my consciousness.

Ian sat shrouded in a dark aura; George was passed out; Alfie, lost in the beat. And there I was, the fog in my head demanding more: more cocaine, more drink, more escapism. It was a cycle that lifted me sky-high only to send me crashing down.

Downstairs, the crowd's voices melded with the pulsating music. The drugs' mood shifted; my thoughts turned to my son - an innocent, joyful being. As I slumped, I knew I'd made a grave mistake in not returning to prison. The law was closing in, its presence poking at my consciousness, as the image of my son's sweet face lingered in my troubled mind.

I'd had every intention of going back, I had the train time fixed in my head and I fully expected to be on it until I wasn't. I needed money, I wanted be a father for my son and I had to have the resources to be able to do that, I couldn't if I was inside, but now it was a half-life. Always looking over my shoulder, constantly paranoid that I would make a mistake and end up behind bars again. The drugs didn't help, they were in part the real reason I hadn't gone back, my mind wasn't focused on the long game, just the here and now and the next deal.

Scotland Yard Flying Squad 1992

Detective Inspector Donald Finch stood on the top floor of the high car park, speaking into the radio. He surveyed the London skyline, his gaze drifting to the bustling streets of North London below.

He listened intently, '...Yes, Gov, we're confident today's the day. We've got eyes on three of the targets and trackers on two others' cars. They met last night in Hoxton... the bike's active...'

His hard features tightened into a look of intense thought and determination.

'OK... don't lose them,' he commanded sharply. 'Today we end this two-year operation.' He inhaled deeply, the brisk wind of the car park's heights caressing his cheeks, tousling his hair. He had a sixth sense for these defining moments.

'Yes. Stay alert. Today, this lot goes down.'

His walkie-talkie now silent at his side, Finch gazed down at the humming metropolis. Memories of long nights foregoing dinner to track the armed robbers on his patch mingled with the demands of family life - a wife yearning for normalcy, a daughter grappling with graphic design at university, a son working late hours, and a personal life overshadowed by the job. At fifty-seven, his world was dominated by the consuming demands of law enforcement.

The team had persevered, laying traps and following leads with little respite. This gang was sophisticated, eluding capture with a disconcerting acumen. He knew they were reaching their zenith, not yet at the pinnacle of London's criminal echelons but alarmingly close. They were learning, adapting. Failure to apprehend them now could mean they'd become untouchable.

The vast expanse of the clear blue sky loomed overhead as he turned to see a colleague in an unmarked grey Audi. Finch pondered the expanse of London, akin to the sky - limitless for those with the right connections and resources. They'd been on a spree, hijacking five Securicor vans, netting over a million in cash, most of it untraceable.

A guttural grunt escaped him as he recalled the terror etched on the guards' faces, recounting the orchestrated heists. The burden of knowing a bug had infiltrated their ranks, listening, while he could utter no warning. The air was crisp in his lungs as he fought back a cough.

DI Finch mentally reviewed his checklist: trackers surreptitiously placed on cars, directional mics capturing whispers, photographs gathered for evidence from various vantages. This gang's tech-savviness meant only the highest level of anti-surveillance measures were employed.

Satisfied with the preparation, he directed his team, some monitoring potential targets, others tracking movements, all weaving a complex surveillance web. He stood, a spider at the centre, oscillating between exhilaration and trepidation - a taut rope, an encroaching trap, and the simmering fear of a missed opportunity.

He glanced down once more at the thrumming city streets, observing a Securicor van merging into traffic - a stream of purposeful ants, oblivious to the impending disruption.

The wind whipped fiercely as he donned his black police cap, marked with the chequered band of the Flying Squad. Stepping back from the edge, he continued to scrutinise the scene, his cap shielding him from the gusts. Staring across the rooftops, he murmured to himself against the howling wind, 'They need to be lucky every time... We only need to be lucky once.'

The Van Heist 1992

The urban male fox paused in the shadows to hone its senses. With a burst of movement, sleek and agile, it darted across the familiar ground under the waning moonlight. Utilising the cover of darkness and blending into its surroundings, the fox nimbly navigated the interplay of light and shadow. It skirted around the sides of the flats, along the road, and into the tree-lined park, thoughts of the vixen in the den mingling with the night's hunt and the most fruitful spots to find prey.

The three men of the armed robbery team lingered back from the open door of the garage. They checked their firearms, ammunition, and surveillance equipment. The day before, a Ducati 750cc had been taken for a thorough test, revved and roared into life. It would soon be time. The four men had separated the previous day after a final meeting in the changing rooms of a swimming pool. Cognisant of potential police surveillance, they had only met three times in as many months. Their communication was through disposable pay-as-you-go phones, used solely amongst themselves and subsequently discarded in an East London canal, replaced anew for further use. The team, well-versed in their assigned tasks, comprised roles spanning police movement monitoring, bugging, vehicle driving, and securing the Securicor vans. Each knew precisely what was required.

In the garage, the trio huddled, whispering in subdued tones, the aroma of oil and petrol pervading the air.

One held the bug, a two-inch round black device with a diminutive aerial, aloft in the dim light.

'Don't forget,' he said, his voice a sharp, clear rasp, 'Instil the fear of God in him, then pacify him. Tape it to the lower part of his ankle. Secure it firmly, aerial upwards. Ensure it's concealed by his trousers and socks. We can't have it spotted, especially by the crew... and stay in proximity to the van on the road. Once we merge into the traffic, the receiver's range is two miles.'

Acknowledgement was silent, conveyed by the resolute gaze in their eyes, now hardened by the impending task. The bike rider donned his black balaclava and blue-black helmet, kickstarted the motorcycle, and eased it out of the garage into the moonlit night. With a nod, the sharp figure gripped the bike, manoeuvring it with assured skill.

The remaining two stood, watching in the obscurity, the fleeting image of a fox catching their attention before it vanished into the dark roadway, becoming invisible. The bike's engine thundered to life; the rider engaged the gear, twisted the throttle, and with one swift motion, surged into the night. The chill of the evening enveloped them; the motorcycle was no longer in sight, absorbed by the darkness.

Scotland Yard Flying Squad 1992

The 750cc motorbike weaved in and out of the traffic, its riders effortlessly settling behind a red hatchback to maintain a steady, unobtrusive pace. The pillion had been collected from a corner in North London under the harsh glare of a streetlight that shattered the embrace of the early morning, cold darkness. Clinging firmly to the rider in front, he concealed within the depths of his black leather jacket a fully loaded Smith & Wesson .38. Propelled forward, the bike sliced through the busy road, aided by the clarity and brightness of the day. As they neared the traffic lights, the vehicles ahead slowed, and they nestled close behind the hatchback. Far down the line, their focused gaze settled on the target: a large, blue-armoured Securicor van coming to a full stop.

Perched high atop a block of flats, the Flying Squad had been observing the unfolding events, their camera capturing the team's early morning convergence and the motorbike's subsequent launch. Two separate trackers, activated at distinct London locations, had also drawn the attention of the officers. Thirty members of the Flying Squad were now mobilised, tracing, surveilling, and drawing an invisible net around the nest of armed robbers they sought.

With another twenty-five armed officers from PT17 in support, they advanced with swift confidence.

'They're on the move again. Targets one and five,' came the hushed update from an officer nestled in the back of a surveillance van, ear pressed to his earphone. The three key suspects had been shadowed since an icy evening seven months prior, when their vehicle's original tracker was stealthily exchanged for a replica. Now, with advanced tracking and audio surveillance active, their clandestine manoeuvres were laid bare - they were inching towards their next heist.

Panic palpably thickened within the armoured confines of the Securicor van. Eyes wide with dread peered through reinforced glass, the cityscape fleeting past them. Escape was a fickle dream.

'We need to report this, Jeff! We've got no choice,' urged the driver's mate, his voice a cocktail of fear and resolve. Tasked with managing the schedule and shuttling money boxes, the gravity of their predicament wasn't lost on him. 'This is bloody madness. What if-?'

But the driver, feeling the unyielding tape against his skin that secured the listening device to his ankle, shushed him with terrified urgency. 'They're listening, Danny. Every cursed word,' he hissed. 'They ambushed me as I got into my car at dawn - forced me at gunpoint.'

The third crew member absorbed the frantic exchange in the van's vault-like rear. He stood sentinel over the safes, awaiting the timed release of keys. 'Someone could get hurt. I'm reporting this,' he declared, defiance threading his whispered tone.

The driver's retort was sharp, slicing through the tension. 'We're not calling it in, alright? They've got Sharon. They know where the kids are schooled,' his voice cracked, laden with a father's terror. 'There was a photo, Danny. A recent one - by the school gates.'

Silence reigned as the van merged with the river of traffic, a single vessel amidst a stream of normalcy distorted by an undercurrent of fear. The mundanity of the city's rhythm belied the storm brewing within.

Then, a reflection of chaos flickered in the wing mirror - the motorbike, a harbinger of dread, barrelling towards them. Clad in black, the riders' intent was unmistakable. The thud of their approach echoed, a prelude to the inevitable.

'Follow us,' the pillion commanded, pointing decisively. The message was unambiguous, the directive chilling.

Atop the car park, Detective Inspector Finch stood beside his car, his grip firm on the walkie-talkie as updates crackled through. 'They navigated from East India Dock Road to Limehouse and on towards the Rotherhithe Tunnel. We've retained audio but lost visual, sir. They're somewhere south, potentially regrouping. They've been referencing an East

London rendezvous. We're adjusting our strategy accordingly. Over.'

The report concluded, Finch stepped out into the blustery embrace of the high vantage point, his gaze sweeping over the urban sprawl below. The enigmatic movements of his targets threaded through his mind, the unyielding winds echoing the tumult of his thoughts. As he scanned the horizon, the vast open sky above seemed to mirror the breadth of the unfolding mystery.

Standing alone, with the city's pulse in the distance and the walkie-talkie's static whispering of a chase in flux, DI Finch contemplated the elusive quarry. What was their endgame? The vast sky offered no answers, only the boundless canvas of possibility. And there, amidst the sweeping gales of London, he waited for the next move in this intricate dance of hunter and hunted.

Unlawfully at large, 1992

The flickering streetlights cast eerie shadows as I leaned against the cold brick wall of the alley, my heart pounding in rhythm with the distant sounds of the city. With trembling hands, I reached into the pocket of my worn leather jacket, withdrawing a small baggie filled with white powder. The familiar scent of cocaine filled the air as I hastily prepared a line on the back of my hand, my breath coming in shallow gasps as I leaned down to sniff.

The rush was immediate and intoxicating, a surge of euphoria coursing through my veins and momentarily drowning out the nagging voice of doubt in the back of my mind. I closed my eyes, savouring the fleeting sense of invincibility that the drug provided, a brief respite from the harsh realities of my life.

But as the effects began to wear off, the shadows seemed to grow darker, the once familiar streets taking on a sinister edge. Paranoia gnawed at the edges of my consciousness, whispering tales of unseen threats lurking in the darkness. Every passing car, every distant footstep sent a jolt of fear coursing through my veins, my senses heightened to the point of agony.

I glanced around nervously, my eyes darting from shadow to shadow, searching for signs of danger that may or may not be there. The weight of my unlawful status hung heavy on my shoulders, a constant reminder of the ever-watchful eyes of the law enforcement officers who sought to bring me to justice.

And then there was Syd, my son, a beacon of hope in an otherwise bleak existence. The thought of being a good father filled me with a fierce determination, but it also brought with it a crushing weight of responsibility. How could I protect my son from the dangers of the world when I could barely protect myself?

With a heavy heart, I sniffed another line of cocaine, the bitter taste burning my nostrils as I sought to drown out the doubts and fears that threatened to consume me. But deep down, I knew that no amount of drugs could silence the relentless voice of paranoia that haunted my every waking moment.

Scotland Yard Flying Squad 1992

The police helicopter had kept the suspect high-powered blue BMW under a close watch. Like an experienced carrion hawk high in the late evening floating winds it had hovered from high altitude using specialised equipment hugging the thermals at times manipulating the cloud cover as it stayed concealed over the city skyline. The car below was moving and going towards the city of London. The call had come. Its three male occupants were fleeing the scene of an armed robbery and were armed and thought highly dangerous. From the docklands in east London, they had observed the car. Tracking, trailing, sometimes in their high-altitude optical lenses, a dot that moved, twisted, turned, and would intensify.

'Bravo six. Sky bound, will soon execute hard stop. Over.'

It was the ground team. They circled and tightened, focused and prepared. A floating group was a twelve-car team of vehicles, all armed.

The echoing hum of the rotors muttered a high noise. In the cockpit, the pilot was answering. A clear, precise, targeted voice trained and fluent.

'Still have eyes, over. Repeat Charlie One still mobile along Princes Street at the back of the Bank of England, copy. Still have eyes. Over…'

DI Finch was in a passenger seat of the four-man car. The chequered caps were on their laps and 38 calibre Smith and Wesson handguns were on their laps. They had missed the van attack by a sheer fluke. They had lost a few of the robbery team earlier in the day. Having spread their observation because of potential targets, they had miscalculated the actual raid point. He asked the driver to steady, to slow down. Soon. The car slotted into the moving traffic behind a bread delivery van. The suspects were far up ahead around a mile in the built-up city. DI Finch's weathered face focused, his determined eyes tightening with the growing pressure in his head. They had the suspects in a floating box now. No escape. Cars and a van, and two motorbikes moved and swung and weaved around them as their car cruised and navigated the heavy city traffic.

The grey, busy pavements were now the foundations of taller buildings as they went deeper into the city's heart. High above them, in a forecast of fresh sweeping winds and slight showers, was the police helicopter swooping now to use their camera equipment for photographs.

'Can't believe we missed them, Gov,' from one of the detectives in the back seat. 'Lucky for them.' He continued.

In the passenger seat, the Detective Inspector made a deep hum. Close to a grunt, but not quite. He was very aware of the blood bath that could have been, and he and his men would have been able to meet it. Four trained guns were no match for thirty, he thought. Out of the side of his mouth, he growled, 'It was another one for the suspects. Let's be thankful for this one. We need to watch the attention at the moment. This lot are very dodgy. I have no doubt if we had caught them cold at the van, it would have been a very dangerous situation. This way is a better solution this time.'

Finch had his hand on his gun in the holster at his hip. He was thinking when to call it. The car flew forward in traffic that picked up speed. The radio in the car crackled. It was a

Detective Sargent in one of the lead cars tasked with synchronising the armed officers and the hard stop of the suspect vehicle. The suspects' behaviour, he said, suggested they were unaware. They had showed no panicky movements or anti surveillance.

He heard the stopping hiss of the bin lorry hydraulics as it braked at the side of them. He saw the monitor and could see images of the suspect's blue BMW. The main operational CCTV team had joined them on request as an arrest drew closer. The car came to life again. Either side of him the tall greyness of buildings tightly enclosed them.

In his mind, he was returning to the information he had been given of the robbery just committed. They had lost the two main suspects they had watched from the early hours. They had also had to pull back close cover surveillance on the motorbike. They had done this to not alert the suspects they were walking into a carefully crafted trap. They had listened on the audio, watched the long-range trackers. The Robbery team had changed their rendezvous at the last minute and gathered at a place in Islington. Clever bastards, Finch thought. There was a feeling deep down inside him. It was frustration he recognised. They had used the weapon of confusion and they had used it well knowing first a crime would have to be committed and for a conspiracy to stick they would need to be woven together.

He spoke sharply into the mike, 'Bravo One, Bravo Two and Bravo Three! This is India Tango. Repeat India Tango. Hard Stop next junction. Execute. Execute…'

His voice hung for a moment in the moving car. The two-year Operation Nemesis was approaching its end.

They came back now. They had understood the call sign from their senior officer. The order to attack, to move with stealth, eagle-like precision, swoop with noise, screeching tyres, and smashing glass and firearms drawn. Three Detective Sergeants were in charge of three separate teams that tracked the separate getaway cars fleeing across London.

Detective Inspector Finch could see the ambush position far ahead of him. A busy three-way cross road with traffic lights wide open spaces and no chance of escape. He was more aware of the heavy black gun now. The other officers had their chequered caps, their firearms ready.

Adrenalin pumped through Donald Finch's body. From a pounding heart, it was quickening, speeding through a labyrinth of arteries and veins. His eyes squinted, and his temples were pulsing. It would soon be the end for them, he thought. Two years of punishing tactical work. The robbery behind them had left three guards from Securicor in fear for their lives. On the fenced, rock peppered waste ground, where grass grew in tufts through large cracks in the concrete, by the thrown rubbish and plastic bottles and old rolled-up carpets and under the closed quiet shadows of a bricked railway overhead, the robbery team had waited for the motorbike to escort the armoured blue Securicor van in. Together, four of them had ordered the guards out at gunpoint, opened the individual safes and cleared it of four hundred and fifteen thousand pounds. Finch was determined, the streets would be free of them. These people who waged fear and toted guns in broad daylight.

The radio squawked to life. 'Copy, India Tango. Message Hard Stop Execute understood, Bravo Two. Over.'

He replied, 'India Tango received. Over. Good luck...'

It sounded in his ears. The car changing gears, the light grey of flitting buildings, pedestrians, passing quickly. The weight of the gun, the top was unclipped now, the fabric of the chequered cap resting on his lap, the adrenalin. He felt it all. The thoughts returned to the quickness of his brain. The robbers had fled the scene as soon as they had taken the money in the crisp plastic Securicor wrappers. Their getaway cars had scattered in different directions. The police safeguards had been activated then. The moving arrows of the trackers had tightly warned and followed while an alert had gone wider. He was happy to remove them to prison, put them away for long years behind heavy closed doors.

'Copy, India Tango. Execute Hard stop. It's clear here. Approaching contact point. Will execute when ready understood. Copy...'

Something pulled at him. Two positioned, he considered. Donald Finch pressed the receiver again and confirmed, 'Received, Bravo One. India Tango, good luck. Over.' Ahead of him, he could just see the suspect vehicle. It approached the ambush point at the junction. The hard-stop ambush was just about to be sprung.

Everyone had their chequered caps ready, one hand on their gun, the other ready to exit the vehicle. It still pulled at him and jostled in his mind. A worm that was eating through the hard thoughts of his subconscious. It was the missing suspects. The surveillance logs had thrown up other collaborators. He knew there were other members of the robbery team. They were suspected. Today they would not be arrested.

It was the last team leader Detective Sergeant. His voice came in clear and precise. 'India Tango, Copy. Execute hard stop. Over and understood. Copy.'

In front of them, the traffic had stopped at the traffic lights. The busy, typical scene of a City of London junction about to erupt. They were out of the car doors, caps raised to their heads and guns raised with them. In unison. In a second. Quickly. A fluent, practiced motion.

'Go! Go!' It was belting on the black hard metal radios in their ears, echoing and shouting in and around them. The blocking cars screeched in front and at each side of the suspect blue BMW. A torrent of mayhem erupted. Shattering glass. Shouts. Screams. There was no chance of escape for the occupants as the Flying Squad Officers smashed the side of the car windows. They screamed and shouted. The police, surrounding the car with their guns trained forward.

'Show us your hands! Shows us your hands now!'

DI Finch was running. His large frame thumped the pavement. He was slightly behind. He watched a superb arrest. Heard his officers' shouts. It was his intention to show authority that he would be there but just arrive at the opportune moment. The suspects had been pulled from the car, were being cuffed behind their backs, spread-eagled on the pavement.

'We're securing the scene, Sir'. It was the young DS. He had the elation of the capture in his eyes, a light brightening his face and cheeks.

He looked at the three suspects on the floor. They would be having second thoughts about the day ahead of them now. He knew them. Three hard and clever and slippery men. Target criminals who had needed a fortune to be captured. But there would be more. There would be tomorrow and more guns and more witnesses and more robberies on his patch in the east end. He prided himself that he was clearing his manor like a powerful hoover that shifted and cleaned hard stains. DI Finch smiled inside, then grunted, his only self-congratulation. He walked round to the back of the BMW. One of the team had opened it.

There is an open and unzipped black holdall, still in the plastic wrappers from the Securicor sorting room, were the piles of banknotes newly taken. Clouds high above him were gathering to close in on the London skyline. They were coming in hard from the west and seeking strength as they summoned an hour's worth of rain. The winds he had felt on top of the carpark this morning were subsiding. He was happy with this day's work.

The three suspects were being taken in separate cars. Their car had been moved to the roadside. He stood a moment, looking at the scene. He knew it had been repeated simultaneously in two other separate ambushes. He listened. The commentary crackled that the other suspects had also been arrested successfully without any casualties. He stood on the roadside a moment, DI Finch, pensive. Today had been a win for Operation Nemesis, but he thought of the other robbers who had not been arrested. The traffic flowed past him quickly. They were out there, he thought. Somewhere they were holed up, still dangerous planning their next robbery.

The police helicopter had kept the suspect's high-powered blue BMW under close surveillance. Like an experienced carrion hawk floating on the late evening winds, it hovered at high altitude, using specialised equipment, at times riding the thermals, occasionally manipulating the cloud cover to stay concealed above the city skyline. The car below was making for the City of London. The alert had been raised: its three male occupants, fleeing the scene of an armed robbery, were armed and considered highly dangerous. From the docklands in East London, they had tracked the car, a moving dot in their high-altitude optical lenses, twisting and turning, intensifying under scrutiny.

'Bravo Six. Skybound, preparing to execute hard stop. Over.'

It was the ground team, circling and tightening, focused and ready - a twelve-car fleet of armed vehicles.

The echoing hum of the rotors droned above. In the cockpit, the pilot responded with a clear, precise, and practised voice.

'Visual maintained, over. Repeat, Charlie One is still mobile along Princes Street, rear of the Bank of England, copy. Visual maintained. Over...'

DI Finch sat in the passenger seat of a four-man car, chequered caps and .38 calibre Smith & Wesson handguns resting on their laps. They had narrowly missed the van attack by sheer fluke, having lost a few robbery team members earlier in the day. Spreading their observation too thin across potential targets, they had miscalculated the actual raid point. Finch instructed the driver to steady, to slow down. Soon, their car merged with the traffic behind a bread delivery van. The suspects were a mile ahead in the dense city. DI Finch's weathered face tensed, his eyes sharpening with the mounting pressure. They had the suspects encased in a floating box now. No escape. Vehicles and bikes wove around them as they cruised the heavy city traffic.

The grey pavements now lay at the base of towering buildings as they delved into the city's heart. High above, the police helicopter swooped, ready to use its camera equipment for aerial photography.

'Can't believe we missed them, Gov,' muttered a detective in the back seat.

The Detective Inspector grunted, a sound teetering on the edge of frustration. He knew the bloodbath they had narrowly avoided, his men more than capable of meeting it. 'Another lucky break for the suspects,' he muttered. 'Let's be thankful this time. We're dealing with a dodgy lot. A confrontation at the van would've been perilous. This way is better.'

Finch's hand rested on his holstered gun. When to make the call? The car surged through quickening traffic. The radio crackled - it was a Detective Sergeant in one of the lead cars coordinating the armed officers for the BMW's interception.

The suspects seemed oblivious, displaying no signs of panic or anti-surveillance tactics.

The hydraulic hiss of a bin lorry braking nearby filled the air. Finch watched the monitor, the blue BMW's image clear. The main CCTV operational team was now linked in, anticipating an arrest. The car, flanked by the impersonal greyness of tall buildings, surged to life.

Recalling the robbery details, Finch noted they had lost the two main suspects they'd been tracking since dawn. Close surveillance had been pulled back, not to alert the suspects to the trap being set. The robbery team had changed their rendezvous at the last minute, meeting in Islington. Clever bastards, Finch in frustration, they had used the weapon of confusion and they had used it well, knowing that for a conspiracy charge to stick, they had to be caught in the act.

'Bravo One, Bravo Two, and Bravo Three! This is India Tango. Hard Stop at the next junction. Execute. Execute...'

His voice resonated in the car as Operation Nemesis, two years in the making, neared its end.

The response was immediate - they understood their senior officer's call sign. The order to move with stealth, precision, and the suddenness of an eagle's strike.

Detective Inspector Finch could see the ambush position far ahead, a busy three-way crossroads with traffic lights, wide open spaces, and no chance of escape. He was acutely aware of the heavy black gun now. The other officers had donned their chequered caps, firearms at the ready.

Adrenaline surged through Donald Finch's body, quickening from a pounding heart, racing through a labyrinth of arteries and veins. His eyes narrowed, temples throbbing with anticipation. This would soon be the endgame, he thought, the culmination of two years of gruelling tactical work. The robbery had left three Securicor guards petrified. On the fenced, stone-strewn wasteland, where tufts of grass pierced through large cracks in the concrete amidst discarded rubbish and plastic bottles, under the silent shadows of a bricked-over railway, the robbery team had awaited the motorbike escort for the armoured blue Securicor van. Together, they had forced the guards out at gunpoint, plundered the safes, and fled with four hundred and fifteen thousand pounds. Finch was resolute; the streets would be purged of their menace.

The radio crackled into life. 'Copy, India Tango. Message 'Hard Stop Execute' understood, Bravo Two. Over.'

He responded, his voice a steady calm. 'India Tango received. Over. Good luck.'

The sounds around him, the gear changes, the fleeting grey of buildings, the blur of pedestrians, melded with the weight of his unclipped gun and the fabric of the chequered cap on his lap. His mind was alight with the chase. The robbers had scattered immediately after seizing the money, their getaway cars vanishing in different directions. But the police were primed, the trackers' moving arrows had warned and followed, an alert rippling out widely. Finch was ready to consign them to prison, behind heavy doors, for years.

'Copy, India Tango. Execute Hard Stop. Clear ride, approaching contact point. Will execute on readiness. Copy...'

His mind momentarily went to the missing suspects, the surveillance logs had thrown up other collaborators. He knew there were other members of the robbery. Pressing the receiver again, Finch confirmed, 'Received, Bravo One. India Tango, good luck. Over.' The suspect vehicle was now visible, nearing the junction. The ambush was moments away from springing into action. Caps were readied, hands on guns, bodies tensed for rapid egress. But it was the absent suspects, those elusive collaborators the surveillance logs had identified, who gnawed at his subconscious. They would evade capture today.

Then came the last team leader, a Detective Sergeant, crisp and precise. 'India Tango, Copy. Execute hard stop. Over and understood. Copy.'

At the junction, the city's pulse paused at the red lights. Officers leapt from their cars, caps pressed to heads, guns raised in a fluid, practised motion.

'Go! Go!' Orders blared from the radios, resounding around them. The tactical vehicles screeched into position, boxing in the blue BMW. Glass shattered, shouts and screams filled the air. There was no escape for the occupants as the Flying Squad officers converged, guns pointed unflinchingly.

'Show us your hands! Show us your hands now!'

DI Finch was in motion, his robust frame pounding the pavement, trailing the swift action. He arrived just as the suspects, extracted from their vehicle, were cuffed and sprawled on the pavement.

'We're securing the scene, Sir,' a young Detective Sergeant reported, his face alight with the thrill of the capture.

Surveying the scene, Finch noted the prone figures. These were the hardened, wily criminals who had long evaded capture. But there would always be more - more guns, more witnesses, more robberies in his East End patch. He took pride in cleansing his manor, as if vacuuming away stubborn specs of dirt. A quiet grunt was his only self-congratulation as he walked to the BMW's rear. The boot was open, revealing a holdall with the loot, still in Securicor plastic, an ill-gotten bounty now reclaimed.

Above, clouds gathered, preparing to shroud the London skyline with impending rain, the winds that had buffeted him earlier now abating. Satisfied with the day's work, Finch watched as the suspects were led to separate cars. The scene was one of three coordinated ambushes, all successful, with no casualties. He stood, pensive, by the roadside. Today had been a victory for Operation Nemesis, yet the remaining robbers lurked in his thoughts. They were out there, dangerous, likely plotting their next move. Traffic streamed past, a reminder that the city's heartbeat continued, indifferent to the drama that had unfolded.

Armed Robbery 1992 Age 21

The early darkness of the evening had enfolded us like a trap. At the bus stop, we readied ourselves, and from a shop preparing to close, carols spilled into the busy December traffic. A choir's soft, comforting melody unfolded, attempting to stir emotions within me. Despite the ecstasy in my system, a remnant from the day's habitual use, my focus remained sharp.

We moved swiftly with purposeful strides, drawn to the lights at the door across the road. As I crossed, the point of no return long behind me, I raised the shotgun from beneath my jacket. The door, a mix of glass and silver metal, yielded to my kick. Connie was right behind me, armed as well.

'Get on the floor!' I yelled, the command slicing through the room's light.

'Armed Police, drop your weapons!' The dread of that shout enveloped me. From the corner of my eye, I saw Connie's silhouette dart away. I was left with a struggle. An undercover officer had emerged from just inside the door where they had lain in wait. He was a large man, broad-shouldered and taller than me, with cropped black hair.

A shot burst into the air, its roar vibrating through the night, sending wadding and zinc skyward. Time seemed to distort as we grappled for control of the shotgun, our movements a frenzied dance. Chaos erupted around me; screams, shouts, the scrambling crowd, screeching cars, and wailing sirens. The officer wrested the gun from me; it jerked unpredictably as we fought on the ground, and another shot ricocheted off the pavement.

I ran for my life, abandoning the gun and the pursuing officer on the lit road. Veering left into Barnet Grove, I plunged into the darkness. Panic surged, sharpening my senses, driving my body into overdrive, my thoughts ensnared by cold fear. The desperate flight from the illuminated road, the abandoned firearm, it all unfolded in slow motion. My breath laboured, my limbs ached, and the cry of 'Armed Police' echoed in my ears.

I zig-zagged down the pavement, discarding cartridges under parked cars. The belief that I might not survive consumed me; I imagined a bullet striking my back. The night's chill, the waxing moon above, I ran, dodging between cars, alongside the towering iron railings of the Turin Street estate. My mouth was parched, each breath a struggle, the drugs in my system were purged by the adrenaline racing through my bloodstream.

No bullet came, but the night was torn by police sirens, a piercing whirr that dominated the dark. I could hear them closing in, a relentless pursuit through the shadowed streets. I slipped through an opening in the railings, dropping a glove in my haste, and darted into the labyrinth of flats, desperate for escape.

Above, the sudden roar of a police helicopter broke the silence, its spotlight slicing through the darkness.

'Show us your hands. Down! Down!' They forced me to the ground, a tangle of shouting, pumped figures pinning me down. The helicopter's spotlight flooded the scene as I was kicked in the face.

'Fucking shoot at us,' they spat.

My hands were cuffed tightly as people from the balconies shouted protests.

'Leave him alone!'

'Get inside,' the police barked back.

The rotor's noise and the downdraft faded into the night. My mouth tasted blood; the blue lights of the police cars flickered around us. It was over. They spoke of moving to a secure location, the high-security police station on Leman Street. My face pressed against the cold ground, numbness spread through me as my adrenaline and terror levelled out.

On the ground, cuffed, my gaze stretched to where Connie Draper was also being subdued. The Flying Squad had monitored our approach on Bethnal Green Road and had been part of the team surveilling us, along with other armed robbery teams. They knew exactly who Stephen Gillen and Connie Slaney were and what they were suspected of.

Detective Steadman, with his clear hazel eyes and a distinctive mole by his lip, surveyed the scene as the helicopter ascended into the night. The balconies were emptying now, the clamour subsiding.

The detectives had found shotgun cartridges and one black woollen glove along the route I had fled. Steadman, who nursed a slight limp, often the butt of jokes behind closed doors, smiled to himself. He had purposefully taken the other glove and a cartridge from me during the search and slipped them into his pocket.

With the suspects now contained, he planned to plant evidence, ensuring it would link me to the crime. As I was led to the police car, he contemplated his next move. A stocking mask would soon find its way into my jacket pocket during processing, and the gloves would connect me to the scene of the gunfire...

Flying Squad 1992

Detective Inspector Finch and DS Truman were just outside the cell, the latch open, their eyes gleaming with a sense of triumph. Finch's voice was gruff, tinged with a note of satisfaction, 'You're lucky, Gillen. You had quite the fortune tonight. I always said your time would come. The world is run by stories, and make no mistake, tonight your story could have ended very differently. The gods were with you. With all those pedestrians around, if we had a clear line of fire...?' He shook his head in mock commiseration.

In the cell, a sense of doom loomed over me, leaving me feeling weak, desperate, and shattered, yet a flicker of defiance still kindled within. The serious nature of my situation was becoming a heavy load to bear, but I faced them with a glare that was more a brave front than true courage, my inner foundation trembling.

'Shooting at police, firearms with intent to endanger life, conspiracy to rob,' Truman interjected, his voice laden with condemnation. 'You're looking at a lengthy sentence... Eighteen years, perhaps.'

Finch chimed in, 'What about the other robberies? The security van heists? Come clean with us. Share the names, the operations. We can advocate for you, get the judge to show leniency.'

'You can go and fuck off. I'd rather eat stones on the road!' I was at the back of the cell. In my white paper-thin forensic suit, sitting on the cold step as far as possible away from them.

DI Finch's eyes appeared at the hatch, hard and icy green, exuding menace.

'I'm going to ensure you and Slaney are put away for a very long time. Remember this, Gillen. Your cohorts in crime, the robbers and gunmen, they're all behind bars. And we'll catch the rest. The East End will be free of your kind. I promised I'd see to it, and I'll make sure you get a hefty sentence.'

As the figure withdrew, Finch snapped, 'DS Truman, read him the additional charges.'

'Gillen, you need to understand the gravity of this,' Truman said, his lazy eye narrowing as he read from the sheet. 'Beyond the current charges, we're also adding unlicensed firearm possession. Do you comprehend? Have you got anything to say, Gillen?'

I approached the hatch, peering through the frame at Truman's mocking visage.

Softly, yet with a hint of insolence, I said, 'I have one thing to say, yes.'

'And what might that be?' he prodded, pen at the ready.

'I'll confess to the firearm charge if you drop all the others.' Despite the pain, a laugh escaped me, a brief respite flashing across my expression, causing their faces to contort from smug certainty to incredulous fury.

The metal flap was slammed shut, sealing me once more in stark solitude.

From the corridor, I overheard them, Truman's voice tainted with disdain, 'These two are serious trouble, Gov.' Finch agreed, 'Indeed, serious trouble.' Their footsteps faded down the hall.

At the end of the corridor, Finch's voice boomed, 'You're in for the long haul, Gillen. We'll make sure of it!'

A sigh escaped me as the walls of the cell seemed to close in further, the starkness and the distant sounds of keys and polished floors merging with the constant hum of a generator. My body was sore, my thoughts in disarray, and I slumped to the floor, overcome by exhaustion.

Reflection

We find ourselves exactly where we're meant to be. It's crucial to acknowledge that our past, with all its tribulations and triumphs, has shaped us. We are the sum of our experiences. They forge us, for better or worse. Some falter under the weight, others navigate the storm and emerge stronger, but our current state is a direct result of our journey thus far.

Humans are complex creatures, capable of great beauty yet tainted by darkness. My salvation lay in transforming that darkness into something creative, positive, and full of light. The figures who've played roles in the various acts of my life, good and bad, are unforgettable. But the past should not be a place of permanent residence. It's a revolving door, and its value lies in the lessons we extract and the strength we draw from it. We glance back not to remain but to learn, to fortify ourselves for the road ahead.

CHAPTER 6

Sentencing

" 'We will have to shut you up where you can't do any more
harm.' They took him away and shut him in prison. "

— H.A. Rey, Curious George

The Old Bailey 1992

The blue flashing lights and screaming sirens of the police escort exploded into the busy early morning of the city of London as the motorcade quickly navigated the tight streets. The white, level 2 escort transportation van holding the dangerous prisoners was bombproof, with distinguishing thick black numbers on the roof and a wide, bright orange stripe along its side, so it could be continuously observed from the ground and air.

Police snipers from vantage points across the road, on top of buildings, watched as the four armed police vehicles and two lead police motorcycles created a floating box manoeuvre, sealed the roads and access at every side of the van as it disappeared into the downward tunnel to the Old Bailey.

We had started out earlier in the day from the high-security Unit in Brixton Prison, South London. We had been searched in the sterile area in the prison, within a prison, taken through the air-locked doors and guided by a bolstered prison staff with barking dogs into the van, which had pulled tight into the side yard. The van had joined the police escort as it left the prison gates, and it had not stopped at traffic lights, just roared and screamed through the early morning traffic. My mind would not settle, and my thoughts moved as though I was skimming through a series of movie trailers. The attempted robbery that had put me here. A hidden shotgun under a coat. Walking the streets, as 'City', my hand in many pies. The cells at the High Security, Leamon Street Police station. DI Finch and the warning of his cold voice through a metal grate in the green cell door.

Then a completely different movie, and this time my mind decided to watch this play out. It was three weeks ago, and I saw it clearly. Could smell the freshness of the crisp air, could hear the softness of the conversation in my ear, and the snap of the young horse as its legs ran...

We were together as we watched the fierceness of the young, black foal run in the paddock. I could see it clearly as my eyes closed against the harshness of the police motorcade and the stabbing of the sirens surrounding me. Arms were draped over the wooden frame of the outer ring, and we talked quietly. Happily, like a father and son, as we studied the progress of the young, wild horse. Showing its youth and immaturity, it ran and pulled and tugged on the rope around its neck, testing the man who held it. Near the centre of the circular training paddock, the man who skilfully worked the rope stuck his heel hard into the soft ground to facilitate the position he needed, the proper leverage against the pull of the horse. The young foal shook its sleek, silky black mane, opened wide hazel eyes, dipped its head with strength, breath snorting fiercely as it bucked and ran.

He stood resting on the wooden frame of the paddock, relaxed beside me. A big, fat man with rich dark hair, a big name and a specialist experience in life, great wealth, and influence. A fighting man known far and wide. A gypsy from the old school who was head of a highly respected family.

'His father was a great racehorse,' he said in a soft voice as he watched the horse stop and steady itself for a moment. 'We have great hopes for him just the same. But he sweats out a bit early. This is how we train them, Stephen.'

I was silent but felt compelled in the company of this man to speak. 'They're beautiful. What an animal. Really something,' I said.

He smiled. A genuine soft smile like that to a young son who was wet behind the ears. I knew behind the smile was a wide, striking, cunning and knowing. A hard upbringing that had forged, moulded, kicked, and polished him toward the finished article that now stood before me. He moved again with an unassuming manner and objective measured eyes.

We turned. We said goodbye to the trainer and strolled to the black Mercedes Sports we had arrived in. I had travelled down the night before with his son, James, who was a professional boxer and a close friend of mine, and I had stayed the night at their family home in Newmarket. I had been welcomed into the house with this unique family that was fierce and wise with no airs and graces, and I was treated like one of the family.

I knew I was being nostalgic, but this was the one place I ever really felt what it was like to be in a family. A genuine flesh and blood family, not one made up of comrades. Bobby used to treat me like one of his sons, I looked like one with my dark hair and Irish heritage, so I fitted right in, and I was welcomed, it was the place in my mind that was safe, a sanctuary from where I was now.

The raging sirens pulled me from the memory. The police and the van manoeuvred through an obstacle in the traffic lanes.

I sat on the plastic box that was my seat. Inside the van, in my cage, a claustrophobic space that you could just about stand in, I watched the police escort outside from my tinted window.

I had a splitting headache as the sirens of the screaming motorcade were worse inside the van. A relentless, vibrating screech that affected the heart and soul hammered your head. I pushed back the bright yellow and green of the prison jumpsuit I was being transported in, revealing my watch. The black and gold round face of the IWC logo shone and glinted. As a category A prisoner, I would only be given my pressed blue suit, white shirt, and tie when safely inside the building.

My watch was a reminder, I realised, of finer things and happier moments in the calm of a hellish storm. Twenty minutes, I thought... It had taken us twenty minutes from Brixton to the City of London. A bloody miracle. I sighed. A long, gasping inhaling sound that helped release the tight muscles in my neck and shoulders. The image played dissipated. The young foal, its playful jumping, the brightness of the day I had spent in Newmarket not three weeks before... was gone. My heart crashed. Hitting waves of despair, it ebbed like a withdrawing ocean on the sand and seashells of regret and longing.

The light of the outside world left us as we drove down into the deep recesses of the building.

At the bottom of the enclosed tunnel, the armoured Category A van came to a grinding halt in the sheltered light as the massive turntable twisted the whole vehicle around towards where we would be walked to the cells.

The dim lights emphasised the greyness and doom. The dark blue uniforms of the prison officer that waited for the handover, the worn, dirty grey of the concrete all around us. The keys that swung and hung and were handled on long key chains. I watched and heard it all. Inside the prison jumpsuit I wore, my heart was heavy. My body ached with stress and anxiety; it was weaker with the terrible diet and sleepless nights. There were three of us in the van. An IRA prisoner linked to bombings and a Colombian drug smuggler arrested with a tonne and a half of cocaine linked to a cartel.

From inside the van, through the little white metal grate on the door, I watched them shuffle past. They opened my door, and I felt gratitude from my legs and body as they gained the opportunity to stretch and move. My feet, in shined, black shoes, hit the concrete of the concourse outside. The aura of old criminals, ancient history, and grim turmoil battered me as I walked up the steps into a holding cell. Then it was up a set of stairs, through more metal, barred gates on my way to the Category A Suite. The sound of keys, banging metal doors, shouts and talking accompanied me. The stale smell of the old building, a damp foreboding nausea attack that mixed architecture, paperwork, rancid food and metal, hit my senses filling me with dread.

In the western part of the City of London, opened in February 1907 and designed by E W Mountford, the Central Criminal Court, also known as the Old Bailey or Justice Hall, was built on the site of the infamous Newgate Prison and over the centuries had been periodically remodelled.

The Cat A Suite comprised six cells. Mostly single cells, with extra officers and additional extra metal gates on either side of a small, tight area closer to the main, most prominent and infamous high-security courtrooms in the massive building. The area was the most secure part of the Central Criminal

Court. The cell door closed behind me. I was in a slightly bigger cell that could hold six people, only two sat on the long wooden bench at the back of a small, claustrophobic space. I stood, exchanged nods with my cellmates, put the see-through plastic bag that held my depositions, strategy notes, and defence correspondence on the bench. I attempted to rub the tiredness from my eyes, my nostrils filled with the damp decay of the building. There was graffiti all over the walls, names and signs and slogans scratched, scrawled and drawn. I viewed the filthy, pale-yellow walls of the cell, the ceiling, and a depressing, painful sigh scattered the energy inside me.

The Old Bailey 1992

The courtroom at the Old Bailey was deathly silent once more, a tactical hiatus in the grand theatre of justice as the Queen's Counsel adjusted his white wig and theatrically arranged the cuff of his black bar jacket.

He directed his gaze to the witness stand, across the crowded wooden courtroom, to Detective Steadman and intoned in a crisp voice, 'Detective Steadman, you are an experienced officer of the Flying Squad, are you not?'

With a flourish, he riffled through the papers before him, surveyed the court, assured of its rapt attention, and continued, 'Twenty years of illustrious service, I note, with commendations. It is reasonable, then, Detective Steadman, for us - the jury and others present - to expect that someone of your standing, who has ascended to such heights within the revered and specialist, Counter-Organised Crime Division of the Flying

Squad, would be an officer of exceptional calibre, is that correct?'

The barrister paused, letting a weighty silence draw out as the courtroom hung on his every word.

DC Steadman nodded, his expression one of concern. His black hair, swept to one side, began to fall across his face, reflecting his discomfort. Adorning his grey suit, his Flying Squad badge glinted on his lapel.

'A decorated officer, no less, and a member of one of Scotland Yard's most esteemed divisions. This, the 'Flying Squad', so named for its unfettered jurisdiction across London...' He allowed his words to linger, his gaze briefly meeting that of the jury - a mix of stern-faced women and attentive middle-aged men - extending an unspoken offer of camaraderie to infiltrate their thoughts. The courtroom's silence deepened for a moment...

'A squad with carte blanche to operate unseen and unbounded throughout the city...'

With theatrical pensiveness, the Queen's Counsel's charisma radiated through the wood-panelled courtroom. His gaze swept over the transfixed faces: the jury, the robed figure of Justice Peterson, the stenographer, members of the press, police witnesses, the public, the black-robed Prosecution QC and his junior, and finally the defendants, Stephen Gillen and Connie Slaney, in the dock behind him. Then, raising his arm dramatically, he announced, 'Your Honour, I call for exhibit 6.5...'

All eyes followed the usher as he carried a small, long, brown paper bag to Detective Constable Steadman. The exhibit was in Steadman's hands for all to see. Yet, as he unfurled its contents - a light grey portion of a woman's stocking, with two small, torn eyeholes - he attempted to wad it into a tighter ball.

The Defence Queen's Counsel swiftly intervened, 'No, Mr. Steadman, display it fully. Let the court see.'

From the dock, I scrutinised Steadman, my blue suit and smart tie in stark contrast to the drama unfolding. Steadman's discomfort was palpable as the stocking mask was stretched over his hand for all to witness. He was lying, and it was evident to everyone.

My gaze swept the courtroom and halted abruptly. In the public gallery, I recognised a middle-aged man with distinctive, hard features, his hair peppered with grey, and his deep green eyes memorable and inscrutable. The man from the bus stop on the night of the robbery, now rubbing his stubbled cheek with a three-fingered hand, remained fixated on a point ahead, unresponsive to the unfolding scene.

'Does this appear to be part of a robber's kit, Detective Constable Steadman?' the barrister pressed.

'Yes,' Steadman's voice faltered, quieter now.

'With your extensive policing background and commendations from one of Scotland Yard's most active units, we can infer that you would have conducted a thorough search of these two purportedly dangerous armed robbers as dictated by your training, correct?'

'Yes...'

The jury, the press, and the prosecution observed Steadman intently as the Defence allowed his next words to resonate with implication. 'Your Honour, I now wish to present exhibit 7.1.'

The usher handed the next piece of evidence - a black woollen glove - to Steadman at the witness stand.

'Detective Constable Steadman, you were charged with searching the scene post-incident, is that correct?'

'Yes, I was,' he stuttered, 'Detective Constable Jones was also present...'

'Please, Detective,' the QC interjected, his tone now edged with sarcasm, 'the questioning is my prerogative.'

The tension was palpable; Steadman's face flushed a conspicuous shade of red, his anxiety laid bare for all to see.

'I'll ask once more, Detective Constable Steadman. Do these items - the stocking mask and the black glove - resemble part of a robber's kit?'

'...Yes, they do.'

'And where did you find them?'

'I searched, Gillen at the scene. He was searched again and a glove was found. I then...'

... 'Mr Steadman, you searched him twice?'

'No, once. There were two gloves. I then'

'Two gloves, Detective Steadman. So, you did search him and you found two gloves?'

'No there was three gloves. I had...'

'There were three gloves?'

'No, I...'

The Queens Council looked around the court. His face smiled knowingly. We knew the officer had been part of moving and planting evidence and our strategy was to expose his lies. The suspense was palpable in the old and aged court room. Its dusty smell had been replaced now by the sweat of the prison officers surrounding us as the court rooms energy raised. From the dock I could feel the jury's confusion and incredulity.

My defence QC pressed home the attack.

'Let me assist you, Detective Constable Steadman... These items do appear to be part of a robber's kit. You are an exceedingly experienced officer. Mr Gillen was searched at the scene, not just once, but three times. Twice at the scene as he was apprehended on the ground, and once more upon his arrival at Leman Street Police Station. I am aware of this because I have the signed custody logs right here in front of me... Detective Constable Steadman, I propose that you did indeed search the defendant at the scene and, being also tasked with securing the scene, you saw an opportunity to cement your precarious conviction by placing the glove and cartridge in the defendant's pockets.

'That is utterly false. I merely...'

'Upon planting the incriminating items, Detective Constable Steadman, you then proceeded to relocate the other glove to the crime scene where a firearm was discharged, further solidifying your fabricated case against my client. I now put it to you that you are fully aware and were complicit in concocting this evidence, Mr Steadman, is that not correct?'

Steadman's complexion turned a lighter shade of purple. He gripped the top of the witness stand tightly, his words emerging in a disordered cascade.

'There were three gloves. I had to log them. I then needed...'

'No, Mr Steadman, there were not three gloves. There were, of course, only two, both discarded by the assailant who vanished into the night. Mr Gillen, my client, was merely unfortunate enough to encounter you and, after being subdued by other officers, you searched him and secreted the glove and shotgun cartridge in his pockets?'

'I didn't... It wasn't...'

'I assert that you are lying, Detective Constable Steadman!'

The courtroom erupted.

From my seat, I observed it all: the police and DI Finch shaking their heads and closing their eyes, the jury tensing, the press fervently taking notes. The Prosecution QC, a sharp-faced, formidable figure of silent legal lethality, had been meticulously selected. He sat, idly turning the other glove in his fingers, a subtle, knowing smile spreading across his lips.

The Judge, a distinguished figure with grey hair and penetrating brown eyes, who would preside over the Millennium Dome Robbery years later, brought his gavel down forcefully, declaring, 'Mr Nathan, that will suffice. Please moderate your language.'

'Certainly, Your Honour, I merely seek to ascertain the truth from the witness.'

'I'm keeping an eye on you, Mr Nathan...'

It was planned I thought this whole business. I had sat here for two weeks, coming back and forth under heavy police guard from Brixton Special Security Unit to the Category A suite here, and like a gripping football match Defence and Prosecution were both scoring goals. End to end stuff. But just when you thought you were winning, the referee, in this case My Lord Justice Peterson would wade in, give a bad decision and save them.

He resembled your closest friend now, my defence barrister, a cunning predator in disguise, orchestrating a trap for the prey.

'Detective Constable Steadman, we have already encountered conflicting versions from you. The reality remains that you must have placed the glove and shotgun cartridge at the scene and relocated the other glove to the attempted robbery site.'

He turned to the jury, drawing them in conspiratorially. Their heads leaned in, captivated by the cadence of his voice and his expressive gaze.

'Members of the Jury, Detective Constable Steadman's extensive experience implies he would have conducted a thorough search of the defendant at the scene, yet no record of these items exists until his arrival at the police station. Additionally, there was no mention of a stocking mask. This item was only introduced into evidence three months later, following forensic analysis of the defendant's jacket.'

He paused, a silence descending, stretching taut across the room, embedding itself in the midst's palpable suspense.

The glaring inconsistency in the police and prosecution's narrative remains unexplained. Despite meticulous searches on three separate occasions, these items mysteriously materialized, evidenced by the custody search record from his arrival at the station, which notably included 'one tiny black button'.

The Old Bailey 1992

The courtroom was silent, a strange, frozen moment where time seemed to stand still. The dusty smell of old, chestnut-stained panelled wood mixed with the rustle of papers and a hint of sweat from the packed attendees filled our nostrils. We stared at the judge.

The trial at the Central Criminal Court of the Old Bailey had been unfolding for four weeks. As the accusations sliced deep into the integrity of the police investigation and sharply cut at the character of their conduct, Lord Justice Peterson's rulings had become increasingly stringent. His mood had darkened, his hawk-like eyes growing sterner and colder.

Now, he leaned back in his chair. It was his moment, one he had awaited with relish. His voice, sure and piercing, cut cleanly through the courtroom air.

'Can the two defendants please stand up?'

A shoe squeaked in the hushed silence. Our hands gripped the brass rail of the dock for stability. The judge's wizened and lined face, crowned with a curled white wig, sat elevated above us, his robes of red, black, and purple imbued with power and ceremony. His piercing eyes drilled into us.

'This has been a long and costly case, concerning a highly organised gang of armed robbers. They appear to have lived in a fraternity with other polished criminals, letting nothing hinder their criminal pursuits...'

The jury and the attending police officers, eager for sentencing, shifted in anticipation, holding their breath.

'…You have both been found guilty on all counts by a jury of your peers, and you have been represented by highly skilled advocates…'

Detective Inspector Finch and DS Truman shared a smile, joined by their Superintendent in full uniform, all present to witness the case's conclusion.

'…The attempted robbery was meticulously planned and vicious in execution, only foiled by the diligent work of a sophisticated unit from Scotland Yard…'

The jury, having returned a ten-to-two majority verdict after intense deliberation, hung on every word the judge said.

'…It was a calculated crime, with two shots fired on a busy London Street teeming with the public…'

DI Finch's lips curled into a sarcastic smile, and DS Truman's lazy eye sparkled with a shared sense of triumph.

'…Two shots, with a deliberate pause between them, fired by the defendant Gillen. Fortunately, there were no injuries or casualties…'

Connie, to my left, faced the judge's damning words, a tremor briefly visible in his steadying arm. Inside, I felt a void, as if the judge's words were meant for someone else.

'…We have heard your defence claim that evidence was moved at the scene, that members of the Flying Squad fabricated evidence, corrupted due process, falsified records, and perjured themselves…'

Stephen Gillen and Connie Slaney exchanged glances, their silent communication conveying a mutual understanding without words.

'...Thus, you have aggravated this court with your accusations, failing to admit any guilt for your actions... Stephen Gillen and Connie Slaney, I have seldom encountered two more dangerous young men. I am convinced you would have done anything to carry out your crime or secure your escape...'

The judge's pause was deliberate, a prelude to the gravity of his next words.

The end was nigh. It was all but over.

'...I have no hesitation in sentencing you both as follows. Gillen, for Attempted Robbery, fourteen years and for Conspiracy to Rob, an additional eleven years... For firearms with intent to endanger life...'

Stephen Gillen and Connie Slaney stood with stoic expressions, absorbing the jury's audible reactions. Emotionally numb, they listened as the judge's voice, resonating through the silent courtroom, began to tally the sentences that would cumulate to forty-nine years.

Category A

John Melton was a confident and assured man, his career a testament to hard work, notable achievements, and the knack for being in the right place at the right time. A Cambridge alumnus with a Master's in Politics, he had briefly contributed to his father's printing business before ascending swiftly through the ranks of the Home Office. His resume now boasted positions such as attaché to the French Ambassador and a senior executive role under the Head of the Prison Service, as well as Chairman of Doc 1 and the Category A committee.

'What level of danger do they pose to the prison service? They are career criminals with targets. Our intelligence paints a very grim picture,' inquired the Superintend Gold Commander, a dynamic, young, dark-haired man from the Met, who represented the police chair. Melton surveyed the long teak table, noting the assembly of experts and area executives from various divisions tasked with the containment and security of the nation's most perilous criminal, narcotic, and terrorist threats.

The Head of the Probation Service, a steely-eyed, middle-aged woman with a calm voice, informed the group, 'We do have records from Gillen's history. He first came to our attention regarding contact with his son, Sid, who is now one year old and living in Bow with his grandparent. Gillen was released from HMP Wayland in August for home leave and failed to return.'

The Police Commander elaborated, 'Our intelligence suggests many troubling details about this gang. They are highly active, involved in armed robberies, tobacco lorry and security van hijackings, and organized crime. The list is extensive and dark; I have it here. They have affiliations with other organized groups domestically and internationally, notably in Spain, Ireland, and South America. They would indeed pose a high escape risk. Her Majesty's Police Service would recommend they be classified as high risk.'

A hushed silence fell over the room.

All eyes turned to Chair John Melton, an unremarkable middle-aged man in a grey suit, with intent grey-blue eyes, a round, well-groomed face, and neatly combed short brown hair.

Melton paused, his neatly manicured hands ceasing their shuffling of papers as he adjusted his blue and red striped tie. His gaze drifted through the expansive bank of windows to his right, over Millbank, and to the River Thames, where a tugboat made its steady progress through the calm waters.

The files before him weighed heavily on his mind. The job's gravity was not lost on him; the responsibility of safeguarding the public and ensuring the security of the state by properly containing and transporting these individuals was paramount.

He took one more glance at the intelligence files. The police were prone to exaggerating the threat, he mused, yet the committee invariably sided with caution. Looking up from the documents, he met the expectant gaze of his colleagues.

With his characteristic precision and a composed, measured voice, he declared, 'I've listened to each of you, and thank you. I have diligently reviewed the background, particularly the security and intelligence files. There is a compelling case for heightened security due to the nature of the offences and their serious crime connections. The clear risk of escape and propensity for violence are significant factors. Therefore, it is confirmed that Case 360, Stephen Gillen, and Case 361, Connie Slaney, do present a substantial security threat. Sufficient evidence warrants their detention under

High-Risk Category A conditions. This decision is predicated on the proven risk they pose to the public, the police, and the security of the state.'

The room burst into a flurry of activity: chairs scraped against the thin grey carpet, papers rustled, briefcases clicked shut.

As Doc 1, the strategic Security Committee of the Home Office, adjourned, John Milton's face remained impassive. Clutching the brown file, he walked to the window. The tugboat was now further up the Thames, widening its distance from Lambeth Bridge, while Millbank teemed with traffic below. Glancing next door at the stark white façade of the MI5 building, he reflected on the gravity of his role. Indeed, it was a responsibility to do the job he did, a job he was determined to execute with excellence.

The man with three fingers felt the cool burning flow of the whiskey rush down his throat. In the cheap but clean bedsit chosen for invisibility in Islington. He burped and rolled to his side on the bed covers and pushed his square green, checked tweed cap to the floor. The morning light was fighting to infiltrate the cracks of the blinds he had closed tight at the window and the deep well of his depression and loneliness had returned to take him again.

He blinked his eyes, gulped. It was the hell that was a double life. The two faces to the world that he kept in place for privacy and protection. The guilt and powerlessness were seeping through him again. Like an aggressive cancer it attacked him when he was at his most vulnerable, at his weakest moments. He groaned and got to his stockinged feet, walked to the little sink and looked at his face in the mirror above it. His green eyes were less angry and bitter today. Like moving winds, they had been replaced by pain, anger, loss and guilt.

He moved, as he tended to, his three fingered hand over the stubble on his cheeks and chin. Bare chested, curled hair covering his upper torso and, in his jeans and stockinged feet he walked to the bottle, it was his fourth bottle of whiskey and he slugged at it hard. The day before he had been at the sentencing of the boy at the Old Bailey. He had missed his chance. He pulled the old, torn, black and white photo from his back pocket. He still called him the boy, although he was the man because that's what the Gardner did and was known for. Taking boys, the broken and unique and hard and lost and troublesome. The strays. Like the twisted and different and slightly broken flowers in the pretty and beautiful bunch. That's what he was instructed and driven to do and because of it they reckoned him an important nuisance and called him the Gardener.

He looked again at the old dogeared photo and the pain like a lifting jet pierced through him and his lungs filled with a rattling cry. He smashed the empty bottle of whiskey against the wall with force. He had slipped on his knees to the wooden floor and with his disfigured hand he clasped the photo. Dizziness had risen within his aching body and heart and the riveting anger was growing again with every present bitterness. The boy, Stephen Gillen who was now a man might be away and out of his reach for a long time but he would be released one day, and when he was he would be waiting. Next time, at the first opportunity, he would make his decisive move and finish this.

CHAPTER 7

Inside Hell

"Imprisonment is as irrevocable as death."

— George Bernard Shaw

Note: This chapter is a little different, as whilst the narrative continues, there are also sections that provide an insight into the world behind bars, that help to paint a clearer picture of how we lived.

Parkhurst Prison 1992

Following my sentencing at the Old Bailey, I was whisked away under a level 2 escort straight to Parkhurst. The operation was shrouded in secrecy, fuelled by fears of a breakout or a dramatic rescue effort coupled by the intelligence that I had tried to smuggle in a firearm to aid in an escape.

The journey to the ferry terminal was one I'll never forget. It was marked by a farcical mishap; the van's starter motor gave out. As the police swarmed around the van, I couldn't help but mock their efforts, "You lot, you're a joke!" I jeered. "You couldn't organise a piss up in a brewery. You've gone to all this trouble, the cloak and dagger, to transfer me like this, and you've norsed (cockney slang) it spectacularly."

With me locked in the back, they scrambled to fix the van.

The ferry ride as a Category A prisoner was another experience altogether. They parked the van right at the ship's stern, the police cordon tight around me, while I remained in shackles inside the van. Staring at the rolling waves, I thought about the Titanic - if we went down, they'd be all for themselves and I'd certainly go down with this thing, there'd be no escape for me.

Charlie Bronson, Parkhurst 1992

Parkhurst, back in those days, was a repository of infamy, housing all the big names - a veritable who's who of the criminal underworld. It was the kind of place where you couldn't set foot on the landing unless you were a 'somebody' your history was known and you were liked. And I had my mates there, armed robbers and organised crime gang members; Perry Taroni, Vic Dark, Dennis and Mehmet Ariff, David Jude, Johnny Kearney, Bobby Green, Eddie Richardson, Billy Gentry, my badminton companion, John Kendall a very close friend of mine and Sid Draper with his notorious helicopter escape, Brink's-Mat robber Michael McAvoy, Bill the Bomb, and a slew of other mafia & organised crime figures. Then there were armed robbers, Kevin Brown, Wayne Hurren and John Dunford, the Pewter brothers and some of the IRA men. People like Hugh Doherty from the Balcombe Street siege, Dingus Magee who shot his way out of the Crumlin Road prison, Franny Pope & Charlie Tozer the 'Wild Bunch' armed robbers, Brixton escapee Stan Thompson, murderer Alan Burn, and armed robber Frankie Quinn; we were like a large, dysfunctional family, looking out for each other in those days there and as a younger guy I felt lucky, as we all did, to be there at that iconic time.

We had a nickname for Parkhurst - 'the rock', a moniker that spoke volumes about its hardened inhabitants and the unyielding life within. As cat A's we'd be in each other's pockets, live together and have get to know everyone well. Other co-inhabitants on the block I associated with were, John Gilligan who was deported back to Ireland for the Veronica Guerin case, Charlie Sega from Liverpool, Valero Vichy the Knightsbridge robber, Kevin Lane a wrongly convicted contract killer, Filippo Monteleone & Francesco de Carlo two key Sicilian mafia guys. They had been thought to behind Roberto Calvi 'God's Banker' who was found hanged under Blackfriars Bridge. De Carlo, a Count back in Sicily, was so high ranking in Sicilian Organised crime, that they later deported him after his brother was murdered. He returned to Italy to be a witness against former Italian Prime Minister, Giulio Andreotti for Mafia collusion. Before he left, he gave me a great coffee maker, so there was a little luxury behind bars.

In the bleak confines of Parkhurst Prison, a place with an Alcatraz-like reputation, I had a very good friend, Dessie Cunningham. A well-liked man, facing a 15-year sentence for armed robbery, he tragically ended his own life later into his term, a consequence of the relentless beatings and abuse within the walls of Full Sutton Prison. His passing sent ripples of sorrow among us, especially following an incident that ignited a riot in the already cramped and tense C wing.

Charlie Bronson was nearing his release from Parkhurst on his first incarceration. With a longing to leave a mark of his legacy, he approached the governor, expressing his desire to contribute something to the establishment. The governor handed him a pick and a shovel and commissioned him to construct a fishpond in the compound for the inmates to enjoy – a parting gift of sorts.

The compound of Parkhurst was our slice of freedom. We had our small allotments, tennis courts, and a modest football field. It was our routine, our small escape. And there was Charlie, the infamous inmate, eccentric as ever, dedicating his last few days to the excavation of this fish pond.

My mate Gary Stags, who stood as the best man at my Whitemoor Prison wedding in the high-risk visiting room, Dessie, and a few others would don their long, grey lifer jackets and stroll around. In Parkhurst, you wore your clothes, cooked your meals, lived a slice of life within confines, but the coats helped you to be picked out when you were off the landing.

But Charlie was always a force to be reckoned with, and one day, a misunderstanding blew up into a fierce altercation. Misinterpreting the actions of Dessie and the others as they roamed around the compound, Charlie lashed out, berating them with "You Cockney fucking gangsters", a rare outburst, as he was generally amicable, a big character despite a notorious reputation for being somewhat unhinged. Charlie got on with everyone, so this was out of character.

The quarrel that erupted was intense. Charlie, known for his physical prowess, became embroiled in a notorious confrontation that left him stabbed multiple times on the compound.

Later, reflecting on the incident, Charlie confided, "Stephen, yeah we fell out, but they didn't have to stab me, to try to kill me!" And I could understand that; but that was the times, it was life and death in there, and reputations were not only valuable, but a must to survival in many instances.

In the aftermath of the stabbing, with the alarm blaring and pouring with blood from many stab wounds, Charlie did something typically Charlie. He walked, unaided and bleeding profusely, back to his cell. He shrugged off his cellmate's concern with a brusque "Nah, nah, I'm alright, leave me alone!" showing a refusal to bow to weakness. He was subsequently taken to the hospital for his injuries, and Charlie being Charlie lived to fight another day.

That incident at Parkhurst marked a turning point for Charlie. He left, but the experience had altered him. It was a stark reminder that Queensbury Rules did not apply in there and extreme violence could come and explode at any moment over the slightest thing. Later, he was apprehended again for armed robbery, a reflection of his troubled state. In those days, his youth was marked by a fierce spirit, a fire that did not align with the expectations of society.

The Big Red A

In the classification system of the British prisons, Category A is the highest level of security for those inmates whose escape would be highly dangerous to the public or national security. Within this category, there are three sub-levels:

- AAA: Reserved for the most dangerous individuals, often top terrorists or crime bosses who pose an exceptional risk.
- AA: For high-risk individuals who are influential, potentially with significant financial resources or connections.
- A: The standard level for those who are considered highly dangerous to the public and the state.

I was initially categorised as AA but spent the bulk of my sentence under A. My journey began in Brixton's Special Security Unit, a place renowned for its tight security - so tight, in fact, that when Nessan Quinlivan and Peirce McAuley, two IRA members, managed to escape, it sent shockwaves through the system. They had smuggled a gun into the church service, taken a guard hostage, and breached multiple gates to gain their freedom, sparking rumours of MI5's involvement due to the audacity and success of their escape.

Brixton Special Security 1992

The Brixton Special Security Unit was a prison within a prison, caged and impenetrable. This three-floor self-contained Unit, with airlock doors leading to the main prison and a separate central locking system for once the doors were closed, along with vibration-proof sensors upgraded since the audacious escapes of gangsters Shaun Moody, Stan Thompson, and IRA bomber Gerald Tuite, was deemed the most secure unit in the United Kingdom.

As I listened with the phone pressed to my ear, I could see the other inmates playing on the small pool table sandwiched between the five single cells on each side of the narrow landing. Our cells, reserved for the top security category A's on protection, were on the very top floor, while the hot plate from where we collected our food was at the bottom of the tight metal stairs on the ground floor.

Lily Draper's soft, soulful voice whispered across the line, 'Stephen, I hope you're okay... I miss you. We've been apart for a while and with all that's been happening, I truly realise what I feel for you...'

A warmth spread in my wounded and battered heart as she continued, 'I miss you all the time and you're always on my mind, in the morning when I wake, throughout my daily chores, and in those quiet moments when my thoughts drift to the image of your face, the touch of your hand...'

'I have thought of you too,' I confessed. 'Over the years, I questioned whether a time would ever come that we could talk like this...'

'Stephen, though you're gone, you're not here, I see your face clearly and I miss your smile, especially when it was free from the pain I can see in your eyes... Looking back over the years, I realise that when I was with you, conventional rules didn't apply. Now I'm left looking forward to the times I can come here, to feel you close so we can talk and I can share my feelings...'

'Lily, it is perilous to love me like this,' I warned. 'You don't understand what you're asking of me, what it will mean for us both...'

'...Stephen, I knew it from the first moment I saw you. I was too timid then. I remember following you and Callum just to watch you...'

'But I could be in this place forever. I'm looking at a long sentence. I can't take those years from you?'

'...I will wait, Stephen.'

'I can't subject you to years of this, the pain, the sacrifice...'

'We can endure it together, Stephen. Together, we're strong.'

'It's too much to ask, Lily...'

'We won't let them defeat us. You'll come home one day. We can be together. Our love will triumph...'

Her voice was a balm, soothing my soul and yet stirring tumultuous emotions within me. I was caged, physically and mentally, the walls pressing in with the weight of emotion.

Softly, like a father to a child, I said, 'I can't ask this of you, Lily. To endure this is a pain beyond words, one that will extend through the years...'

'...I'm ready, Stephen. We can do this. It's my choice. I'm not leaving you there.'

'How is Callum?'

'Callum is fine. He has his family. I have no one, only you... You're all I need...'

'Can you finish now, Gillen?' interrupted a prison officer. The staff were already locking cell doors, collecting the snooker cues, and gathering the pool balls.

'Lily, are you certain? Do you understand what you're committing to?'

'I do. You know what I'm like when I've made up my mind...'

The guards watched me, their annoyance palpable, keys jangling impatiently.

'Lily, I'm sorry, I have to go. My God, you've given me much to think about. All these years, I didn't know... I must go now. Send my regards to Callum. Take care... you're in my thoughts. Despite the pain, bars, keys, and uncertainty, I can see you and feel you as if you were here with me...'

I could sense her smile, her laughter, 'Remember, Stephen, I'm with you. Take care. We're like two peas in a pod, okay?'

The phone still against my ear, I heard the finality of the doors slamming shut, their echoes confining me once more within the high-security block's narrow confines.

'Yes, I will. Two peas in a pod...'

The Blue Book

Category A, Section A - it's like a chessboard. they even said as much. They have bespoke, tailored strategies for handling all the cases, their treatment, their movements, all that. It's about wearing you down, containing you, controlling the intelligence. That's the crux of it. And breaking you.

There's no rehabilitation in such a system because you're written off as a lost cause, the worst of the worst. It's about security and containment. This is the origin of the 'blue book'. You're on the book because there's that red 'A' in front of your door, branding you. And at the top, 'HR' screams *High Risk*. But wherever you go in the prison, at any time, there's a blue book with your photo and a big red '**A**' in it. In the offices, on visits, the book follows you, and you're signed over like a package to ensure they always know your whereabouts.

Prison Currency 1992

In the dispersals, tension was the default, a silent pressure that hummed through the corridors. Surrounded by individuals whose minds were labyrinths of violence, unpredictability was the only certainty. A casual morning greeting could be a prelude to an outburst, if you misread the subtext or glanced the wrong way, it could spell trouble. Petty squabbles spiraled into life-

or-death confrontations, and you learned to sense the precursors to chaos. Violence was never a matter of if, but when, and it escalated with frightening speed. My way was to come forward when a real threat presented itself and send a clear aggressive and violent message. In this to me there was kind of safety as others would know and be weary of trying something later.

Cruelty was another layer of this harsh existence. Guards would tamper with your food, finding sadistic pleasure in spitting in your meal, or they'd play mind games with your personal correspondence, weaponising your anticipation and hope. They manipulated situations, positioning you within striking distance of your fiercest adversaries, orchestrating conflicts with the precision of puppeteers. It was all part of this warped, unnatural crazy existence.

Currency inside took many forms. Fortune had me often on the receiving end of these prison economies. Corrupt officers turned smugglers, sneaking in phones long before they became commonplace. The later years of my sentence saw these devices as lifelines, a means to maintain contact, influence, control. Drugs were trafficked under their watchful eyes, the prison's veins pumping illicit substances as a form of capital.

But the trade wasn't restricted to narcotics. Tobacco, a seemingly innocuous luxury, was as valuable as gold. I ensured I was flush with resources - money, cannabis, food, toiletries anything that could be bartered. My survival hinged on my ability to procure and peddle, to live as best I could within the constraints of my cage.

I stood out on the landing, one of my East End crew coming over to chat. 'New shipment's on the way. Got to keep the wolves at bay.'

Mike turned so no one could hear him or read his lips. 'Phones again? How you keeping the screws quiet?'

'They get their share. It's not about money; it's about keeping the peace. Their silence is part of that.'

And smokes? You know it's what keeps the tempers down in here.' I could see the hope in his eyes and knew he's been gaging for a fag for a few days now.

'Sorted. It's all about leverage. Tobacco's the oil; keeps everything running smooth.'

Mike looked relieved. 'What about the gear? The screws can't be liking that.'

I shrugged. 'They turn a blind eye. They know the score. Without the gear flowing, this place would go up in flames. Besides, what are they going to do… lock us up?' I winked at him 'Half of them are the ones bringing it in. We go down, so do they.'

'This whole block's a ticking time bomb.'

I nodded, 'That's why we need the gear, the smokes… and the booze. It's not about comfort; it's about control.'

'Control, right. Because in here, you're either the hammer or the nail.' He mimicked bashing someone's head in.

'Exactly. And these,' I gesture to the hidden contraband, 'make sure I'm not the one getting hit.'

The screws had their price, their integrity sold for a few crumpled notes. They'd slip vodka in water bottles, the clear liquid passing unnoticed, a small reprieve from the relentless grind of incarceration. In that economy of contraband, every transaction was a lifeline, a way to cling to a semblance of power in a place designed to strip you of it.

Breaking Free, Wormwood Prison, 1992

They sat in the front seats of the parked car, rain lashing against the windscreen on the slender side road near the main supermarket close to Old Kent Road.

'It's all there,' said the driver, passing a small shoebox to his companion.

The man in the passenger seat, a serving prison officer, opened the green box. Inside, he saw a .22-calibre handgun and ammunition rounds, neatly black-taped, beside two small mobile phones, orderly arranged.

'Okay. Now no one's going to get hurt? This was my one condition... As long as no one gets hurt...'

The prison officer replaced the lid on the box. With a decade of service behind him and his pension on the horizon, his past was not forgotten. A former Royal Marine commando, he had served in the Falklands, witnessed the battle of Goose Green amidst the chaos of burning ships and skies filled with lead and tracer rounds. He was all too familiar with the destruction firearms could wreak.

The driver glanced over, fleeting yet firm. 'No one will get hurt. We just want him out. We need him out. Here's your payment.'

A brown envelope exchanged hands.

'Alright, I'll get it to him. But it will be on my terms. Security's always tight. I can't say when I'll manage it.'

With the transaction complete, the prison officer, burdened by gambling debts and rent woes, pulled his collar high against the rain. He stepped out of the car and vanished around the street corner.

In the oppressive silence of a high-security prison, the night closes in on the inmates like the calm before a deafening storm. Encased within are compartmentalised souls and minds, sorted for control, security, and the efficient operation of the institution. Regardless of the crime or the individual, the tumultuous well of emotions within them – tearing, shuddering, surging – presents an ongoing battle for control. Amidst the various scenarios playing out in their minds, some as tiresome as old B-movies on repeat, a profound longing always lingers at the surface: the yearning for freedom, for the sun's warmth on one's face, the feel of the wind, the grass beneath unrestrained feet. The desire to revisit past times to forge different plans, take new paths, to reclaim the life left behind, and to relish once more the sweet taste of unbound freedom.

Letters, Wandsworth Prison 1993

In the stark simplicity of my white-walled prison cell, with morning light straining through the round, aged bars of the high window, I penned a letter, my emotions tempered by the gravity of this situation.

Your last letter arrived, Lily, a beacon in the bleakness of my days here, amidst the cacophony of clanging keys and raucous calls. It's a strange existence, isolated from you, facing a future that's indistinct, its years unfurling before me like an endless road. They say the full weight of a sentence like mine takes years to sink in. After twelve years, I wonder who I'll be then, how I'll change...

My senses seem heightened in captivity. Last night, they transferred me from Brixton to Wandsworth, South London. Such is the lot of Category A inmates – always in flux, never privy to when or where we'll next be taken. After the ritual of searches and the donning of sterile clothes, the journey begins anew. We joke that the Home Office's best-kept secret is the next move of a 'Cat A.'

As I passed through London under police escort, the city seemed more vivid, life outside more tangible. I caught myself fantasising about turning the corner onto our road in Bethnal Green, greeting you with a smile. But now, I understand that the most profound beauty in life is felt, not touched. My fear is that time will wear me down, Lily, that even my memories might fade, making my imprisonment as much about losing myself as it is about being confined...

Life in here is bearable; there are those I can call friends.

You're in my thoughts constantly – from the moment I wake, throughout the day, and until I drift off to sleep. I cherish the memory of your touch, the sound of your voice, the look in your eyes.

We'll endure this side by side, for I am resolute in the face of this ordeal. Time will pass, and I believe our love will endure and strengthen with it...'

Setting down my pen, I approached the window, breathing in deeply as sunlight touched my face. Resignation was not in my nature but a plan was taking shape, with threads reaching beyond the prison walls. A quiet, determined smile graced my lips; the ache in my heart eased and my gaze grew firmer. I was reminded that bravery often shapes fate. My destiny, I resolved, would be back in my hands. Freedom was not an if, but a when – and I was ready to seize it.

Prison Senses

The thing about prison, you see, is the noise. It's always there, these echoey clatters, the jangling of keys, metal against metal. The banging, the voices, the tramping boots of the screws on approach. The activity creates an echo, an acoustic reverberation that hangs in the air. And the smells - they're something else. A mix of cheap, hospital-like, institutional odours of stale food, disinfectant, dirt, mops, and urine. A miasma of smoke pervades everything. It's peculiar because amidst all this, after a certain time at night, it falls deathly quiet, and you could hear a pin drop. Everyone's left alone with their thoughts, wrestling with their own demons - the past, the present, the future. It's all turning, churning inside, you know?

These sensations, they permeate the soul. The feelings, the thoughts, the smells, the sounds - they're timeless, unchanged, I'm sure of it. It's like being in a land devoid of colour and sound, a land of shadows, like a hall of mirrors that warps and twists you emotionally, mentally, spiritually, and physically. It's an unending torture of desperation, where everything seems to close in on you. You feel like you're adrift in the middle of a tempestuous sea, perpetually in motion, like being cast into the

Atlantic with nothing but a life jacket, no land in sight, no hope. Only darkness, grey sky and watching the sea knowing it will turn turbulent, rise crazy and you'd better be ready to navigate it.

Behind the Façade

Within prison walls, individuals wear a multitude of faces. There's the facade on the landing - the one that declares 'I'm coping, don't mess with me.' This mask of resilience signals a readiness to resort to violence if provoked, not out of desire, but as a necessary evil for survival. Then there's the visage for family during visits, in letters, and phone calls, where the semblance of normalcy is desperately maintained. Yet, behind the cell door lies the most private countenance: moments brimming with desperation, lost in fear, consumed by worry for the future, confused by past choices, and questioning the path that led there, as well as pondering the way forward. People are complex. In there the complexity multiplies silently and translated quickly simply as that's all there is to hang on to.

Wormwood Prison, 1993, 5am

The night before, the prison officers - a specialist squad trained in control, restraint, and riot management - had been briefed by the Security Governor. Gathered in a spacious room on the first floor of Wormwood Scrubs, with the Principal and Senior Officers in attendance, they had been informed about intelligence concerning a gun smuggled into the prison, intending to facilitate a Category A prisoner's escape.

Clad in full riot gear, helmets and shields at the ready, the ten-strong team had been acutely aware of the need for silence as they entered the hushed environment of A wing's bottom landing. The only sound was the echo of their boots on the gleaming floor tiles as they ascended the metal stairs to the second floor. In formation at the door, they lowered the transparent visors on their black helmets, gripping their shields tightly.

With keys inserted into the cell door, they waited. A glance at the Senior Officer, a nod given, and the spyhole flicked open revealed the inmate, LR 3246, Gillen, still in bed.

On command, they burst in. The cell was filled with sudden noise and shouts as the officers, like a tempest, surged through the door. They overwhelmed me with the shock of their entry, pinning me to the bed as I awoke and struggled, attempting to evade the press of shields and bodies. Despite my efforts to push and pull against the overpowering force, I was swiftly cornered, subdued on the floor, and secured in wrist and headlocks before being transferred - bound as tightly as a Christmas turkey - to the segregation unit.

Wormwood Prison 1993

It was a deep dark dungeon and I knew it well. In the strip cell, sat naked on the floor in the corner of the cell with a small heavy blanket draped around my shoulders, I focussed on the terrible bruising I felt on my arms, shoulders, legs and my genitals. They had dragged me from my bed and down the stairs, and when outside in the corridor away from the sight or hearing of other inmates had really hammered me. Unable to move because of the wrist locks they had kicked, punched and pulled my hair. One of them had grabbed my balls and twisted and squeezed them hard. The pain had nearly made me pass out.

The banging of a truncheon hard on the outside of my locked cell door invaded my thoughts and interrupted the silence.

They were back.

Every ten minutes they would bang the door to give me no rest.

Outside, the spy hole moved, and an eye looked in at me and disappeared. It was another one of their tactics. It awakened something inside me. Deep in the depths of my soul, in place of unmitigated pain was a factory that turned suffering into anger and loneliness to rebellion. It was working now, a smooth and fast process that converted my pride and the physical, mental and emotional torture I felt, into rage and stubbornness.

I moved. I could not stand as the fresh wounds would not allow it. I remembered what had been said in my ear, spittle flecking the side of my face as they held my head down dragging me to the strip cell, cutting my clothes from me, holding me down as they ran vacating the room in a burst of movement and closing the door.

'Getting a gun are you!' Their angry voices were in my head. 'You fuckin see where you'll end up. Think you're a wide boy do you. You'll rot behind the door for a long time. See what you get. Like our little visit this morning, want more? We can give you that every hour on the hour…'

The spyhole outside the door moved again.

The voice was soft, kept low and aimed at me and into the cell through the side of the cell door.

It said, in broken rushed tones. 'Look, I'm sorry for what they done to you. I had no part in it. I'll know you'll get the gun in eventually. I've read your record. But I'm just a family man…I had no part in it…I must go they're coming…I'll do what I can for you.'

…The voice was gone. I heard the movement of keys on the landing, heavy boots, an exodus of movement, coming towards my cell like a herd of travelling elephants.

My instinct told me they were coming. My body braced, readied my mind and hands so I could defend myself. The door flew open. They stood there, a sea of dark blue uniforms and white shirts that blocked completely the entrance to the cell.

'Gillen…'

It was the Governor. A bald man in a grey suit whose head and shoulders strained to see me through the mass of prison officers.

'You were removed from the wing this morning for the security and smooth running of the prison.' He stopped a minute and looked. A burning glance that faltered at the end of our locking eyes.

'We know, Gillen. We've had intelligence of a proposed escape attempt. You will be held down here while an investigation is carried out.'

'I want to speak to my brief?'

'…You will not be speaking to that brief or anyone else for a long time as far as I'm concerned, Gillen…'

The screws glared. They blocked and protected him at the door. A gaggle of attack dogs primed and ready to be unleashed.

The Governor peered at me one last time.

He said, 'Let me tell you, Gillen. When you try stuff like this you see what will happen. You will see where you will end up. Shut the door!'

He had indicated to them. I sat silent, back hard against the cold wall. I stared as the door to the strip cell slammed shut.

In the depths of the prison, I knew the dungeon-like strip cell all too well. Seated naked on the floor, a small heavy blanket my only cover, I focused on the severe bruising marking my arms, shoulders, legs, and genitals. They had yanked me from my bed and down the stairs; once out of sight and earshot of other inmates, they had unleashed their fury. The wrist locks rendered me immobile as they kicked, punched, and yanked my hair. One officer had viciously twisted and squeezed my balls, the pain almost rendering me unconscious.

The relentless banging of a truncheon against my cell door jarred my thoughts, shattering the silence.

They had returned.

Every ten minutes, the banging resumed, denying me any chance of rest. An eye peered in through the spy hole, then vanished – another one of their intimidation tactics. The relentless intimidation sparked a reaction deep within me. The pain kindled a fierce response in my core, transmuting suffering into a burning anger and solitude into a resolute defiance. This internal alchemy was at work, refining the raw hurt and humiliation I had borne into a steadfast resolve and unyielding rage.

I shifted my position; standing was not an option with fresh wounds protesting. The memory of their words hissed in my ear, spittle landing on my face as they dragged me to this cell, cutting away my clothes, pinning me down before vacating in a swift exodus and sealing the door.

'*Getting a gun, are you? You think you're a clever one. You'll rot in here. Enjoy our little visit this morning? Want more? We can do that every hour if you like…*'

The spy hole fluttered open once more.

A voice, hushed and hurried, reached me through the gap in the cell door. 'I'm sorry for what they've done. I had no part in it. I know you'll get the gun in eventually. I've seen your record. But I'm just a family man… I had no part in it… I must go, they're coming… I'll do what I can for you.'

The voice disappeared. The sound of keys and heavy boots approached my cell with the thunderous momentum of a stampeding herd.

My instincts screamed an alert. I braced myself, preparing my mind and hands for defence. The door burst open, revealing a mass of dark blue uniforms and white shirts.

'Gillen…'

The Governor, a bald man in a grey suit, peered over the sea of officers.

'You were removed from the wing this morning for the security and good order of the prison.' His burning gaze faltered as it met mine.

'We're aware, Gillen. Intelligence suggests an escape attempt is planned. You'll be detained here during the investigation.'

'I want to speak to my solicitor.'

'You won't be speaking to your solicitor or anyone else for quite some time, as far as I'm concerned, Gillen...'

The officers stood firm, a wall of guard dogs at the ready.

The Governor gave me a final look. 'Remember, Gillen, when you try things like this, you see the consequences. You see where you end up. Shut the door!'

With a gesture, he commanded them. I remained silent, my back against the cold wall, eyes locked on the doorway as the cell door slammed shut.

From Parkhurst Prison Isle of Wight - The Ghost Train 1994

At Prison Service Headquarters, John Milton sat at his desk in a blue pinstriped suit, scrutinising the report marked 'Urgent' that had arrived via the fastest, encrypted Security Intelligence channel. The document had interrupted his salad lunch and musings about returning to the squash court and his daughter Isabella's new show jumping lessons.

His eyes narrowed as he read.

Outside, as the fawning grey clouds threatened to engulf the waning light over Lambeth Bridge, he recognised the name in the report and digested the text with concern.

Inmate 360, Gillen Stephen.

Prison: Parkhurst

Rank: Governor 2 (Security)

Intelligence Report.

Threat Level: 1

Details:

An Officer, targeted by internal Security for suspected contraband smuggling, was arrested on the 21st of May. A search of his car yielded three ounces of cannabis resin and two phones with SIM cards taped together. The Officer, suspected of smuggling contraband for up to two years, confessed to facilitating a plot by the aforementioned inmate to smuggle a firearm into the prison and escape via a bin lorry.

The inmate is categorised as a high-risk Category A prisoner. Daily observation logs, prison audio listening devices, and monitored phone conversations are being collated.

Actions:

The inmate has been transferred to the segregation unit by control and restraint and remains compliant. However, he continues to be a significant security concern and a drain on resources.

Please Advise.

End Quote.

Milton felt a tightness in his chest. The recent IRA escape from the Brixton Special Security Unit, coupled with press speculation of British Intelligence interference, had put his department under scrutiny.

He glanced out the window at the MI5 building, musing bitterly about their relative freedom. A bead of sweat formed under his collar, symbolising the worry that now threatened his career.

A bloody nightmare. The situation had been a catalyst for lingering indigestion, late-night reading, and pulsating headaches. Relief came with the confirmation that the threat had been neutralised, and he welcomed the fresh air streaming through the open window.

Managing Category A inmates was like a complex chess game, each individual presenting unique challenges requiring constant vigilance and suppression. He acknowledged their cunning; the battle had raged for years, and victory lay in unwavering control, schemes to divide their ranks, and sharp intelligence.

Pen in hand, Milton annotated the report with further instructions, signing and dating his directive:

Further Action:

Inmate 360, Gillen Stephen, to remain in closed and segregated conditions under Rule 34 (Continuous Assessment) until otherwise directed.

End Quote.

Setting the pen down, he loosened his tie. The Continuous Assessment would keep Gillen in almost perpetual solitary confinement, shifting him anonymously through the prison system.

Milton leaned back, anticipating that Gillen would ride the 'ghost train' for at least two years. It irked him that such a threat could undermine his authority. His thoughts drifted back to squash, and the possibility of spending extra time with Isabella at her show jumping events to rebuild their bond.

* * *

The 'Ghost Train' was a continuous assessment in segregation, used for the most disruptive prisoners to ease the pressure on the prison system. You'd end up in the locals, kept in the block because you were already a fixture there. My respite with great friends in Parkhurst had come to an end.

I was shuttled between so many different prisons, like pieces on a chessboard. Oddly enough, I didn't mind it that much. It was a change of scene, kept things fresh, gave me new stimuli. Even though I was always in the block, the environments varied, different faces, different routines. I could still get my visits, feel a different vibe, witness their unique ways of running things, new visuals, feelings, and experiences.

By the time my stint ended I'd been through a fair few, Strange Ways in Manchester just before the riots kicked off, Lincoln, Wandsworth twice. Leeds was particularly bleak, like an old castle with a damp, oppressive air, and a strict, barren feel to the whole place. I was stuck on the northern circuit for four years. It's a tactic they used to grind you down, especially since I was from East London. It made everything tougher, not just for me but for my family and folks too, being so far from familiar ground.

By deliberately keeping me up north, they prolonged my punishment, and those four years are etched permanently in my memory.

Riding The Train 1993-1998

The echo of my footsteps was swallowed by the grim walls of the Category A prisons, the so-called dispersal jails, each a fortress with its own notorious reputation. There are six dispersal prisons, Belmarsh in London, Whitemoor in Cambridge, Full Sutton in York, Frankland up near Durham, Long Lartin Worcestershire and Wakefield West Yorkshire - names that reverberated with the tales of those held within. Here, I was more than a number; I was a chess piece in a lethal game, shifted from one high-security prison to another in an effort to quell the gang wars that raged like persistent storms and to lessen the burden of violence I was involved in against the system.

My time was spent amongst the infamous and the feared. I shared spaces with the likes of Warren Slaney, Peter Fury, Michael McAvoy, and Gary Nelson, leading Mafia & Cartel figures, top IRA men and the cleverest, most notorious and know villain's and criminals in the country. The network of alliances and enemies was intricate and volatile, a single misstep could spiral into chaos, and often did. Peace was impossible and normality was a different universe. The gang wars were not just disputes; they were protracted battles of survival, where allegiances were as sharp as the shivs we concealed. In this harsh realm, the passage of time mattered little. A feud ignited over a trifling matter could evolve into a vendetta that lasted fifteen years, its flames fanned by every fresh incident, each assault, and every whispered threat. The prisons themselves became arenas where every corridor turn, every mealtime, was a potential battlefield.

The transportation from one prison to another for Category A inmates was a clandestine affair shrouded in secrecy. Sterile clothes, the heavy scent of fear, misdirection and confusion, and the barking of dogs marked the transfer. We were commodities of violence, handled with extreme caution, our destinations hidden until the very last moment. Peering through the van's barred window, every sign on the motorway was a clue to these hidden destinations, every turn a potential prelude to a new battleground.

In this treacherous world, your strength was measured by your allies. A familiar prison could be a haven, surrounded by comrades from the streets, the inside. But the real test came when you found yourself isolated, outnumbered by foes who circled like wolves, waiting to pounce at the first sign of weakness. It was in those moments that the reality of prison life crystallised – it was do or die. There were no second chances and fortune always favoured the brave and crazy.

The threats were not idle; they were as real as the steel doors that slammed shut each night. A fallout could ignite a war over the smallest infractions. They'd come for you with knives drawn, with scalding oil, with any means to extinguish the threat you posed. And when they came, it was with the intent to kill, to remove you from the equation, to ensure you were no longer a menace. I had great friends, people who would stand or fall with me, bound by threat, respect and loyalty. But in the world of Category A, life hung by a thread, every day a gamble, every interaction a potential death sentence.

Full Sutton Prison 1994

The prison escort this time came to move me to another institution at an unusual hour. Just as I had settled after eating my teatime meal, the cell door burst open. It was the usual drill. Strip search, change into the bright yellow and green jumpsuit used for transport, belongings packed, bagged, logged and cable tied. They double cuffed me. One set of cuffs on both hands, then another set which handcuffed me to an officer. Quickly, with a rush of movement I was escorted down the metal stairs, out the back door of the segregation unit to where the Category A van waited, uncuffed from the officer and locked into a cubicle.

The van moved. The big double gates in front of us leading to the gate house swung open.

Unbeknown to me, this time I was being transported to Full Sutton in York.

Vincent Meer fancied himself the original gangster. Towering with a thick-set, muscular frame, he bore the robust genes of his Jamaican father from Tivoli Gardens. Serving a twenty-five-year sentence for two shootings and cocaine importation, his history of impulsive violence traced back to the days when Dudus's father, Lester Coke, held sway over Kingston. In his cell on D wing of the high-security Full Sutton prison, alongside the three close associates he ran with, he twisted the short, tight plaits of his hair and gazed out the window over the tall fences dividing the compound from the prison yard.

Vincent saw himself as a man of style and sophistication, a far cry from his humble beginnings running errands back in Jamaica. The years of incarceration had cut him deeply, yet like his carefully crafted image of superiority, he shielded his vulnerabilities behind a facade of aggression, never fully revealing his wounds. It was the rage that fuelled him, allowing him to feel significant even in the bleakest depths of prison, demanding respect for his capabilities. Stephen Gillen, a name that travelled with him in his thoughts along with others on a list as he shuffled through the UK's prisons - a list of scores to be settled upon sight.

His Breda offered a joint, but Vincent declined with a wave. He seldom indulged; his image of aloof discipline was paramount, distinguishing him as more authentic than his peers. His first encounter with Gillen had been a brief intersection at the Special Security Unit in Brixton while on remand, awaiting trial. They had taken an instant dislike to each other.

Vincent kissed his teeth and chuckled. He understood the undercurrents, it was about dominance, a clash of two alpha males, raw and ravenous from their respective conquests. The tension between him and Gillen had erupted beside the pool table, culminating in a brawl that summoned the entire staff to quell when the riot alarm blared.

He had dispatched a message through the gym's grapevine to Gillen, now on a different wing, upon learning of his transfer. Concealed behind a cushioned chair was a metal stiletto spike, one of many weapons he secreted throughout his realm. The weekend's communal exercise period in the vast yard, minimally supervised except for the watchtowers and with a restroom outside the cameras' line of sight, presented an opportunity.

Vincent clicked his teeth again, a long, sibilant sound accompanying his exhalation. The weekend loomed close. He and his crew would confront Gillen and his associates, intending to end their feud once and for all...

Full Sutton Prison 1994

The two makeshift knives were secured down each side of my back, positioned for swift access. Shane and I moved with deliberate speed along the prison's lengthy corridors that led to the football fields where inmates assembled for the weekend exercise.

Clad in the coarse grey coats issued to lifers, our hearts thrummed with a fierce rapidity. Midday sunlight streamed through the windows lining our path, illuminating our figures as we shielded our vital organs with magazines tucked into our waistbands, armouring against potential stabbings. We spoke in hushed tones, our words barely leaving the sides of our mouths to evade the ears of nearby prisoners.

'Stephen, keep sharp. They'll be in their usual group of four, aiming for a sly attack,' Shane cautioned.

'Absolutely. There's no alternative, Shane. If we don't confront this head-on, they'll take us down individually. That can't happen,' I replied firmly.

Shane walked on, his nod betraying the fear and anxiety within. A faint flush of apprehension spread across his face and neck. Like me, he understood the stakes: fight or fall. Escape was a fantasy; the only path forward was one fraught with violence and the spectre of death. We had to advance, to claim our right to space and time, even if it meant facing brutal violence or our end.

We scrutinised the other inmate groups for signs of an ambush as we stepped into the sprawling, sunlit yard. My senses were heightened, tuning in to the laughter and chatter of prisoners, the jangle of guards' keys as they secured the gates behind us.

As we emerged onto the open rugby field, the sun's intensity beat down on our heavily garbed, magazine-padded forms. The towering watchtower cast its gaze over the razor-wired fences, while prisoners meandered in small clusters around the green expanse of the secure compound, basking in the scant light and freedom.

There they were.

It was instantaneous. They were poised, waiting. We peered intently, not wanting to overlook them, simmering with high-intensity energy and striving to maintain an unassuming presence. Three black figures and one white stood in front of the outdoor toilet building, their expressions taut with seriousness.

We circled, striding far up the field with our hands buried deep in the pockets of our grey jackets, our eyes sharp, minds racing, preparing for what was to come.

Vincent Meer was unmistakably there. I spotted him, his lips forming silent commands. They retreated, a strategic move before the clash. They withdrew into the changing rooms, biding their time for our next circuit.

'They've ducked inside, Shane...'

'Yeah, they've clocked our padding, our jackets. They know we're armed.'

'Right. I'm not sure how many blades they've got, Shane. Be ready for anything. I didn't see any armour on them.'

'They've stashed something in the loos.'

Armed with two knives each, we drew closer to the toilet block. A mix of panic and exhilaration surged within me as adrenaline flooded my system. Nearing the open door, every instinct screamed to flee, but I pressed on, steeling myself with determination.

We entered the dimly lit, stale-smelling space, passing through the deserted changing area into the toilets. My heart hammered, sweat sheened my neck and began to bead on my forehead. I reached for the knives at my back and drew them forth.

'Hey, lad. You're done for. Last time was luck. Today, you'll both pay dearly!'

It was Meer, wielding a metal bar and a sharpened spike. His crew flanked him, poised like hyenas ready to pounce, their makeshift weapons glinting dully in the subdued light.

Shane stood firm at my side, our faces set and determined. With a burst of force, I stepped forward and roared my challenge.

'You think we give a damn? We don't need this, not here. But if it's to be, let's finish it! We end it today, even if it means dying together! Come on, then. These knives will have their say!'

A sudden stillness fell. On the cusp of cataclysmic violence, everyone halted, caught in a tense standoff as our gaze bore into theirs, challenging their resolve. Our desperation was a fortress, etched with the insanity of reckless intent, and it seemed to sap their vigour.

Vincent Meer's eyes narrowed, a mocking smile playing on his lips.

'You've got guts, Gillen. Bold move, walking in here like that. You've done one thing right...'

We retreated, our weapons still at the ready, moving back towards the sunlight streaming through the doorway.

His voice trailed after us. 'That's it, Gillen. Not today... Take your little sidekick and run along. We'll leave it for now...'

We passed back through the changing room, out into the open where the air could envelop us again. We'd do a few more laps on the field before returning to the wing.

Meer's taunt echoed from the toilets.

'Not today, Gillen... But one day, just remember that, one day...!'

Dangerous Men 1994

In those halls of cold steel and relentless surveillance, I navigated the treacherous undercurrents of gang wars, fit-up guards and my own sanity - and these conflicts were not fleeting – they were entrenched vendettas that stretched across years, sometimes over a decade. The corridors of Full Sutton became battlegrounds, echoing with the clang of makeshift weapons and the shuffling feet of us – men ready for confrontation at a moment's notice. The main yard and football field where all the wings could congregate was the place of high conflict, where all firms would meet, ambushing when they could as people made their way there.

Amidst this chaos, I encountered men like Ferdinand. His legacy was one carved from violence; he'd worked as a doorman until he'd gutted a punter on the doorstep of the nightclub. he wore his scars like badges of honour and was in their for life. His weapon of choice was as concealed as it was constant, a long sharp stiletto hidden beneath the innocuous guise of a tissue box. I remember his figure, a monolith in the prison yard, always prepared, always armed. He was a bully and a thug and he didn't care who he took out. I'll never forget the day he threw boiling oil over a screw in Whitemoor – it was a moment that etched itself into the fabric of prison lore. The officer's screams as he ran down the wing and tried in vain to peel away his uniform with his face half melting, will remain a stark reminder of the brutality that governed our existence behind those walls.

This was a world where your strength was measured by your ability to survive the next ambush. Allies were your shield, your strength in numbers. To be isolated was to be exposed, vulnerable to the swift and often lethal justice meted out by those who deemed you a threat. Every movement through the prison was a calculated risk, every new face a potential assassin. The stakes were life and death, and we played the game with a fervour born of desperation.

In the grey confines of Long Lartin, I found myself in the communal TV room, a small, cramped space barely holding the ten of us.

One of the other prisoners of the block turned to me 'Have you notice the lads hanging about today? Something's going down I can feel it.'

I nodded, 'I think it's Ferdinand.' I gestured subtly with my head to where he was sat like he was holding court. Payback's coming,'

Suddenly, the door was flung open, four figures clad in balaclavas barged in. One brandished a pan, the liquid within glistening ominously. Knives glinted in their grips as they zeroed in on Ferdinand.

Chaos erupted. The scalding oil arced through the air, finding its mark.

'God, that's gonna stick with him... the oil, it's burning right through!' I'll never shake the image: the fabric of his jumper melding with his skin.

'They're on him! Knives out and everything!' Exclaimed the guy next to me as we backed away giving them room.

The assault was frenzied, a pack descending with precision and ferocity. Despite his size and strength, Ferdinand was overwhelmed, brought to his knees in a struggle as primal as it was vicious. The assailants were relentless, their knives finding him again and again. His struggle was lion-like, but outnumbered, he was eventually subdued.

The aftermath was grim; Ferdinand was on the brink of death, not once, but twice, as they rushed him to the hospital. He'd crossed the wrong people – a younger member of a Liverpudlian firm who demanded retribution. It was a brutal reminder of the lawless governance behind bars, where violence could erupt and be over in moments, leaving behind a chilling silence as thick as the tension that precipitated it. Nothing was ever what it seemed, you couldn't take anything on face value.

Hull Special Unit 1996

The prison dog handlers supported the six prison officers as they walked me through the back closed yard of the prison, through four sets of locked gates and into the centre of the prison where the special Unit was. Totally self-contained, a three-floor building enclosed by the green mesh and razor wire of a tall fence, it was a prison in a prison and held some of the country's most dangerous prisoners.

The main doors to the unit's entrance were unlocked. I was escorted in.

It was the smiles of the officers that hit me first. The calm way they introduced themselves and the softness I was treated with.

The escort was told to undo my cuffs.

'Hi, Stephen. How was your trip? Have you had something to eat? We cook all our own food here. There are two TV rooms. We have our own gym fully equipped. Our own visit rooms. It's totally self-contained. It holds twenty, but we like to keep the numbers down. There's eight here at the moment.'

The officer wore the blue jumper of his uniform. With smiling eyes, in a soft middle-aged face with wavy black hair he continued, 'We have some friends of yours here at the moment, I believe?'

I followed him. Hull Special Unit was a small square. A fishbowl that was an experiment. The main office was on the second floor where you came in. This floor also housed the cells that mirrored each other across the opposite side of the building. Upstairs reflected the second landing with rows of cells that no one used and where the recesses were covered in bird shit left by resting seagulls in from the docks. The ground floor housed the kitchen. Situated in an open corner, it was complete with hobs and fridge-freezers where we would put our food tied in cloth sacks. On the ground floor there was also a perfect gym with free weights, an Olympic bar, a running machine and squatting stack that could be used to bench-press. The door to the visits was around the corner, and to the side of the gym were two TV rooms with soft chairs that were situated on either side of the ground floor landing by the outside gates to the exercise yard.

I had friends here. Good staunch men I had met around the system who had travelled the segregation units and dispersal prison as I had.

'Who is here?' I asked. Following him. It was a place of light blue, green and grey. A weird energy hung in the air. Like all was good but great trouble bubbled just under the surface. I could smell the richness of food being cooked downstairs. Spaghetti Bolognese made well with a hint of sugar and good tomatoes.

'Oh, people you know. They knew you were coming today. They've been asking for you. I'll take you to your cell, Stephen. It's different here. Not like anything you've experienced in the system before. Everyone here calls everyone by their first name. I'm, Keith, Stephen and if there's anything you need, anything I can help you with, just give me or one of the other officers a shout…'

He left me. It was May, 1996.I put my bags of belongings on the floor by the small cupboard. It was a normal cell, like any and many I had been through and stayed in. I sat on the bed a moment and looked out of the barred window. The afternoon sun was streaming in to freshen and greet me and the sea gulls were squawking. I felt my life was on a train. It travelled in the night going through echoing tunnels which all looked the same. Forward it thundered on its route, going I knew not where. Its not the pain, I considered that destroys us. It's what we do to avoid its embrace, the fullness of its march. I started to unpack my belongings. It was a new start for me. I would grasp it with both hands…

In the special unit, which was a prison within a prison, I was housed with the most disruptive prisoners of the day. It was a place where notorious names like Alan Lord from the Strangeways riots, Kevin Brown a top league robber from

Bermondsey, and Frank Birley, the Leeds mobster, were my companions. Frank was a good friend who sadly, when he was released years later, got caught up in a series of killings in Leeds and was shot and killed. Gunman, Keith Pringle, who had been shot in the throat by a police sniper, was there too. And then there was Ian Steel, notorious for multiple murders and prison escapes, who was extradited back to Australia.

'Frank, we've got a problem with Ian. He's mouthing threats, thinking he's untouchable, he needs a wake up call.'

Frank's eyes darkened 'Yeah he's a dickhead that one, needs servin' up.'

'He's cornered himself, really. We just need to drive the point home. Time to snuff out those threats.' I snarled

'Okay, here's the plan,' said Frank, 'dead-end corridor by the showers. No ears, no witnesses. We make it clear, his next threat could be his last breath.'

'Exactly. We box him in, set the record straight. Ian's got to understand the price of his words.'

Frank gave me a nasty smile 'What if he's too dense to take a hint?'

'A taste of fear should sharpen his mind.' I said with a cold, hard edge to my voice.

'I'll get what we need. Enough to scare him straight without drawing too much attention.' Frank headed back to his cell.

'Keep it sharp, keep it silent. We're not here to cause a scene. Just a little chat to remind Ian of the rules.' I murmured.

'He'll get the message. We'll make sure of it. Either he walks back on those threats or he doesn't walk at all.'

We were good to our word and gave him the battering he needed. Sorted his mouth out as he couldn't talk for a while anyway.

Hull was unique; it housed only eight of us at a time. Unlike the harsher prisons, Hull's approach was different. You were on first-name terms with the guards and could cook your own meals. They even allowed visitors on the unit.

However, when Colin Ireland, the serial killer, was placed with us, tension escalated. He didn't fit in with our microcosmic society, striving for some semblance of normality despite our dark backgrounds. He had to go or there would be real violence.

I entered the TV room to find him Colin by himself watching videos of 80s pop stars, the ones with the men all wearing makeup. He glanced up at me and nodding to the TV, "You know, if they let me out I'll do it all over again.'

He turned his attention back to the TV and went back to watching the videos with a very strange expression.

His presence was disturbing, and that's a lot coming from me. He only lasted two weeks in our unit, we saw to it that he was moved.

Living in Hell 1998

Winston Green in Birmingham stands out as one of the grimmest stays despite it being Cat B. They had a hit squad in the block, a team of ten brutes lying in wait for the likes of me. They didn't just manhandle; they aimed to shatter you, piece by piece.

Wandsworth was another hellhole, but Wakefield, Wakefield was the abyss. You'd avoid the block there, notorious for housing the vilest offenders. But it was the control unit and the cages that you'd really dread, the same cages where Charlie Bronson and Reg Wilson spent their days. My time there was a brutal dance, a constant battle against the heavy hands that governed the place, not giving an inch as they waged their war of attrition to break me.

Up in those cages, life was doubly confined. A barred gate followed by a mesh, each a barrier to the wider world. Every interaction, every necessity passed through a hatch, a small portal to a semblance of humanity. The cell was a world in itself, complete with a shower and a sliver of a view to a television, watched through bulletproof glass, flanked by curtains that rarely drew back. It really was like being Hannibal Lecter, your world was reduced to these walls, except for a meagre hour's exercise in the yard. Prisoners like us were only confined to the control/segregation unit. But I knew the wings were full of nonces and I felt a barely controlled rage the entire time I was there.

These cells, they haunt me. The hooks embedded in the concrete bore witness to straitjackets and screams from another era. The atmosphere of Wakefield was thick with malevolence, the stench of corruption and despair. It was more than hatred for the place; it was a visceral loathing for the very air that filled my lungs, for the stain it left on my soul, for the brutality that hung as heavy as the chains they used on others before me. I hated the place, detested the monsters housed on the wings and the crimes they had committed, resisted with everything the bully screws who were there every time the door opened.

Charlie Bronson 1998

My initial encounter with Charlie Bronson occurred in Wandsworth block, where I was transferred following the allegation of smuggling firearms into the Brixton unit. The journey between the Old Bailey and the block was marked by a formidable police escort and the flurry of flashing lights. Once there, I found Charlie housed next to me. Our rapport was instant; we connected as soldiers might in the trenches, bound by the commonality of our treatment. A kinship forms in those depths - a mutual support system against the onslaught of punitive measures.

Charlie was an individual of many layers, his comedy a beacon in the dreariness of incarceration. We'd spend hours engaged in conversation, his tales from Broadmoor and various exploits painting a vivid tableau of his life. His humour was as sharp as it was dark, but he held steadfast to a code of old-school values, with a vehement disdain for those who preyed on children or women.

Yet, his temperament was mercurial, capable of swift and drastic change, though I was never on the receiving end of such a switch. He reserved his volatility for others, not for those he deemed the 'real faces' or the stalwarts of the old school. It was a matter of respect, a line he wouldn't cross with certain individuals. But for the rest, vigilance was paramount; Charlie's intensity was such that he seemed ever poised to pounce, to bend iron doors with sheer will to reach those he targeted.

He was one of the fittest men I've ever seen. He would train constantly. He's in the Guinness Book of World Records for doing press-ups with people on his back and such. He was like an old strong man at the circus, and he talks like that, too. Camaraderie was solid from the outset and has remained so throughout the years. On occasion I receive cards from him wishing me well, which I treasure. I find my name etched in his life story, '*Bronson*', on three occasions, a testament to our enduring bond. Additionally, I feature on a page of another of his works, '*Living Legends*', a chronicle among a compendium of notable figures.

Nonce 1997

As I mentioned, Charlie couldn't tolerate anyone who'd hurt women or children, it went against every code that he had.

At one time me and Charlie were together in Wakefield Prison, with a nonce in the cell next to mine. He was a sadist, and he loved to play it up. I'd tell him through the walls between us, 'See you, skinny boy, when I get my hands on you, I'm going to break you like a plate.' He'd taunt me back, thinking the screws wouldn't dare put him in the same yard as me, but he was in for a shock.

The screws, as twisted as they were in Wakefield, despised him as much as we did, so they left me to it, which whilst perhaps not right, worked for me.

One morning we headed out to the yard; there were two gated arches, one to the right and one to the left. We usually went through the right gate since the cages were to the left, and that's where Charlie was, so we had the opportunity to chat.

That morning though, as soon as we stepped out, I noticed that all of the screws were there. They opened the right door for the nonce, and as soon as he saw me, his eyes filled with terror. I gave a nasty smile and said, 'This is brilliant, let's end this charade today.'

I listened for the clang of the gates closing behind me. As soon as they did, I walked over to him and bang! Bang! I laid into him, putting him down on the floor. Shouting obscenities as I did. Like most nonces, he was all mouth, could only feel big when his prey was smaller and weaker than him. It didn't take much but I laid into him quick and hard.

The screws gave me a moment, watching as I tuned him up, but eventually, they had to pull me off him. As they did, I said, 'See you, skinny boy, I told you I'd get you, wrongan', not giving it now are you?'

I was overjoyed getting my hands on him; he was truly vile. As they dragged me away, I said, 'I fucking told you, you're the scum of the earth.' In defiance he spat at me. Clearly not a quick learner.

Honestly, it was one of the best things I've ever done, as he was a real monster. A Category A sadist, he'd spent his life abducting women in Manchester, torturing them, and worse. The little victories were what kept me going. I felt this one major, it kept me going for weeks.

Charlie was in stitches the entire time, couldn't contain himself. The next day, the nonce had two, big black eyes, and Charlie, chucking things at him from the window, kept shouting, 'You've got two big black eyes, like a panda! Stephen gave you a right good going over. Two big eyes like a panda.'

Charlie then turned to me, laughing and he yelled, 'Stephen, well done! Look at the state of him.' Laughing his head off again.

Even the screws, whom I'd been at odds with, appreciated it. They thought he was the scum of the earth too. They came up to me, saying, 'Saw you the other day in the yard, looking like a real boxing champion.'

I thought, 'Are you having a laugh?' But it was too good a moment to play deaf, normally I wouldn't engage with them or their comments. I had to smile to myself because it was those little moments of camaraderie that made it all bearable.

Bronson and the PR Trail Present Day

With Charlie Bronson, it's a clear example of the prison service's knack for pigeonholing people, crafting PR campaigns around them, especially when they're struggling. It's one of their tactics. The saddest part about Charlie is that he's never lived a life outside, never achieved anything of note in society. In prison, though, he's someone - 'Britain's most dangerous prisoner' and all that. It's a life worse than a dog's, the way they've treated him, it's wrong. But in some ways, Charlie has played into their hands. It's more than that, though, it's a response to the appalling treatment, repackaged by the prison service like some slick PR firm, justifying their actions.

Charlie deserves rehabilitation, just like everyone else. Reflecting on my own journey, the survival mechanisms, the depth of what long-term incarceration does to a person... They need support to overcome the effects of long-term imprisonment, violence, and segregation. There's a stark disparity in the conditions of Category A prisons compared to B, C, or D, which offer more opportunities for rehabilitation. The idea is to progress from high-security Category A down to open Category D. Charlie's never been afforded these chances. There's growing evidence, even psychologists agree, that the likelihood of violence from prisoners like Charlie drops significantly with age and he's in his 70's now. They've certainly made a statement out of him.

For all that is said about him, Charlie's got a big heart. He's a talented artist, a prolific writer, and contributes to charity. There's much we can learn from him. The issue is the prison service's failure to see this, losing individuals like Charlie, and me, in the system and demonising us. But it shouldn't be like this. Charlie's never taken a life; he's not serving a life sentence. While people must pay their debt to society, the other side of that is rehabilitation, integrating them back into society once they've served their time. This is crucial. It's not something he's ever been afforded and I support his son's campaign to see his father free from prison.

More than a Number 1997

Inside the worst prisons, desperation clings to you like a second skin. It's an emotional rollercoaster. Take Wakefield, for example, down in the block, clad in prison garb, they'd deliberately issue clothes that didn't fit, stripping away your identity. It was a method of disempowerment, reducing you to a nonentity, just a number. You'd be handed these ill-fitting jeans, or more often, flimsy slippers, light blue, cheap t-shirts paired with a feeble sweat top, or blue and white pinstriped shirts, all rough to the touch.

'Look at us, dressed in rags like we're meant to forget who we are.'

Tom looked at me and laughed, 'Certainly not headed for the cover of GQ looking like that City! That's the game though, isn't it? Break us down, make us numbers instead of men.'

I laughed without humour 'These slippers, they're a joke. And the jeans, they might as well be chains the way they're hanging off me.'

'You missing your Armani? It's all part of their control, mate. Wear you out by wearing you down.' Tom looked down at his own mis-matched outfit.

I smirked at him thinking back to my days on the street, always looking sharp, 'But they can't take what's up here.' I said tapping my temple, 'They can't dress down our thoughts.'

'True. But you see some of the lads, losing a bit more each day, it's like watching someone fade away.' I knew Tom was thinking about some of the men that had been in longer than us, especially those back in Wandsworth.

'Not us, though. We keep each other sharp. Can't let these Northerners grind us into nothing.' Tom had been on the street with me, here in the North, we were a couple of East End lads against the tide.

Tom laughed, 'It's like Dunkirk, right? They can take our clothes, our comfort, but not our spirit!'

It was hard to remember that at night though in the cell, with just the coarse green blankets and sheets that were like starched paper, just unbearable.

I carry this with me even now, I cannot sleep unless the bed is very firm and the pillow hard. Softness is a luxury that feels alien to me, all because of those years, those memories.

Tiny Luxury

The food in prison is akin to tasteless pulp, akin to cardboard, serving as nothing more than a rudimentary means to sustain life. It's slop, devoid of colour or flavour, boiled down to an indistinguishable mass, offering no nourishment beyond the bare minimum required for survival. It's why food becomes such a coveted commodity, and having your own is a luxury - a stark contrast to the daily fare. But when you're at odds with the institution, such privileges are the first to be sacrificed.

I was on the unit with Alan Lord, he personified resilience. He was as tough as anything, as unyielding as iron, he chose to sleep directly on the floor, eschewing even the basic comfort of a pillow. His rationale was rooted in defiance; by owning nothing, by embracing austerity, he left them nothing to take, nothing with which to torment him further. In this stark existence, we were trained, programmed with such discipline that deprivation became our armour, an impenetrable shield against their attempts to break us.

In this environment, the minutiae of life becomes monumental. A spoonful of sugar in your tea transforms into a daily highlight - a small, savoured luxury amidst the bleakness. Years of such existence mould you, not just to survive but to navigate the darkest aspects of captivity. It warps the mind, pushing you to spiritual, mental, emotional, and physical extremities no person should ever encounter, and then it drags you back through the abyss repeatedly.

This crucible of incarceration tears you apart, only to stitch you back together, teaching you about the depths of your soul, the capacity for despair, and the resilience within the human spirit. Even shrouded in darkness, you learn to seek out the faintest glimmer of light, to find happiness and peace in the simplest of things. This journey wires you with trauma, but it also forges a formidable strength. Once you've traversed this gauntlet, once you've been shaped by such relentless pressure and heat, there is little left in the world that can truly phase you. The torture becomes a transformative process.

Personalities 1998

In that place, you learn to read people fast. It's a skill you get when you're locked up with all sorts - crazy, smart, and everything in between. You see every part of what makes a person tick, the good bits and the bad, and you've got to get real good at figuring out which is which. You've got to know when to hold your ground and when to keep your head down, when to push and when to pull back. You also get good at spotting a hair trigger and know when to pull it.

Creating relationships with the toughest ones, steering clear of the loose cannons - it's part of the daily grind. And it's not easy when you're up close with that kind of unpredictable all the time. But it sharpens you, gives you this ability to see right into the heart of people, to know what they're about, how they'll react when things hit the fan. It's a brutal way to learn about human nature, but in there, it's the only way.

I was halfway through a set of push-ups when Jacko dropped down beside me, his voice a low growl. 'Stephen, got a minute?'

I pushed up off the floor, wiping sweat from my brow. 'For you, Jacko? Always. What's eating you?'

He glanced around, his eyes darting to the corners of the room where shadows loomed. 'It's the new guy, Sid. He's been shooting his mouth off, saying he knows you from the outside. Reckons he's got dirt that could stir the pot.'

I kept my face neutral, but inside, gears were turning. Sid, Sid... the name didn't ring any bells, but in this place, that didn't mean much. 'Yeah? And what have you heard?'

'Words, just words. But words are like shanks here, ain't they? They cut deep if you let 'em.' Jacko had a point. Rumours in here were as dangerous as any blade.

I sat down on the bench, my mind racing. 'Listen, Jacko, you know as well as I do, talk is cheap. Sid wants to make a name for himself, let him. But if he crosses a line, come find me.'

Jacko nodded, the tension in his shoulders easing a bit. 'I hear you, mate. It's just... with your rep, you've got more to lose. You've got to watch these mugs.'

I stood up, clapping him on the shoulder. 'Appreciate the heads up. But I've walked tighter ropes than whatever Sid can spin. Keep your ears open, yeah? If he talks out of turn, we'll deal with it.'

As Jacko walked off, I turned back to my workout, each push-up now fuelled by a new focus. In here, you had to be ready for anything. That was the game. I had no friends, didn't want any and watched everyone. And I wasn't about to lose.

Wakefield Prison, 1999

My existence was a relentless sequence of painful, spartan, concrete cells that ensnared my true humanity, warping my thoughts, feelings, and emotions into jagged distortions. These caricatures whittled down my essence, moulding my soul into grotesque forms that struggled for control. I wandered, bereft of feeling, in a world suffused with internal agony and external monotony. Days became mere markers; nights, fragmented. As time marched on, my memories of life beyond these walls were usurped by a darker self, clinging to sanity and reality.

For the initial ten days of my incarceration, I strove for composure. But soon, they began to torment me, meagre and chilled meals, delayed exercise times, penetrating stares, and growled remarks. The deprivation of showers was just the beginning. The nadir was reached when I was overlooked at breakfast. In defiance, I shredded a towel, defiled a plastic wash basin, and smeared the walls with excrement. The foul stench, the uncleanliness, the risk of infection, it all served as a primitive but potent weapon against the regime, a safeguard against beatings and violence. The guards detested the 'dirty protest', but it granted me a measure of power.

Sequestered in a double-doored grey cell, reinforced with a heavy mesh and a secondary iron door, I huddled in the one untainted corner. Here, I ate, slept, and contemplated my choices. Two weeks into the dirty protest within 'the cages', I stood against my treatment and indefinite segregation, fighting for survival against the Prison Officers.

Now, three and a half years into my sentence, subjected to endless assessment on 'the ghost train' for over twenty-eight months, I felt dehumanised. To my right, a bulletproof screen concealed a curtain and a dormant television. My beard grew unkempt, itching incessantly. Gazing outside, I glimpsed passing feet through the window, signifying solitary walks in the exercise yards. My throat was parched, yet my sinuses were clear. The appalling odour of my own waste had dulled for me, but for the guards, it lingered.

During this time, I'd been shuffled among twelve prisons, predominantly in the North, distant from my southern home. Leeds, Winston Green, Leicester, Full Sutton, Frankland, Bristol, Whitemoor, Strangeways, Parkhurst, Cardiff, Walton - I knew them all, some repeatedly. It was a strategic battle, designed to tame and break me. Despite attempts to conform, solitary confinement exacerbated my reputation as a disruptive inmate. My fate seemed sealed, my resistance ingrained. They refused me the normalcy of general wings, playing with me like a predator to its prey, evoking a primal ferocity within me.

Outside, the same walking shoes passed by. My body remained robust from daily cell workouts, but my heart ached. The ten officers who supervised my cell openings taunted me, draining me of the beautiful emotions that once resided deep within - an empty shell. My existence was now punctuated by the sounds of the metal dinner trolley and the consumption of substandard food, all to maintain a semblance of strength amidst mental turmoil.

In the clean corner of my soiled cell, enveloped in despair, I sought my smouldering rage. In my life I had met many difficult characters. Narcissists, psychopaths, sociopaths, the violent, the lost and the plain stupid; I had engaged with them all in their better and worse moments and I learned one thing, that there were two types of violent people. One, the majority, who would rather avoid violence but saw it and used it as a tool when needed and their security was threatened. The other, a darker breed stamped with the iron of a twisted insanity, revelled in it and thrived on it with a ferocious appetite. Hollowed out, my humanity was now a refuge for primal instinct, shrouded in stubbornness and rage.

The storm of my resolve was building. They would never conquer me. As my freedom and future were stripped away, so were my life and dreams. All that remained was my self-respect, the core of my being that I guarded fiercely, I would die before I yielded. Invigorated by a resurgent spirit, the echo of the silent cell and the clatter of metal trays accompanied my vigil.

Then I heard it - the rush of boots and the jangle of keys, the resounding thud of heavy footsteps on polished floors.

The heavy cell door swung open. Escorted by guards, I was led to a cell down the landing.

'...Okay, Sir. There he is. We're just up the landing; let us know if you need anything.'

They left him, a cluster of Prison Officers that stayed within reach.

From the chair he gestured to, in the freshly-painted cell still echoing with the scent of new paint, I observed him across the wide, grey table adorned with his papers and pen

'...Stephen Gillen. May I address you as Stephen? I am John Milton, from Prison Service Headquarters. I sit on the Category A committee and I'd like to have a word. Is it alright if we talk here, Stephen...?'

He sat alone, clad in a finely tailored blue suit, his face partially obscured by a white mask stretching over his nose and mouth. A silence fell, dense and heavy. I could sense his discomfort, the veneer of normality failing to conceal his recoiling tension. He inched his chair back.

'Can we talk, Stephen? I've travelled quite a distance to see you...'

'...Why are you here?'

'It's a matter of necessity, I'm afraid. To convey a decision we've made.'

I responded sharply, 'I am done reasoning with you people.'

He shifted uncomfortably, hands meticulously arranged before him. 'We find ourselves at an impasse as to how to proceed with you...'

'Are you going to remove me from 'the Book', take me off Cat A?'

'...Sometimes, Stephen, individuals are downgraded, yes. But there are occasions when intelligence, either internal or external, prompts us to reconsider.'

'You call it a 'different view'. You've kept me in solitary all these months...'

'You have been exceptionally disruptive, Stephen. You're deemed a very high security risk. It's akin to a chess game, managing the movements of Category A prisoners.'

'Can I be moved to the wing?'

He hesitated, clearly grappling with the foul odour and the scene before him.

'We've resolved that you are to be transferred to Hull Special Unit. They offer a distinct approach, very supportive. You'll enjoy more autonomy within the unit, prepare your own meals, and have educational opportunities...'

He waited for a reaction, which I deliberately withheld.

Rising to leave, he added, 'Hull is pioneering a novel initiative. We're seeing promising outcomes. We trust you'll fare well there...'

The guards were summoned. The chair was reclaimed. They stood by the door.

Impulsively, I asked, 'When do I leave?'

'Soon. I cannot provide a specific date; you understand the reasons.'

'Is there a chance I'll be removed from the Book?'

As the guards arrived, he approached the cell door. They formed a protective circle around him, an assembly of white shirts like sentinels guarding a treasure.

Milton, behind his mask and patting down his now sullied suit, looked gravely at me.

'Gillen, a caution regarding your Category A status. Continue this path and you'll be released with it intact. Close the door.'

Whitemoor Prison 1997, 2.17am

Huddled under a thin blanket in the cell's darkness, my feelings, tormented by prolonged confinement, had morphed into a despair so sharp, it cut deeper than anything I had previously known. The silence of the segregation unit hung heavy around me. Whitemoor, a dispersal prison in Cambridgeshire, tucked its segregation wing away in a detached, secluded section, overshadowed by the formidable walls of the Special Security Unit. My fifteen-month stint in Hull's Special Unit had passed without incident, and for the first time during my incarceration, I felt a glimmer of progress. Hull's more relaxed regime, coupled with rigorous training that sculpted my body, had temporarily quelled my anger and imbued me with a forward-looking desire to swiftly navigate the remainder of my sentence.

Then, without warning or explanation, I was uprooted. One morning, an escort team materialised and whisked me back into segregation.

On the third floor, the darkness echoed around me, punctuated by the floodlights from the yard and the harsh glow from the Special Security Unit, which cast eerie, unnatural shadows across my window. A sense of desperation dragged me further into a chasm of acute torment, a pit that seemed to have no bottom.

The descent into depression had been stealthy yet relentless. It began tentatively, like a snowball of grief and yearning for freedom that swiftly gained momentum on a downward slope, signifying a life entrapped with no foreseeable future. Then the boulder of fear and anxiety hit me, hurtling down, propelled by self-pity, dragging me deeper into its depths. The crushing solitude was compounded by the violence of my circumstances and the turmoil of my mind, my desolation about the direction my life had taken, pulling me inexorably towards an abyss.

In the midst of this maelstrom, I strained to hear the quiet. My breath filled my ears, short and laboured, each inhalation a rushed and shallow battle. The walls of isolation seemed to draw nearer. And within the nightmare, as my thoughts spiralled towards how to end the torment, I heard a voice. It cut through the web of sadness that ensnared me, a sliver of clarity in the engulfing gloom. Once, with a soft clarity that belied its strength, it offered a succinct directive: 'You must endure this…'

'Why?' I responded, my voice a mere whisper. 'Why must I endure this living hell?'

The voice was steadfast, echoing once more in my mind, 'You must go through this.'

Tears blurred my vision in the stark chill of the cell. I curled into myself, seeking solace in the foetal position, a childlike instinct for warmth and comfort in the frigid air.

I was aware of my deteriorating health, yet too far adrift in my despair to care. Ending it all seemed a mercy, not just for me, but as a reprieve for everyone. It would be swifter, gentler.

The voice had come from deep within my psyche, but I doubted its sanity. The relentless waves of sorrow continued their assault, while torment and anxiety wove through my being like a venomous thread.

Detached, as if in an out-of-body experience, my consciousness seemed to hover in the stillness above me.

Visions flashed before me: violent episodes from my past interspersed with moments thick with emotion. My son perched on my knee, Callum's grinning face, the grip of a little girl from a children's home years past, the cherished yellow Tonka truck of my youth, a spiky towering tree, and the tender hands of my Aunt Margret. The memories hurtled by like a runaway train, their collective force stirring a tempest of piercing emotions, drawing more tears.

'Oh God,' I murmured. 'What will become of me after twelve years of this?'

In that solitary place, I faced my darkest hour.

Then, without warning, it arrived a gradual, yet insistent presence that descended from the pitch-black cell ceiling, carrying with it an overwhelming sense of love and protection. I took in a sharp breath. Its luminous aura brightened my surroundings, dispelling the shadows that had haunted me, yet its gentle light was not blinding. It enveloped me, its warmth seeping into my very essence, quelling the chill that had taken hold. My mind and body halted their turmoil, yielding to this pure, comforting assurance. Eyes wide, heart momentarily unguarded, I surrendered to the profundity of its embrace. It lingered, a silent guardian, and then receded as gradually as it had appeared.

Darkness reclaimed the space. In the silence that followed, I pondered the nature of the experience. Beneath the blanket, although my inner wounds remained raw, a sense of rejuvenation washed over me. I swallowed, moistening the dryness in my mouth. The encounter had reignited a spark of hope and faith within me.

Prison change 1998

There is a defined hierarchy in prison. In the tight-knit world of the prison's dispersal system, we were a unit, a collective of the 'cream of the crop'. As gangs, we had our ranks and territories - Birmingham, Manchester, Liverpool, but the top, strongest firms came from London. We were at the top because of the armed robbers, the true 'faces' and other hardcore criminals, how we led and stuck together, our dominance and quick ways of being. Together, we pooled resources for what we called the 'food boat', contributing cash to ensure we ate well. The screws would covertly shop for us; it was one of the concessions made to maintain a semblance of peace.

Our camaraderie extended beyond meals; we trained together, shared homemade hooch, and threw the occasional party. Protection was a given - you never left a mate exposed. We paid back any slight, kept tight together, and defended each other ruthlessly. Long Lartin was riddled with shadowy nooks perfect for ambushes. The furniture outside the cells, the hidden corners away from the prying eyes of cameras, became strategic points for attacks. Every man was armed, every corridor a potential battleground.

But the system was failing, the screws were scared, and the equilibrium was shaky. Decisions were made in whispers, all to prevent an eruption of violence. Amidst this, drugs flowed freely, keeping some placid, others on edge. Prisoners ran the jails and the screws conformed to keep things quiet.

It was about halfway through my sentence, five years deep, when the tide turned. They introduced the incentive scheme, dividing us into standard, enhanced, and basic regimes. This move splintered our unity, segregating prisoners based on behaviour, sentence, and disposition. Suddenly, privileges like visits and association time became currency, leveraged to induce compliance. It was a game-changer. This new system, by offering and withholding perks, managed to tame the chaos that once defined our existence behind bars.

John Steed, Full Sutton Prison 1998

Locked up in Full Sutton, on the block, Charlie Bronson's cell was next to mine. That's where the story unfolds, with John Steed, notorious for his crimes. He knocked on the wall, on the pipe, as we all did, it was how we communicated, he was talking through it to me 'Who's that?' I'd asked, cautious as always.

He replied 'I was always kind of like you guys. I was always going to be a villain.' Trying to blend in with us, it set off alarm bells.

'Who are you then?' I asked.

'Oh, I'm John Steed.' Once he said his name, I knew - he was a Cat A, The M4 Rapist, the worst of the worst.

Once he said his name, it confirmed what I already knew, 'You're in for what?' I pressed, my tone dark as the cell around us. When he confessed - rape, murder, my rage boiled over. 'You fuckin slag, don't you fuckin talk to me or bang this wall again you're a wrong un.' I spat with venom.

His reply was twisted, 'You fucking Cockney gangster, you think you're all that.'

You killed a woman, that makes you nothing more than a fuckin' coward.' I snarled.

'Yeah well, she disobeyed me, needed teaching a lesson.' His response was so twisted. 'I'm like a Viking from the old days, rape and plunder.'

Charlie and I, we gave Steed hell from then on, made sure he felt the weight of our contempt. We'd communicate during the day throwing lines out the window, they were rolled-up paper, like a kind of dart. We'd make a line from the green blanket and we'd tie it the paper and then we'd throw it out. Someone further down the wing, would throw their one out over that and we'd pull them up together and we'd make a line so we could pass stuff back and forth. Every time we were passing the papers back and forth, Steed would jump on the papers and try to take them. He was desperate to cut off our lifeline of communication.

So, we made his life a misery. That's what happened when you caused problems.

Weeks later, the stark reality hit – I was lying in bed when I heard 'Rigour Mortis.'

Rigour mortis, I thought *what the fuck is that?*

Then the screw came to my door and lifted the flap, and looked at me, his eyes wide.

Steed was found dead, suicide by hanging. Strangely Steed thought himself a Buddhist, and he's picked a religious day, knotted up his sheet and hung himself that night. It was so strange as I hadn't heard a thing.

The block went silent as the screws took their time with him, leaving his body as a morning's grim spectacle. Eventually, they wrapped him up like a mummy, carted him off the wing, while the block erupted into jeers. There was a funny kind of feeling coming from the cell, but you're just so dehumanised that you don't recognise what it is.

Watching from the window a week later, I saw an old man, a stick in hand, a woman at his side - Steed's family, I reckoned. It's not usual to see visitors come into the segregation unit, They were shepherded right to where he'd spent his last moments. It was then, amidst the shouts and scorn, I caught a glimpse of the pain he'd inflicted, stretching far beyond his cell, beyond the block. I recognised the pain that he would have caused his family.

Months rolled on with Charlie and I mulling over the depths of life and death inside these walls. No matter how dark a soul, we never wished that end on anyone. As the block returned to its hard rhythms, we were reminded - in here, justice has its own twisted path.

The message should be clear. I've seen men serving full life terms, men who believe they have nothing to lose, and that mindset breeds more violence, more danger. It's a self-perpetuating cycle that sends the wrong message and fuels more crime, despair, and expense for taxpayers. More people return to prison, more prisons are built; it's become a business.

There needs to be a balance, a fair and effective system that truly rehabilitates, sending the right message for the sake of fewer prisons, less violence, and a safer community. Another significant issue is the red tape in the prison service, the bureaucracy. It's slow, compartmentalised, archaic. And they often miscategorise people. Many inside shouldn't be there, they have mental health issues, or they belong elsewhere. They're thrown into this 'University of Crime', marked for life, when they could instead be redirected to become productive members of society.

You'll Never Break Me 1998

I spent most of my sentence on the Ghost Train, I endured five years of solitary confinement, recognised as one of the UK's most disruptive prisoners. Witnessing others broken by the system was a daily occurrence, yet I clung to an indefatigable part of myself - they may have stripped me of hope and freedom, subjecting me to relentless torture of every kind physical, emotional and spiritual, but I resisted. They branded me with a reputation that justified their treatment, attempting to erase my identity and silence me. But I refused to be just a number, to be lost in their system. This, too, was part of their strategy, their twisted public relations exercise - to dehumanise and discredit. I would hold on to the anger, thinking how I'd pull my tormentors apart piece by piece. The anger and rage kept me going when I had nothing left.

Woodhill Prison 1998

The newly operational Close Supervision Centre (CSC) at Woodhill Prison, constructed at considerable expense, was designed as a prison within a prison. Its mandate was to manage, contain, and correct the behaviour of the nation's most challenging, disruptive, and dangerous inmates. Modelled after a high-security prison control unit in America, the CSC operated on an incentive-based tier system. Compliance would be rewarded with increased privileges and a more bearable existence. Non-compliance, on the other hand, would result in a stripped-down, exceedingly austere life. With four self-contained units intended to house around ten prisoners each, the aim was to start most prisoners in the middle and standard level of the system, with the capacity for up to six tiers.

Back at his desk in the lofty expanse of Clelland House, with the relentless wind still whipping the Thames into a frenzy and the windows rattling persistently, he perused the list of seven inmates already placed in the CSC. A twinge of concern flickered within him. The HM Inspectorate of Prisons was pressing to visit the facility, and they were far from ready.

With a fluid, almost creative motion, he penned and signed the directive order for the next inmate to be transferred to the CSC with immediate effect. His gaze fell on the sheet listing the names of selected inmates in bold. Below the name Charlie Bronson, he added the next prisoner: Stephen Gillen

Move to Woodhill 1998

Woodhill was based on Marion Prison in the States, Charlie Bronson was the 7th to be 'selected' as they called it and I was the 8th. Charlie had been moved there after famously smashing up Hull Special Unit and taking one of the teachers hostage.

In the depth of the new prison designed for the most serious of us, life was carved into three distinct tiers, each a step on a torturous ladder. There would be up to ten prisoners in each tear at any time depending on behaviour. It would also be the location of a murder, as two friends I knew well would clash; Matthew Wainwright would kill Lenny Tierney on the stairs one day crushing his skull with a pp9 battery in a sock. I write this remembering the brutality of life and how everyday objects were turned into lethal weapons.

On the lowest rung, I was faced with a regime so harsh it bordered on the inhuman. My 'bed' was a sloping concrete plinth, a design so cruel it guaranteed the numb agony of dead limbs and the relentless torment of sleeplessness on a skinny mattress that may as well have been cardboard for all the comfort it gave.

The 'standard' tier offered a sliver more of dignity, a semblance of normality with slightly improved food and the barest increase in comfort. Yet, it was all still under the shadow of constant control, a life measured out in the scantest of increments.

The top tier, however, was a different world within the same confines. Here, I could cook my own food, enjoy additional visits, and embrace those few comforts so starkly absent from the tiers below. It was a carrot dangled before us, the promise of a more humane existence that could be snatched away at the slightest infraction.

This structure, this building was not just a prison of walls and bars; it was a psychological crucible, a place that tested and broke the spirits of many. Every moment was a calculated move by unseen puppeteers, every privilege a meticulously placed piece in a game of compliance and control.

But the prison was insane, run by psychologists, with every method employed to manipulate us. I vividly recall the Fridays when they served fish and chips, a small pleasure in an otherwise grim life. We'd be wary of the guards, avoiding conversations to not give away our thoughts as they were always watching, always evaluating.

I remember one Friday, they brought the food on a cardboard table, placed right in front of my cell. It looked like they'd given us salt for the chips, but it turned out to be sugar, ruining the meal we all looked forward to. Frankie Quinn, in the cell next door, was livid, hurling his food against the wall in frustration I heard him screaming 'You fucking slags' at the top of his voice.

I didn't react, though. I ate those sugar-covered chips without complaint. I knew they were trying to provoke me, to justify further punishment. It was all a mind game to them, mental torture at its purest. My rule was never give them what they wanted, no matter what that was.

It goes without saying, my time within those walls was a relentless seesaw of highs and lows - down, up, and down again, mirroring the fate of many others. For two years, I languished towards the end of my sentence, until necessity dictated my move to the normal wing for a semblance of rehabilitation.

I'd been there only two months before they decided to deliver one final blow, transferring me to Durham. That place was the very definition of desolation, bitingly cold to the bone, it felt like even the polar bears would weep in search of warmth. The high-security Cat A women's wing just across from my window only added to the darkness that permeated the place.

The atmosphere in Durham was oppressive, a strict, bizarre world painted in shades of freezing grey. It lacked the familiarity of London, filled instead with faces from the north and Scotland, none of whom had any love for a Londoner like me. Each morning was heralded by the grating sound of chains dragging through bins, a deliberate addition to the day's grim soundtrack. But the stay there was finite, and eventually, I was shifted down to Belmarsh. With just four weeks left, still a Cat A prisoner, it felt like a respite, a slight easing of the shackles as my time edged closer to an end.

A day in the life 2000

Navigating each day in prison required a distinct approach, whether on the wings or in the solitary confines of the block. On the unit, a semblance of structure dictated the daily routine: breakfast, gym, educational pursuits, and moments of camaraderie with fellow inmates during visits or while watching television. I'd indulge in writing, perhaps engage in some form of education - always ensuring there was a subject to pique my interest and sustain me. Life on the wings was more dynamic, punctuated by movement, yet still governed by periods of being 'banged up' - locked in a cell during afternoons and nights, with occasional breaks for association or work duties.

Segregation stood in stark contrast, embraced by silence, a comfort and a curse, where one is left alone with the depths of their own psyche, wrestling with thoughts and feelings that churn relentlessly.

Writing became my sanctuary; it was where I embarked on a literary journey. Shakespeare's sonnets, Dickens' narratives, and the classics became my escape, a way to transcend the confines of my cell. Factual literature too played its part in my self-education, serving as fertile ground for a mind seeking liberation. I wished to become a screenwriter, but now, in later life I have achieved much more, being successful both sides of the camera and in writing, producing, and distributing my own content, TV and film work worldwide.

Physical training was another cornerstone of my daily life. I'd execute relentless circuits within the cramped space of my cell: a thousand push-ups in sets, interspersed with brief intervals of pacing. Six hundred squats, dips using the edge of a chair, and leg raises became my regimen to maintain strength and resilience - not just physical, but mental and spiritual too. These exercises fortified me against the reality of confinement.

In quieter times, I'd pen letters, sketch, allowing creativity to flow as another means of maintaining sanity. Each discipline, be it intellectual, physical, or artistic, was a vital thread in the tapestry of my daily survival, weaving a barrier against the encroaching walls of my environment.

Millennium, New Year's Eve, 2000

On my knees, in the subdued darkness of my cell within the Close Supervision Unit - a stark place that had claimed two years of my existence - I listened to the distant sound of fireworks crackling in the late evening sky. With my eyes closed, the weight of my years in confinement pressing upon me, I offered up a prayer and made a solemn vow.

'...Dear God, the universal force behind all things, I ask for forgiveness for my shortcomings, for failing to make better choices. Through suffering, I've come to understand this world, and as the falling years of my imprisonment have stripped away all emotion, in the deepest pit of my despair, I've been led to the great courage of my unyielding resolve to alter the course of my life for the better... I humbly ask you to help me with this, show me the next steps forward...'

As the world outside celebrated the dawn of a new millennium, the air charged with hope, I found it fitting, in quiet humility and with resolute strength, to connect with the collective spirit of humanity from my cell. On bended knees, I sent forth my prayer and vow.

Outside the window, against the backdrop of a moonlit sky, fireworks burst forth, their reflections ephemeral against the yellowed, floodlit concrete of the exercise yard and the enclosing fences and walls that held my freedom captive. Nearly a decade had passed since my incarceration as a Category A prisoner.

The truth was clear to me: the harsh years of high-security imprisonment had mercilessly stripped away my emotions, as if stolen by a thief in the night. My humanity had been pilfered. Anger had served as my sustenance, rebellion as my compass, and I had been tempered into a figure of gritted resilience. The vow I had murmured echoed once more in my mind. With less than eighteen months until my release, a part of that vow, held close and untold, reserved for the sanctuary of my own heart, was a commitment: to not let anger or bitterness ensnare me, to seize any chance for change, to aid others, and to reach ambitiously towards becoming the best version of myself...

Reflection

Life, as I've come to understand, is riddled with paradoxes. The more I've witnessed its complexities, the more I recognise the power of simplicity. True wisdom lies in distillation - finding the essence within the convoluted. The simplest solutions, ideas, or answers often bear the greatest impact, capable of changing the world and serving as a foundation for expansion and refinement. Life thrives on paradoxes, on the cycles and patterns, the formulas that dictate our existence. It's structured and coded, a test to gauge desire, authenticity, and one's place on the path of growth, success, and happiness. It's a navigational challenge laid out for each of us.

Reflecting on my own narrative, it's the ultimate irony that my current standing is a direct result of my past afflictions. This journey, with its missteps and lessons, highlights that the true importance lies not in the destination but in the growth that occurs along the way. It's a realisation that the path to becoming more is paved with openness to learning from our errors. The essence of existence isn't merely about where we end up but about the transformation within us and the impact we have on the world around us. It's an internal endeavour, a responsibility to leave the world and its inhabitants better than we found them.

On tour in America 2021

*In Make-up for Gangs
of London 2022*

*Filming on my Canadian tour with human right's
lawyer Joseph Neuberger 2022*

Good Morning Canada breakfast show 2022

Filming and directing a feature film in our studio 2022

Production With YouTubers Beta Squad 2022

341

Cover for Muscle & Health Magazine 2023

36 With Irish Champion Peter Doherty 2023

With former caporegime of the NY Colombo Crime Family, Motivational Speaker & Author, Michael Franzese on his UK Tour 2023

A challenging interview with two politicians for GB News 2023

Daphne interviewing me
Past, Present & Future 2023

With Syd, my grandson Ronnie, Lucia & Stevie 2022

*With the legendary Sir Trevor
McDonald 2023*

*With Sky News Presenter
Kimberley Leonard 2023*

*With Daphne, my
angel 2023*

*With ex-gangster Dave Courtney
just before his tragic death 2023*

Filming The Search for the Mafia with Ross Kemp 2023

With ex-gangster, 99 year old Bobby McKew (Billy Hills right hand man) and Ross Kemp

With Bobby McKew, Michael Emmett and Ross Kemp

Me with Lucia & Stevie 2023

With broadcaster and journalist Carole Malone 2024

With Daphne winning an award for Philanthropy 2024

With friend and TV presenter Nana Akua after appearing on GB News 2024

With my mini-me Stevie, boxing 2024

With retired professional boxer and actor, Joe Egan 2024

The old life behind me, now in 2024

CHAPTER 8

New beginnings, The Same Mistakes

"You have to believe in yourself."

— Sun Tzu, The Art of War

New Gangs 2001

The barber shop was a slice of Istanbul nestled in the heart of Manchester, the buzz of clippers harmonizing with the murmur of city life. I took a seat, the leather creaking under my weight - a sound reminiscent of the time I'd served. My eyes met his in the mirror, a nod enough to acknowledge the mutual respect between us.

He was a top player from Manchester, his presence alone demanding respect, his reputation as solid as the steel he trafficked. I watched him through the mirror as he approached, his reflection an echo of my own life - hardened by the streets, polished by the game.

Stephen: 'Alright, mate. Good to see you outside of the usual circus.'

Gary Mulligan nodded, a small smirk on his lips 'Stephen. Always a pleasure when business brings us together.'

The barber draped a towel over his customer and excused himself, sensing the air had thickened with something other than steam.

I settled into the chair. 'So, Amsterdam's on the cards. Guns and gear, the usual dance. It's a smooth operation, but it's getting hotter. The heat's not just from the coppers now; it's international.'

Gary was cool as he sat in the chair. 'Aye, it's a tangled web out there. You've got to keep your wits sharp. Amsterdam's a gateway, but it's also a spotlight. You've got eyes on you from all angles, not just ours.'

I leaned back, the blade cool against my skin as the barber started his work, a silent audience to the covert discussion. 'I'm not blind to the stage we're on. But the rewards are worth the spotlight.'

'Just watch your back, Stephen. You've got the charm and the muscle, but those can only take you so far before you hit a wall.' Gary cautioned.

I gave a laugh, edged with the confidence of a man who's stared down darker threats than words 'I appreciate the concern. But I didn't come this far by being careless. We do this clean, no mess. We keep it tight, right?'

Gary gave a slow nod, his eyes never leaving mine in the reflection before us. 'Clean's how I like it. But remember, every job's got its shadows, and some of them bite. You're good, Stephen, one of the best. But even the best can fall.'

The conversation was a dance of words, a choreography of the life we led. As the barber finished up, I rose, my reflection now sharper, the lines defining me more precise. It was a metaphor not lost on me.

'Then we don't fall. We fly, mate. We fly high and make sure we're not the ones to land first.'

We shook hands, the grip firm, an unspoken contract sealed with the understanding of the life we were bound to. I walked out into the Manchester drizzle, the weight of the impending job a familiar friend on my shoulders.

Under Observation 2002

The Interpol Agent spoke to his National Crime Squad contact 'We've got eyes on the target. Gillen's en route to Dover as we speak. His activities in Amsterdam haven't gone unnoticed. It's time to bring him in.'

NCS Agent Jones replied 'Agreed, Eriksson. Our intel suggests he's been a key player in the smuggling operations between here and the Netherlands. Weapons, drugs - you name it, he's been involved. Do we have confirmation on his transport?'

'Yes, we've tracked his vehicle leaving Amsterdam. According to our Dutch counterparts, he's driving a black van. It's believed to be carrying a significant haul.'

'Good work. We've got teams positioned at Dover. Surveillance is in place, and we're coordinating with the port authorities. There's no way he's slipping through the net this time.' Jones replied.

'What's the plan once he's on UK soil? Direct apprehension at the port, or are we tracking him to a secondary location?' Asked Eriksson.

'Direct apprehension. The moment he steps off that ferry, our teams will move in. We've got enough evidence to detain him on multiple charges. This operation needs to be clean and by the book - we can't afford any slip-ups.'

'Understood. We'll ensure our international teams are on standby for any fallout. Gillen's connections are extensive; his arrest could shake up networks across Europe.' Said Eriksson, a touch of hope and excitement in his tone. Unusual for Interpol but he'd been on this gang a long time.

'Exactly. That's why this has to go smoothly. We're not just after Gillen; we're using this as a stepping stone to dismantle the larger network. Once he's in custody, we'll press for information on his associates.' Jones thought deep down it was unlikely they'd get anything out of Stephen Gillen, but you never knew.

Eriksson nodded to himself, 'I'll relay the details to our teams. Everyone's on high alert. Today could mark the beginning of the end for this smuggling ring.'

'Let's hope so. We'll touch base once the operation is underway. And Smith, let's make sure this is the end of the line for Gillen. It's time he answered for his crimes.'

The End I hadn't Seen Coming 2003

Being away from the high walls that had caged me, the taste of freedom and Lilly was the life I'd convinced myself I wanted back. A straight life. The life that, deep down, I knew I was ill-equipped for. The world had moved on, but I was in a time warp, a man out of step with time but marching to a familiar drum.

The connections I'd made inside, they weren't just names in a book. They were lifelines to a world that understood me, a world where I wasn't an ex-con but a man of respect. Within a few months, Amsterdam became a second home, a haven of vice that welcomed me with open arms. The city's canals reflected back a life of counterfeit money, of drugs that promised the night and weapons that whispered power. Interpol and customs were shadows in my peripheral vision – I knew they were there, but they seemed like ghosts, powerless to touch me.

Lilly... she watched me. There was no need for words; her silence was louder than any argument. She didn't want the late nights, the whispered phone calls, the ever-present danger that hung over us like a chandelier, beautiful but threatening to crash down at any moment. She's grown up in this world, knew the risks it brought and wanted more for herself.

I was flush with money, the jobs were big, and my reputation was solid. It was a perfect storm, and I was the eye of it, calm and central while chaos raged around me. The buzz of it all, the sheer 'Fuck you' to a life that had dealt me hard blows, was intoxicating. I'd been beaten, bent, and bruised by life's fists, and now I didn't feel beholden to its rules.

But there was a cost, a toll that the lifestyle exacted with silent precision. Lilly and I, we were drifting on a sea of my making, and the currents were strong. The end was written in the lines of tension that framed her face, in the sleepless nights and the unspoken fears.

I was fighting a double-headed monster: the law on one side, my own demons on the other. Each day was a battle, each deal a skirmish in a war that I was starting to realize could not be won. The rules I was flouting weren't just society's – they were the fundamental laws of what it meant to be human, to live with honour, to love and be loved.

And in the midst of it all, I could feel the tide turning. The freedom I thought I had was an illusion, bars of a different kind that were just as confining as the ones I'd left behind.

New Organised Crime 2003

The two detectives assigned to the National Crime Squad, an organisation tasked with tackling national and transnational organised and major crimes, had been alerted through their specialist channels when the target, Stephen Gillen, left his home. Disguised as tourists donning baseball caps and backpacks, they blended seamlessly into the crowd on the grass verge of East London's Victoria Park. The cameras draped around their necks, doubling as long-range directional microphones to capture conversations, were inconspicuous as they feigned casual chatter with non-committal gazes fixed on Gillen. He was scattering pieces of bread to the ducks from a bag he carried.

The sunshine coaxed dense crowds to the park, facilitating the detectives' integration and manoeuvring to prime positions for their surveillance operation. Gillen, who as a boy had dared adventures on the small island across the lake, now stood in solitude by the water's edge, silently feeding two towering swans that had elegantly approached him. Unbeknownst to the park's casual onlookers, these detectives were but cogs in a larger investigative machine that was monitoring a criminal network spanning four UK cities and three continents, now stirring into action.

Two months had passed since Gillen's return to the streets and he and another individual were subjected to a search in their vehicle at Dover, moments before they could embark on a ferry to mainland Europe. Their journey was shadowed across the Channel to Calais, then on to Dunkirk, through Ghent, reaching Antwerp and Breda, and finally crossing into the Netherlands at Rotterdam. A different surveillance team had trailed them further to Utrecht and Amstelveen, culminating in Amsterdam's centre, where they were observed engaging with known international criminal figures in Leidseplein.

Now back in London and hugging the lakeside, Gillen was on the move once more. He strolled along the water's edge, his phone in hand.

The detective adjusted the lens of the camera, which doubled as a directional listening device capable of capturing conversations with clarity from five hundred meters away. Amidst the bustling wildlife scavenging along the bank, he blended in effortlessly, the picture of a photographer in search of the perfect shot.

He hunched over, simulating a keen eye for the optimal lighting. Recent briefings had cautioned them: vans had been spotted departing and returning, heavy with contraband, at various strategic points along the motorways from London to Manchester. With the anticipation of an artist awaiting the decisive moment, the detective from the National Crime Squad (NCS) kept a watchful eye on Gillen, who was nonchalantly clutching his mobile phone. The ducks and swans orbited the unsuspecting man, their movements a natural camouflage for the surveillance at play. Should Gillen activate his phone, the detective was primed to eavesdrop and document every word.

Possession of a Firearm 2003

In the world I traversed, a gun wasn't just a tool; it was a part of me, as essential as the air I breathed. It was a brutal truth, one that underscored every step I took on the streets where reputation and respect were currency. Brendan and I, we weren't just playing at this life; we were embedded in it, career criminals by any standard, our names known in the shadows we frequented.

The day they finally caught up with us on Bethnal Green Road, it wasn't for lack of trying on their part. They'd thought they would grab me off the ferry in Dover, but I'd had a funny feeling and at the last minute decided to hire a car and come back by myself. I'd have loved to have seen their faces when they realised I wasn't in the van. The authorities had been baying for my blood ever since. They wanted to see me go down, to lock away the menace they saw me as, forever if they could. But the world doesn't always give you what you want. They could only pin the firearm charge on me, despite the myriad of sins my name was tied to.

The gun in my pocket was damning evidence, irrefutable. It was a lifeline in the chaos of my world, but in the hands of the law, it was the anchor that sought to drown me. The plea deal was a bitter pill, a strategy played in a game where the odds were stacked against me. Five years - it was a concession, a nod to the fact that while they couldn't cage the beast entirely, they could clip its wings.

Brendan, standing beside me, faced his own demons. The identity parade, a flawed attempt to stitch him into the fabric of a crime he hadn't committed, was a glaring misstep in their crusade against us. His acquittal, months later, was a testament to the flimsy case they'd built, a house of cards that couldn't stand the scrutiny of justice.

For me, the deal was a calculated retreat. I knew the game, knew when to hold and when to fold. The sentence handed down was a leash, a way to keep me bound within a system that loathed the uncertainty I represented. Wormwood Scrubs was to be my penance, my exile from the freedom I'd so fiercely guarded. Incarcerated again as a Cat A on the book.

As I stepped into the confines of my cell, the reality of the situation settled heavily on my shoulders. The plea deal, the sentence, the gun - they were all chapters in a story that was far from over. They'd wanted to bury me, to erase the threat they saw. But in their haste, they'd forgotten one thing: even caged birds remember the sky.

The narrative of my life, marked by the law as a career criminal, was not ending with this sentence. It was merely pausing, gathering breath for the next chapter. And as the days in Wormwood Scrubs began to blur, the resolve within me sharpened. I was down, but far from out.

Back Inside 2003

This time around, the walls of Wormwood Scrubs seemed to close in on me with a suffocating embrace. The familiar defiance that had fuelled my previous bids for survival had dwindled, leaving behind a raw, exposed nerve. I was a broken man, haunted by the echoes of freedom and the relentless passage of time. The fight against the regime, the battles waged within these walls, had taken their toll. My cocaine addiction was tearing at my mind and I couldn't face another stretch with the same hardened resolve. Desperation called for desperate measures.

So, I embarked on a new strategy, one that demanded as much from me as any physical confrontation had. I decided to play mad. It was a performance that required me to shed every last vestige of dignity. I stopped washing, let my hair and beard grow wild and unkempt, a tangled mass that masked the man beneath. I spoke to phantoms only I could see, engaged in one-sided conversations that filled the air with my voice and nothing else.

My walks in the exercise yard became a spectacle. Counter-clockwise I roamed, against the flow of my fellow inmates, a lone figure wrapped in his own world. I muttered to myself, laughed at jokes unheard, and gestured to empty spaces. To any onlooker, I was a man lost to his own mind, a soul unmoored by the harshness of prison life.

The guards watched, their scepticism plain to see. They huddled in their groups, casting glances my way, their murmurs a low hum that I pretended not to hear.

'He's putting on a show, has to be. No one goes crazy that quick.'

'Yeah, but have you seen him? Talking to the walls, laughing with the air. It's convincing.'

'Convincing or not, it's his word against the doc's. And who's gonna believe a career criminal over a psychiatrist?'

Their doubt was a threadbare cloak that barely concealed their uncertainty. They questioned, but a part of them wondered if the strain had finally broken Gillen, the unbreakable.

The culmination of my act was the rope, a twisted sheet of desperation and deceit. I wove it openly, a challenge to their disbelief, a tangible proof of my descent. It hung from the bars of my cell, a noose in search of a neck.

Yet, even as I crafted my facade, I remained acutely aware of the eyes upon me, the minds behind those eyes weighing, judging, searching for cracks in my performance.

'Look at him, with his rope. Thinks he's clever, but we're not fooled.'

'But what if we're wrong? What if he's really lost it?'

'Then he's the best actor we've got in here. Either way, we keep an eye on him. Crazy or not, Gillen means trouble.'

In their watchful gaze, I felt the weight of my ruse, the precarious balance between freedom and further damnation. To 'play the fool to catch wise,' to outwit those who held the keys to my cage, was a gamble of the highest order.

And so, my days became a tightrope walk between sanity and its imitation, each step a calculated risk, each act a plea to the unseen judges of my fate. In the depths of Wormwood

Scrubs, amidst the mad and the broken, I played my role, waiting for the curtain to fall, for the verdict to be delivered.

The Flying Squad, London, 2003

'Oh my God. The shit has hit the fan.' The Detective barely had time to express his shock before the phone was snatched from him, the handset forcefully replaced on its cradle, and he was instructed to remain at his desk in silence and refrain from touching anything.

They arrived like a relentless swarm, buzzing and organised, akin to predatory hornets descending upon a coveted beehive. Amidst the midday hustle of the office and under the leaden skies of South London, which were now ominously promising rain from the east, the most clandestine division of the Metropolitan Police's anti-corruption unit - dubbed 'The Ghost Squad' - executed a sweeping raid on the offices of Scotland Yard's S08 Flying Squad, East London branch.

From his back office, a vantage point from which he could oversee the main floor and his squad at work, Detective Inspector Finch witnessed the encroaching tide of the anti-corruption officers as they poured in. His gaze fell upon the black-and-white chequered baseball cap on his desk, and a surge of dread at the prospect of exposure coursed through him. He realised it was already too late. A phalanx of both plainclothes and uniformed officers advanced, halting his team's activities and commencing the collection of evidence, seizing paperwork, files, documents, and computers.

He reclined in his chair. Outside, his team members were being shepherded from their desks, lined up against the wall, and interrogated. The officers from the standards division were unyielding, assertive, and methodical. Finch grunted - a sound more akin to a snarl - as the murky depths of the force would, as always, call for shadowy resolutions. Heads would roll, and the spectre of revoked pensions loomed ever closer. He opened the drawer of his desk, retrieved a cigarette from the concealed pack, and lit it, inhaling deeply.

For nine months, he had waged war against the lure of nicotine. It had been yet another sacrifice in his noble quest to rid London of its gangster scourge, akin to his failing marriage, the endless nights, and the crippling sciatica that caused his muscles to quake. Now, as they conducted their search, his office filled with the dance of cigarette smoke, he watched them uncover some of the 'fit-up kits' - the term his squad used for the sets of replica handguns, gloves, and masks they planted on suspects when concrete evidence was elusive.

'Jesus, Mary, and Joseph,' Finch thought. The forthcoming disgrace would decimate his hard-won reputation, just as he had secured a senior position on the murder squad. He drew another breath of nicotine into his lungs, coughed, and spluttered. He, along with a few others, were doomed. His aspirations were disintegrating. Rome was ablaze, the rats were already scurrying to salvage what they could, and the architects of this new regime would be merciless in their reformation.

For one of the first times in his distinguished career, Donald Finch felt a stark, polarising terror. They would make an example of him, and beside him, in his plea for leniency, would stand the six other officers complicit in these deceptions.

The remaining nineteen members of the squad, though culpable for their tacit condoning of such unsavoury practices, he surmised, might escape with lesser consequences.

The room was now thick with cigarette smoke. Watching the systematic stripping of operational notes, briefings, and photographs from the walls, observing his subordinates being corralled into a room at the corridor's end, and noting the dark rain clouds gather over Walthamstow, Detective Inspector Finch realised that The Ghost Squad was methodically saving the worst for last.

He rose slowly. Through the expansive windows of his office, he could see them - two high-ranking officers leading a dense group of plainclothes operatives.

He snapped his attention to the live and unfinished cases, their details crammed into the brown folders that cluttered his office. Bulky volumes housing dangerous men, hardened recidivists whose violent narratives demanded swift conclusions.

It marked the end of an era.

'Detective Inspector Donald Finch?' The room filled rapidly, the space shrinking as they spread out.

Finch gave a terse nod, 'Yes, that's me. May I inquire who's asking...?'

The grey-haired one, tall and unmistakably in command, dismissed his query with a brisk wave. 'DI Finch, your rank and operational status notwithstanding, rest assured they will not impede our duty here. I am DCI Keith Johnson from the

Department of Professional Standards. We are conducting an anti-corruption investigation into your actions and those of your squad, both past and present...'

Finch tensed, his defiance waning as they read him his rights and moved to handcuff him. Standing erect, he declared, 'I'll not be cuffed.'

Beside Johnson, DI Owen Whitter experienced a fleeting pang of sympathy, a sentiment that dissolved as quickly as it had appeared. He advanced with determination. Having built his reputation within the ranks of the Police Complaints Office, he had attended enough 'grip and pace' operations to understand that a handful of corrupt individuals could taint the overwhelmingly professional police service.

'I'm afraid, DI Finch, you have neither influence nor authority here and must comply,' Whitter insisted.

'It's alright, DI Whitter,' interjected his senior, DCI Johnson. 'He may walk. For the service he has rendered, that dignity we can afford him.'

They encircled him. With his cheeks aflame from embarrassment, and under the watchful eyes of his squad from their confinement, Detective Inspector Donald Finch took his final stride across the expanse of the Flying Squad office he once commanded - a walk filled with pride.

His days as a serving officer were unequivocally over. Reaching the end of the hallway, he descended the stairs surrounded by the team, and then announced, 'I believe I'd like to speak with my solicitor.'

DCI Johnson responded, 'That would be exceedingly prudent, Detective Inspector Finch. Exceedingly prudent indeed...'

Woodhill Prison, 2004

As a Category A prisoner with only nine months remaining on my sentence, the armoured van surged onto the motorway, bound for London. Confined to my cubicle and tightly handcuffed, I squinted through the heavy rain that blurred my view and drummed incessantly on the tarmac and the landscape beyond. The world outside, shrouded in bleakness, seemed unchanged, yet the long, soul-destroying years of violent incarceration had instilled in me a lesson to never take anything for granted. I retrieved a brown envelope from the blue folder resting on my knees, containing my most recent correspondence. Within the larger envelope, which had arrived only yesterday, was the document I had been eagerly awaiting. Issued by the Crown Prosecution Service, it detailed the re-examination of my case from years ago, revealing an investigation into DI Finch and a corrupt cadre of officers by their internal anti-corruption unit.

The rain's relentless assault against the van's bodywork and the window of my cubicle, accompanied by an expanse of grey clouds, fringed with the nimbus of a silver lining, filled the afternoon sky as we journeyed towards London and my impending freedom. My attention remained fixed on the document before me, where at the top of the page in bold typeface, it read: 'Operation Wasteland'.

Cat C 2004

After enduring ten gruelling months within the confining walls of Wormwood Scrubs, a sliver of light pierced the relentless darkness that had shrouded my days. The judge's review of my case, a process I'd barely dared to hope in, bore unexpected fruit. The verdict came down like a hammer shattering chains: reclassification to a Category C prisoner. It wasn't just a change in designation; it was a lifeline, a breath of air to lungs starved of hope.

The transfer to Belmarsh prison marked the beginning of a new chapter. Belmarsh, with its relative freedoms compared to the suffocating constraints of Wormwood Scrubs, felt like stepping from a night into dawn's early light. It was still prison, the bars just as cold, the doors just as locked, but the air carried a different weight here.

I thought to myself *I can't believe this is happening. Feels like I can finally breathe again.*

The move allowed me fragments of autonomy I'd forgotten were possible. Here, the regime was less about breaking the spirit and more about managing risks. I found solace in the small liberties afforded to me; access to better facilities, more time outside, even the opportunity to engage in work and education programs offered a semblance of normalcy, a reminder of the man I wanted to be.

For the first time in a long while, I allowed myself to entertain thoughts of the future, of a life beyond the prison gates. The move to Belmarsh was more than a change of scenery; it was a shift in mindset. The oppressive despair that had clung to me, fed by the isolation and the ceaseless churn of my thoughts in Wormwood Scrubs, began to recede.

Recognising The Demon, 2004

In the confines of my cell, amidst the tumult of my own making, a decision took root. The drugs, my constant companions through thick and thin, had to go. It was a clarity that pierced the usual fog, a moment of truth I could no longer ignore. The thought of Lilly, steadfast and enduring, flashed through my mind as I picked up the phone to call her, my heart heavy with the weight of my confession.

'Lil, I've been doing some thinking. I'm going to quit the drugs. It's not going to be easy, but it's something I need to do. Not just for me, but for us.'

The line hummed with her silence, a pause that felt like an eternity. When she spoke, her voice was a soft balm to my frayed nerves. 'Stephen, that's... that's wonderful news. It's a big step, and I'm here for you. We can get through this together.'

Her words were like a lifeline, a glimmer of hope in the darkness. Yet, I could sense the unasked questions, the concerns she harboured about our future.

'I know it's going to change things, Lil. And when I get out, maybe we need to sit down and really talk about where we're going, what we want.'

'I think that's a good idea. There's a lot we need to figure out, a lot that's changed. But knowing you're making this decision... it gives me hope, Stephen. We'll have that chat, look at everything with fresh eyes.'

Her cautious optimism was a balm, a gentle acknowledgment of the road ahead, fraught with challenges yet ripe with possibility.

'I appreciate that, Lil. More than you know. It's going to be a hard road, but just knowing you're there, that we can talk about it... it means everything.'

'We've been through so much, Stephen. This... this is just another part of our journey. Let's take it one step at a time, see where it leads us.'

As the call ended, the silence of my cell felt less oppressive, infused with the possibility of redemption and the promise of difficult yet necessary conversations ahead. Quitting drugs was the first step on a long path to recovery, a path I would walk with Lilly's support, our future a canvas yet to be painted.

In the days that followed, as I faced the demons of withdrawal and the reality of my situation, the thought of that future conversation with Lilly, of the chance to rebuild and reassess, became a beacon guiding me forward. It was a journey we would embark on together, our love and commitment the compass navigating the uncertain waters of change.

Belmarsh offered a platform, however shaky, from which I could start to rebuild. The freedom within its confines allowed me to confront the demons that had driven me to the brink, to start the arduous process of healing and self-discovery. It was here, in the unlikely setting of a Category C prison, that I began to truly serve my sentence, not as punishment, but as a period of transformation.

Chelmsford Prison, 2004

When the tortuous madness began to seep into my mind, it came as a slight, sparse wind meandering through the corridors of my consciousness - announcing its presence without leaving a tangible trace. It twisted and writhed, a strangling vine that took hold quickly and surely. The scene around me was tinged with an unnatural hue, the colours too vivid, accompanied by thoughts and half-heard voices, eyes that deceived, and non-lucid moments that prodded at my sanity in terrifying ways. This was the onset of a mental illness that would rapidly spiral into a living, walking, dreaming nightmare. I was thirty-eight years old.

The cell was a chaotic throwback to the bygone slop-out days of my youth, devoid of sinks or toilets, just an old bucket in the corner. The walls were a patchwork of filthy grey and green, the paint peeling back to reveal uneven brickwork. Two little shelves jutted out, a solitary cupboard stood, and the blue-framed metal bed was draped with the same old green cotton prison blankets.

It began in earnest during the early evening bang-up, as the sun's yellow disc dipped below the horizon, heralding the approaching night. The voices that soon infiltrated my solitude spoke of vile acts, chopping, butchering, conspiracies, plots, murder. They promised death in whispered tones, detailing the methods they would employ.

Perched atop two white pipes running along the cell wall, I peered out at the fading light in the empty exercise yard, alone with my swirling thoughts, fears, and growing confusion.

The voices seemed to emanate from outside, a cacophony of laughter and taunts, yet they resonated inside my skull, loud, then soft, whispers giving way to raised speech. They morphed into conversations between phantom people before coalescing into a single voice that spoke directly to me.

A slicing, freezing fear took hold within. These voices, unfamiliar yet occasionally adopting the accents of figures from my past, delivered terrible content in a sinister lull.

'We will kill you,' they hissed, as if whispered directly into my ear, the words tumbling and circling in my head, rendering me powerless. 'Your time is now. No one escapes. Not you, no one.'

Huddled in the corner of my cell, the voices seemed to come from both within and without. The arched ceiling above appeared to spin, casting the shadows in a twisted dance. 'Oh God,' I thought, hands clamped over my ears, eyes squeezed shut, yet still, the voices penetrated. They waxed and waned like spectres in the dark, ever elusive.

The shadows stretched further across the cell floor. Time distorted, what felt like an hour had, in fact, been an entire night. I had flicked on the cell light, but the voices only grew louder, more insistent. So, I retreated to the darkest, safest corner to wait, to listen. They were laughing again- a haunting mockery that twisted a paralysing fear into my fragmented thoughts, reducing them to whispers.

The prison officers, the voices suggested, were plotting my demise. They spoke of past atrocities where others like me had met their end, strangled with twisted sheets, dangling from the cell window. My troubled mind was awash with terror, my gaze fixated on the cell door, the spy hole that seemed to flicker with movement. The imagined sound of creeping shoes on the landing outside amplified my dread.

There was no escape, the voices assured. Daylight would never come again for me; the screws intent on fulfilling the voices' prophecy were en-route, their measured steps echoing on the polished floors below.

Broken, I knew something within the labyrinth of my mind was amiss. I grasped for clarity, for a semblance of sanity, but it remained just out of reach, my thoughts and emotions grotesquely contorted. It was akin to being trapped in a psychedelic nightmare, awash with serotonin and auditory hallucinations. Cowering in the corner, wracked with pain and a terror that mocked me, I screamed silently in my mind - a heart-wrenching cry that lingered too long in a void where no sound escaped.

Chelmsford Prison, 2004

The prison doctor, a slender figure with short grey hair and horn-rimmed glasses, listened attentively to the report from the Senior Officer in his surgery office. The file labelled 'Stephen Gillen' lay on the MDF table before him.

'He shows signs of illness, Doctor. His moods fluctuate dramatically, indicating something is amiss. Initially, we suspected manipulation, given his extensive history, former Category A prisoner, stints in Special Units, prolonged segregation, a background of drug misuse, and a substantial security dossier. He's under close surveillance.'

The doctor, meeting the gaze of the reporting officer - a seasoned man with a pale complexion, bald head, and dark beard, asked, 'What about his family situation?'

'He receives visits. Has a partner, Maria, and three children: Syd, thirteen; Stevie, one; and Lucia, two. He's slated for release next week. Observations on the wing suggest possible schizophrenia, confirmed by previous medical consultations.'

The doctor noted in the file, 'And drug use?'

'Believed to be an issue. He has a history with Class A substances. The Principal Officer and I agree on the necessity of a comprehensive assessment before his reintegration.'

'Understood,' the doctor responded, penning further notes. 'I'll see him immediately. Bring him in.'

The night had been an enduring ordeal of solitude, confusion, and agony, following a day lost in a fog of light and motion. In the calm of my cell, I fought for sanity amidst the chaos of my illness, where delusions blurred reality and fantasy. Moments of clarity were stealthily usurped by confusion, as my mind oscillated between euphoria and despair, haunted by contradictory voices and besieged by hallucinations.

The cell door swung open. Despite my pleas, only the medics had attended to me, leaving me to grapple with my fears and pain in isolation.

'Doctor's call, Gillen,' announced the guard.

I stepped out to the landing - a bleak expanse of metal, wire, and towering floors, echoing with the cacophony of prison life. The scent of disinfectant, old soap, and polish clashed with the distant, dull aroma of mass-cooked food.

Led down to the ground floor, my thoughts were a tumult, even as memories of a recent visit from Maria and our children - Lucia and Stevie, offered brief solace. Their presence had momentarily steadied my turbulent mind. Yet, the respite was fleeting; my condition soon worsened.

Guided through the prison's outdoor spaces, the tranquillity of the day clashed with the turmoil within. Mere hours before, paranoia had convinced me of imminent threats, leading me to makeshift defences against non-existent attackers. Alone, I realized the depth of my mental fracture, a legacy of sustained violence and trauma.

Entering the hospital wing, the sterile scent of the dentist's office enveloped me, a stark contrast to the prison's grim atmosphere. The prison officer knocked.

'Yes,' muffled.

'Gillen, Sir…?'

'Let him in.' Clearer. A cut-glass voice that indicated sharpness. The door opened. I was an emotional wreck. In a weakened state, frantically trying to hold onto my sanity, I walked in.

But there was something within me, for my own sanity, that refused to capitulate. That persistence saw me through. I was different in that respect. I would've rather died than give in. That refusal to submit fuelled me. The animosity propelled me, in many ways. I recalled being in the unit in Woodhill Close Supervision Unit in 2000, on my knees over the millennium, uttering a prayer to change my life, to make something of it. I recognised that the anger, the violence that had sustained me in some twisted way had left me like the living dead, devoid of all human emotion, a walking corpse. I was imploding. If I didn't find my way back to myself, to some semblance of humanity, I had no chance at all in life. I had to change, or I was lost forever.

Reflection

Living under constant scrutiny inside, I learned about the depth of observation. Cells and common areas, bugged to capture snippets of conversation - all part of the game within the game. The intelligence gathered wasn't just about maintaining order; it was a chess match played with human pieces.

The hand we're dealt can dictate much of our path. Many of us start outweighed down by negatives that seem insurmountable: poverty, broken homes, violent streets. These are the seeds of a future wrought with challenges. The road built from such beginnings often leads to destruction, the kind that's hard to veer away from. But it's not immutable.

CHAPTER 9

Breakdown & Rehab

*"The supreme art of war is to subdue
the enemy without fighting."*

— Sun Tzu, The Art of War

Maria 2005

The first breath of freedom was supposed to be sweet, but mine tasted like dust. I'd been out before, but this last stretch of 2.5 years hit different – it was the one that cost me Lilly. She'd done her time on the outside waiting, but a woman's got a right to want more than a life tethered to visiting hours, censored love letters and the promise of a crazy lifestyle fraught with dangers.

I found myself in a clean house in Stepney, a stone's throw from the chaos of my past. The government's idea of a fresh start felt more like a halfway house to a life I didn't recognise. No drugs, no crew, no heists – just me trying to fit square pegs into round holes.

Maria came out of nowhere. She was the girl with a family from sunnier places, pouring coffee in a cafe on Commercial Road, not asking who I was or why my hands were calloused in ways that didn't quite match the workman's boots I'd started wearing. She had her own story, I could tell, but she kept it locked away behind that smile that said, 'We've all got scars.'

With her, I wasn't the ex-con, the Category A ghost, haunting East London trying to deal with his issues and rise again. I was just a bloke trying to keep on the straight and narrow, brick by brick, on a building site that tested my resolve daily. She was a momentary solace, a distraction from the itch of cravings, past traumas and scars that were never fully scratched away.

Lilly and I – we ended with a mutual nod, an understanding that life had to be more than what we'd been dealt. She'd always be the one who knew me behind the bars, the wonderful woman who was the keeper of my first shot at forever. But forever's a luxury not made for men like me.

Now, it was about the small victories. A day without looking over my shoulder. A night where the ghosts of my actions didn't crowd the bed. A pay check earned with sweat, not schemes. Maria didn't fill the void Lilly left behind, but she stood with me at the edge of it, a testament to the possibility of something like normalcy.

The old me would've laughed at that – the job, the girl, the too-quiet evenings. But that laughter would've been hollow, the sound of a man falling apart. I was still piecing together what it meant to live without the noise, without the rush. It wasn't easy; sometimes I felt like I was walking a tightrope above the life I knew, and it wouldn't have taken much to tumble back down.

But every morning, I got up. I faced the mirror. I went to work. Building something – not just the structures on the site, but a new version of me. It wasn't a fairy tale, but it was a start, and it was enough.

What Goes Around… 2005

In the grubby bedsit he rented in a third floor two bed flat just off the Walworth Road, Mr Windmill grunted and swung his tired and aching legs to the side of the bed so he could take a sip of the flask of coffee he always carried. At eighty years old, the small, cramped room, painted in a calm lemon with dirty walls, was his latest sanctuary from the world. He pushed out with his wrinkled hand, scattered to the floor the porn magazines stacked on his one piece of bedside furniture. Money was tight. In his mind he cursed them all. The services, the police, the public, his family…

He took the piece of newspaper clipping from his dirty jeans pocket. It said, in bold print: Vile Abuse in The Children's Home Nicknamed 'The Prison'.

He was up, and he snorted his disgust. He kept the clipping and looked at it every morning so his anger could be fed, and his old body get the jolt of adrenaline it needed to get moving. The years of service, of controlling delinquents had meant nothing. They were only the children that no one wanted, his efforts for society were not thought of as a service. He put on his unwashed blue parka jacket, and he felt it, a stirring in his groin, arousing him and sending lewd, illegal images to his mind. There was still life in the old dog yet.

He closed the door to the bedsit, confined the wafting smell that caused his neighbours problems, and ventured down and along the tight run-down landings and concrete steps.

Back behind him, from the second floor of the mirroring flats across the way, 'Oh…Oh, fuckin nonce. Fuckin die nonce. You wait till we catch you!'

Windmill looked up, peered out from the hood of his parka. It was the teenagers from the estate. He raised his elbow, cowered back behind a car close to him, regrouped. Quickly, Mr Windmill again focused his shattering thoughts and hurried out of the estate.

A New Family 2005

The clean slate I was handed felt like a chalkboard, every new day a man's fingers scraping down it. I missed the highs – not the chaos they caused, but that feeling of being untouchable, like I was made of Teflon and nothing could stick to me. That's what the coke did; it smoothed out the edges, made the ordinary extraordinary, and I was just a bloke trying to feel normal in a world that kept reminding me I wasn't.

Maria was a live wire with a laugh that echoed the clink of pint glasses and the crackle of rolling papers. She had the East End in her veins, a proper girl from my patch, not scared of the shadows, but one who found comfort in their familiarity. She liked that I was rough around the edges, a hint of danger wrapped up in worn leather and calloused hands. There was no judgment in her hazel eyes, just the gleam of someone who's seen the darkness and flirted with it.

But her bloodline? That was another story. Her mother, a tough-as-nails moneylender from the old country near Sicily, had roots that dug deep into the East End's community and underworld. They were linked to and ran gambling clubs on Commercial Road, places straight out of a mob movie, thick with the stench of smoke, cards, dice, the movement of stolen goods and fast-moving money. Her brother, Ton Ton, was a well-known figure in East London, he was thought of as a big-time dealer and had often been targeted by the police. Clever, lucky and innovative he was always one step ahead in his life and we got on well. It was the usual stuff. I was playing with fire, just being around the scene, feeling its gravitational pull.

I'd pass by sometimes, after a shift at the site, telling myself I was just taking the long way home. But those places were like gravity to a man trying to fly straight. In London, specifically the East End, every street holds a memory – not all of them healthy, good or progressive.

You can slap on a fresh coat of paint, but the cracks will always show through, the triggering deep inside reminding you of piercing emotions linked to powerful nostalgia. That was me - looking the part on the outside, muscles from honest work bulging, a glint of sweat on my brow from a day's graft. But inside? Inside was a battlefield. My head was a mess of thoughts, a tangle of what-ifs and the whisper of 'just one hit' echoing around the skull. I would need to constantly take the fight, stand guard to my own mind and feelings, sometimes second by second, hour by hour to navigate the right way forward.

It was inevitable, really. One slip, one line, and the dominoes started tumbling again. It wasn't even about the escape anymore. It was about the fear. The fear of going back to what I was, the torment and darkness that gripped me and spelled destruction, the life of crime that whispered my name like a lost lover. I could see the path stretching out in front of me, paved with good intentions, but lined with the skeletons of my past, the need to lay to rest a reputation that was still intact.

I was a lamb to the slaughter, and the slaughter was me – every line, every deal, a step back into the abyss. I was dancing with my demons again, and the music was sweet, even as it heralded my downfall.

What Goes Around... 2005

As London stirred into wakefulness, the River Thames calmed, its late-evening whirlpools and tides gently subsiding. The phone call about something suspicious had been routed through just as the city's thoroughfares began to pulse with the early signs of the day's congestion. The woman, an investment specialist accustomed to running the 2.3 miles from Putney Bridge to Battersea with her dog each morning before work, had reported her concern, the anxiety palpable in her voice.

Police Constable Newman felt frustration grip his heart, a clenched fist of regret. He had served in the Marine Policing Unit of the Metropolitan Police, formerly known as the Thames Division, for seven years. As their rapid-response Targa 31 sliced through the fresh, murky green waters of the stirring Thames, he adjusted the boat slightly to the left, peering through the dissipating smog. The echoes of a slammed door and the remnants of an argument with his girlfriend clouded his thoughts, but his attention sharpened as the object of their search came into view. Drifting near the embankment's break, where a small pebbled beach lay exposed, was a form bobbing against the river's edge.

His colleague, perched at the bow with binoculars pressed to his eyes, called out, 'I see it, Harry. Just downstream from where we expected. The current's taken it a bit further. It's a body, Harry. Looks bloated.'

PC Newman advanced the throttle, and the boat surged, bow lifting as they hastened towards the shore. A metal coffee flask bounced off the hull, bobbing in their wake, as two officers waded into the water. The patrol boat neared the clothed, swollen corpse. As they flipped the body, the tell-tale signs of vascular marbling on the face, neck, and hands became apparent, and the dark discolouration of the skin suggested significant putrefaction. The body had been in the water for some time.

Despite their training, the officers recoiled at the pungent odour. One officer, seeking identification, unzipped the drenched blue parka. Inside a ripped pocket, he retrieved the deceased's wallet, bringing it to light. Tucked behind a sodden newspaper clipping in the wallet was a card bearing a name: Mr Rodney Windmill.

Addiction 2006

Each line was a betrayal – to my parole, to my new life, to my family, who never asked for more than I could give. But the white powder was a masterful liar, promising strength while it hollowed me out from the inside. The more I used, the more I lost myself. I'd look in the mirror and see the ghost of the man I used to be, wondering if he'd ever been real at all.

The streets of East London were no longer just streets; they became a chessboard where shadows moved like rooks and bishops, each one a potential threat. Paranoia became my constant companion, honing my perception of people and places into a hair-trigger vigilance. The harsh lessons of my past had ingrained in me the necessity of watching over my shoulder, yet the edge of cocaine fine-tuned this wariness into a darker, more acute awareness—a chilling tingle that perpetually whispered of danger at the nape of my neck. Assassins seemed to lurk in every shadowed nook, every gaze that lingered too intently. I was hurtling down a perilous slope, careening toward an inevitable crash with relentless, breakneck speed.

Paranoia crept in and ruled like damp in an old house - silent, persistent, destructive. The police had been a distant threat, a possibility I could rationalise away. But now, fuelled by my unravelling thoughts, they morphed into omnipresent watchers. I could feel their eyes on me as I moved from site to cafe to the clean house that felt more like a stage with hidden cameras in every corner.

I'd walk the streets and see the flash of a camera, the glint of binoculars from a window. Every phone call I overheard was a wiretap, every new face a plant. My world shrank until it was as small as it had been inside, a cell made of my own making.

Maria saw the change. She must have. The way I flinched at sirens, the way my eyes darted to exits every time we entered a room. But the party never stopped for her; she lived in the moment, always chasing the next high. And I, drowning in my delusions, was desperately trying to keep my head above water.

The building site, once a symbol of progress, became another place to look over my shoulder. I'd lay bricks and see them as potential hiding spots for listening devices. The clang of metal was a gun being cocked, the whistle of the foreman a signal to someone unseen.

I was losing it, losing the grip I had fought so hard to maintain. The coke wasn't an escape anymore; it was a trap, springing closed on me with every heartbeat, every snorted line.

The paranoia was a riptide, pulling me away from the shore, away from Maria, away from the semblance of sanity I'd cobbled together.

I'd lie awake at night, listening to the city breathe, each exhale a possible whisper of conspiracy. I was teetering on the brink, a man suspended between two falls – the fall back into crime, or the fall into madness. And the worst part? I wasn't sure which scared me more.

I turned to Maria my voice edged with a tension that didn't quite belong in the dim comfort of her living room. 'Do you ever feel like you're being watched? Like there's eyes on you, even when you're alone?'

Maria laughed softly as she looked up from rolling her joint, her hands skilled and sure.) 'Only by you, babe. Why, you getting jealous of the wallpaper?'

I tried to smile but it's a grimace. 'It's not a joke, Maria. I'm serious. I can feel them, the cops, they're out there, waiting for me to slip up.'

Maria glanced up her hazel eyes searching my face. 'You're being paranoid, love. You're out, you're doing good. No one's watching you.'

'You don't get it! They're never gonna let me go. Once you're in the system, you're in. It's like... it's like I'm still in prison.'

Maria sighed as she put the joint down, she reached for my hand. 'Stephen, you're scaring me. This isn't you. You're letting this stuff mess with your head.'

I pulled my hand away and stood up abruptly, my eyes darting to the windows, the door. 'You don't see it. But I do.

There's patterns, there's signs. That car parked across the street for too long, the same bloke on the corner every morning...'

'That's just the city, babe! It's just East London. It's not about you.' Her voice was firm, insistent.

I paced, the words spilling out of me like water from a burst pipe. 'They took everything from me once. They can do it again. They're just waiting for me to fall, and I can't... I can't give them that.'

'Listen to me, Stephen. You're not giving anyone anything. You're free. But if you keep snorting your life away, you're gonna end up giving it all away.'

I turned and looked at her, really looked at her, and for a moment, the paranoia receded, a wave pulling back from the shore. 'I don't want to go back, Maria. I can't.'

Maria spoke softer now, a whisper that barely carried over the noise in my head. 'Then stay with me. Stay here. We can get through this. Together.'

It was my twenty-one-year-old son, Sid, whom Maria had called. In a late-evening, urgent phone call, she conveyed that my delusions were escalating out of control. No one could reach or reason with me as crippling schizophrenia had clamped down on my mind. Her voice, etched with worry and tears falling freely, feared I was a danger to myself. Could he come and take his dad to the hospital?

'It's okay, Dad...' His hand rested on my shoulder, his words a reassuring balm as we entered the Royal London Hospital in Whitechapel. At the reception, 'Can I help you?' Syd regarded the woman before him. He had matured into a fine-looking young man, exuding solid, wiry strength, his hazel eyes alight with understanding, his handsome face chiselled, his intellect sharp. Behind the glass, the receptionist in her blue hospital uniform tapped her computer keys.

'Yes, I phoned earlier. My dad is not well. He's hearing things and is extremely unstable. We're very worried about him. Could he be seen promptly?' The receptionist glanced past the glass at the man beside the young speaker. The well-dressed figure seemed to shift and sway awkwardly. Tall, with dark black hair, clad in grey trousers, black shoes, and an expensive-looking blue coat, his movements were staggered. He stood there, turning now, his eyes wide, surveying everything around him.

'He's unwell. It's urgent he sees someone... he's been acting very peculiarly.'

'Does he have a history of mental illness?' she inquired.

'No, he's mentioned things, been having problems recently. I try to talk to him, but it's like he can't truly grasp what I'm saying. He's physically here but not present. I know my dad, and he's in a lot of pain and not himself.'

'Has he had any diagnoses, any schizophrenic incidents?' she queried, now on the phone.

The receptionist, adept at detecting urgency, observed as the well-dressed man muttered to himself, jabbing at the air before him. 'I'm getting someone now, please wait.'

'Dad...' he anchored me, guiding me to stand by some doors away from the busy throng scattered across the hospital's vast, austere foyer. I recognised him; it was my son. Yet my mind conjured and whispered fallacies. My gaze scoured for assassins. My paranoia insisted they were tailing us, waiting for their moment. Apprehensively, I scrutinised the passers-by, a procession of diverse figures, nurses and doctors, orderlies and patients, beds wheeled towards elevators. I surveyed them all with suspicion, a tumultuous sea of perceived threats.

I closed my eyes briefly, attempting to suppress the torrent of anguish swirling within. My emotions were a tempest, surging and plummeting erratically. Anger soared, then plummeted into rage, paranoia, and fear. They were lurking; I was on alert, vigilant and braced for their onslaught. 'Are you Mr. Stephen Gillen?' Two doctors, in their late fifties and clad in starched white coats, approached. One was white, of average height and stout, with stern eyes and a ruddy complexion; the other was Asian, with greying hair and a stethoscope draped around his neck. 'No, I'm Sid, his son. My father's here... Dad?'

He had my elbow, a gesture of comfort as I remained on guard. They were here, the 'assassins', biding their time. I could see the men in white coats ushering us through the corridors, through sterile halls bathed in bright light where everything seemed suspicious, and the illumination could dim at any moment. He still held my elbow, an instinctive assurance. We were ushered into a side room, a space redolent of disinfectant, with doors shut and locked, where more figures in white coats converged around me. I sensed it then – the acute paranoia of entrapment as the lock clicked shut.

The doctor with the stethoscope stood before me, shining the beam of a light into my eyes. 'Stephen? How are you feeling?' the doctor tried again. Fear joined my rage in the core of my being as the sensation continued upwards, coursing across the contours of my back... The other doctor affirmed, 'He's showing signs of an episode. Stephen, can you hear us? We're going to help you, take you to a place where we can assist...'

I saw his face, but the words were lost on me. My mind perceived a trap, the guns I was convinced were concealed behind their pristine white coats. The rage within me was still gaining momentum, fuelled by fear. Pain spiked in my shoulder as I twisted and threw a punch at the approaching doctor. He managed to partially evade, but not completely - my fist grazed his face. Almost instantly, multiple hands seized me from behind, forcing me down to the ground with overwhelming force.

I struggled against their grip, my survival instincts kicking in, yet their weight was unyielding. In a frantic effort to escape, I tried to kick free, to swing again. My cheek pressed hard against the icy, unforgiving linoleum as insults and curses burst from me in ragged breaths. A sharp prick in my leg suggested an injection, swiftly administered, and my resistance began to fade.

Then I saw my son. The worry etched in his gaze. He was near. His proximity brought me a semblance of comfort. I heard his gentle voice as my consciousness started to wane.

'It's okay, Dad. I'm here. Calm down; I'll make sure you're all right...'

Breakdown, London 2006

In the closed psychiatric ward of London Hospital Whitechapel, a self-contained unit specialising in various forms of mental health, particularly schizophrenia, the doctor and senior male nurse traversed the shiny, burnished white and soft cream corridor.

'His son Syd is with him now, visiting. It's a compelling case. The patient has a history of long-term imprisonment, violence, and other traumas, including drug abuse. His psyche has been severely strained by his lifestyle. Upon admission, he was lucid but believed people were coming to take his life. Then, over subsequent days, he seemed to withdraw further from the present. Currently, he shows no signs of engaging with stimuli. The lights are on, Doctor, but seemingly, nobody's home. We're administering antipsychotics...'

The doctor, a youthful man with black hair and a moustache, nodded in agreement. 'It's indeed a very intriguing case. I wonder what triggered his detachment from reality?'

Approaching the patient's room, they found him sitting silently in a wheelchair, hands resting on his lap as he stared out the broad, curtained window.

The patient's son stood. 'Hi.'

The doctor shook his hand. 'You're Sydney, Stephen Gillen's son?'

'Yes...'

The doctor scanned the room briefly. Everything was immaculate – the metal bed with its pristine blankets, the bedside locker with a jug of water, a locker for personal belongings. It was all clean, sanitised, and minimalistic, just as he preferred. On the far wall, a vibrant, large mural burst with colours, reminiscent of Picasso's style, a deliberate choice to brighten the room and potentially draw the patient out.

'So, how has he been with you, Sid? Any response?' asked the doctor.

'No...'

The doctor noted the worry in Sid's voice as he stood beside Stephen Gillen. 'Is he going to be alright, Doctor?'

As the doctor examined Stephen's open, unblinking hazel eyes with a light, he gently prodded, 'Stephen, how are you today? Your son's visiting. He's happy to see you. Isn't that marvellous? What do you think of that?'

Only silence followed.

The patient remained still, gazing through the window, unresponsive, a shadow caught in stasis.

The doctor gently pinched the patient's forearm, searching for any reaction.

Again, nothing.

'Is he going to be okay, Doctor? Will he come back to us?' Sid's voice echoed near the curtained window, his face half-illuminated, worry etched deeply into his features.

'Stephen, your son Syd has some wonderful stories. He's a remarkable young man. Surely you remember the first time you saw him? What did you feel on that day?' The doctor continued, seeking a connection.

They stood close in the small room, united by the heavy silence that enveloped them. The doctor observed Stephen

Gillen's pallid complexion, noting the waxy pallor and the troubling hollow look in his withdrawn eyes. Silent and still, Stephen had retreated to a place deep within, inaccessible, seemingly absent from the world around him.

Breakdown London 2006

'Dad, Dad…Dad, are you there. Can you hear me Dad, it's, Syd? I'm here. I miss you Dad. I so wish you would come back. Be here with me so that I may not be alone and things can be as they were. I forgive you Dad. I understand how it was. I know that in this life sometimes we do what we have to and we can think of no way back…'

Syd Gillen kissed his father softly on the forehead. He had busied himself with making the room more comfortable. There was a vase of fresh Lilies, a blue bathrobe from home, new toothbrush, toiletries and oranges, grapes, apples and blackcurrant juice. The curtains were open and his father, a solitary, vacant figure who resembled an unmoving block, a carved statue with no recognition, stared unflinchingly out through the sunlight into the little yard with wooden benches and a circular pond which held Koi carp.

He washed a flannel, squeezed it and dabbed his father's brow.

'Is it good where you are, Dad. Are there great birds and flowing rivers and high mountains? Or is it city streets…Am I there, and your grandson, and little Stevie and Lucia. Is it nice weather? Speak to me, Dad…I have been coming most days after work. Every day, wind, sleet or rain…You would laugh,

Dad. You would say don't worry Son, you can't keep a good man down. Old soldiers don't die they just fade away…'

…In the hospital foyer the man wearing a tweed jacket and cap, who had travelled through the night as crushing winds had hit the north of Ireland, moved silently through the crowd at reception. He kept his three fingered hand tight in his trouser pocket so as not to leave a trace of his passing and walked head down and stealthily, unremarkable down the corridor toward the psychiatric unit. His mind was focused. A laser beam that saw one mission, one cause, an ending. People passed him on the long white hospital walkway. He did not make eye contact, did not put out the energy of presence. Diligently, so as to become invisible and unnoticed he navigated forwards. His training, learned long ago and deeply embedded inside him, was to be able to move without a trace of his passing and walk through thunder without leaving footsteps.

He was turning, following the sign for the ward he wanted, nearly at the place where an ending could be found. From the corner of his piercing green eyes he saw the door beside the entrance to the ward open and the doctors coming out. Before it closed he caught sight of the grey metal lockers inside. He pretended to study a poster on the wall, waited till it was clear. He would need a white coat so that he could blend unseen.

It was the doctor's job to watch from a far. It was important that from a private place of seclusion he could study his patients' movements, responses and impulses from a place that could be unsullied and relied upon.

The sun from the little yard, where the patients would sometimes sit, streamed through the window into the room painting folded and gleaming light on the side of the patient and the wheelchair he sat in. Stephen Gillen was an interesting case. He had read the file and it had kept him enthralled for hours into a long Friday night. He had seen cases like this before. Hard, forged life journeys that wielded the experience of a litany of harrowing trauma. The mind, an amazing machine, was wired for safety at all costs and with so much consistent and latent abuse the chemicals released to combat these traumas alone could be a cause for concern. Add other imbalances and drug abuse and it was a recipe for the finite threads that set the boundaries for the conscious mind to unbalance.

The other doctor beside him, said, 'What do you think…?'

He watched the patient's son. He tried to administer a sip of water to his father lips.

'Oh…If you had a beautiful violin, how would you play it?'

'I'd play it to the best of my ability.'

'Yes, but 'how' would you play it. How would you get the best out of it?'

'By learning from a good teacher, practicing…'

'The answer is to play it sweetly…'

The doctor, silent a moment as he watched the unresponsive patient and his son, nodded. He looked at the patient, he was only forty.

'If you had this beautiful violin. Would you hide it from the world or should it be played?'

'…It should be played to audiences, yes.'

'I disagree. I think it should be played to the world. Shared as god intended and played sweetly so it was enriched and respected and elevated…Somewhere in Mr Gillen is the locked sweetness that can return him to the world so his soul may play again…'

'…Dad…Dad, I must go. People to see and planes to catch.' Syd Gillen smiled, but inside him he could cry. It was a hard task, and troubling, for him to see his father vulnerable and distant like this.

'…Bye, Dad. Don't let the bed bugs bite. I'll be back tomorrow, probably after six.'

Syd lingered, by the solitary figure of his father. A man in a distant place that no one knew. He looked at the wide print on the wall. An abstract, and painted in sections, it resembled moving clouds that pulled you in to unravel hidden figures. He could make out a chin, lips a face. With your mind you could see also a bird that soared, the shape of a fish that dived. All in brilliant bright and vibrant colours. Crimson red, blue, yellow, sharp whites and blues and oranges, browns and greens.

His father was behind him now and he nodded to the two doctors who had been standing outside. He was comforted his father was alive. This alone was a miracle. But he would be back and persist as he just knew if he kept on the father he knew would one day return. He pressed the button to leave the ward, waited for clearance to leave. At the open door he saw the orderly who nodded with his head down. He carried a bucket and mop for the shiny floors. Sid's mind winced as he noticed the orderly in the white jacket carried the bucket with a hand that had only three fingers.

He had sat for a while, gazing at the motionless figure before him. The days had turned into weeks, and the weeks had melded into years. Brief, intense flares of pain had given way to a persistent ache, a dense knot of longing that led to stretches of depression.

They were both enveloped by the soft light, its gentle warmth and brightness overtaking the quiet of the moment. His initially uncertain voice found its rhythm, settling into a meaningful, easy flow.

'...And the great Monkey Puzzle Tree bore witness to the passing years. There had been times of struggle, moments when it stood resolute against the morning light, and times when it wept. Erect and dignified, it endured the harshness of the weather. Its roots clung tightly to the earth, yet the severe storms sought to displace it. As history ebbed and flowed, the Monkey Puzzle Tree learned to conceal its sorrow, burying it deep within its mystical core... The wind roared on the mountainside and through the darkened city streets. The rain cascaded, swelling the lakes and rivers, while magnificent thunder orchestrated flashes of lightning that illuminated the land. Men scoured the mountainside, armed with axes and blades, hunting for the magical trees deemed a threat, their magic enshrined in the sap of their bark, misunderstood. Their leader, a man of hatred with burnished golden hair, led the charge against the elements, relentless in their pursuit of the Monkey Puzzle Tree. Close calls abounded, whispers told of near misses with sharp axes...'

He paused to catch his breath, overwhelmed by emotion and the memory of a long-lost face.

'...But there was a woman on the mountain, one with the forest and the bogs and the winding stone streets, her knowledge unparalleled. An ancient soul with a mane akin to a lion's and eyes of bottomless turquoise, she had entered the fray with a purpose,

allied with the spirits of nature, ageless as the wind itself. She watched the malevolent men, mist and shadow her allies against their advances. One day, a young man from the city found himself lost in the fog, a child born into a world of fleeting shadows. As the mist, sent to confound the wicked, engulfed him, he wandered lost as dusk fell upon the mountain.'

Tears streaked his cheeks as he continued the tale, the droplets soaking into his hospital jacket. Yet his voice remained firm.

'...The boy, teetering on the brink of death on the mountain's edge, was saved by the Monkey Puzzle Tree's intervention. Invisible, it became one with the rock, warning him of the danger that lurked. Voices of men echoed behind the veil of fog, their malicious intent clear. The boy, slipping on wet earth and tangled grass, delved deeper into the mountainside, seeking sanctuary and a path home. The man with golden hair, sensing the boy's knowledge of the tree's hiding place, rallied his men for pursuit at dawn...'

The Gardener had been a silent witness to the turning seasons and the melding of years. He now felt a lifeless but warm hand beneath his own. His narrative had been one of pilgrimage, of visiting an Uncle in Belfast, of seeing a Monkey Puzzle Tree standing tall in a small garden and of hearing the boy's love of old stories.

As his eyes brimmed with tears, he persevered with the story.

'...In his desperate dash for safety, the boy found himself ensnared in the mountain's labyrinth. Yet a flickering light, sent by the ancient guardian of magic, beckoned him onward. With dawn splitting the sky, they pressed ahead, guided by the spirit's luminescence...'

A subtle twitch, a faint stir under his hand caught his attention.

'...As the first light of dawn split the sky and morning dew gathered, they pushed onward, the men's pursuit close at their heels.

The Gardener noticed it – a twitch, the subtle movement of the hand beneath his.

'...It's said the woman of the mountain commanded the trees to feign death, blocking the path of those men. But the harsh man with burnished golden hair, he knew the mountain's trails well...'

Wiping away tears, the Gardener sensed a stronger, more deliberate movement. It was as if a dormant flower was stirring, ready to face the day; Stephen Gillen's hand moved, fingers now tightly clenched.

Rising, the Gardener collected the bucket and mop he had set aside. As Stephen's head turned and his eyes met the Gardener's, a moment of recognition passed between them. But without lingering for another glance, the Gardener walked to the corridor, not looking back.

Breakdown 2006

They say in the eye of the storm, there's a calm - a deceiving lull. My storm doesn't have one. Every moment is a relentless assault, a barrage of suspicion and dread. Cocaine psychosis, they've got clinical terms for it, but what do they know of the terror? Hospital walls close in, whispering of conspiracies, each shadowy corner promising doom. Losing my mind was the most frightening thing that had ever happened to me through it all.

Inside my head, it's chaos. I'm not silent by choice; it's a silence born of fear, a silence because my reality has splintered into fragments too sharp to touch. They think I'm not thinking, not seeing, but my mind is alive with a grotesque carnival of horrors.

I'm fighting, though. Not out loud, not where they can see – this is a silent, internal battle, a man wrestling with spectres only he can see. My fists clench at phantoms, my eyes dart to track the movements of apparitions that vanish when looked at directly. They're after me, all of them, or so it seems.

The medication is a fog at first, a blanket thrown over the jagged edges of my psyche. It doesn't feel like it's working until, one day, the edges begin to blur, the figures start to wane, and the voices... they're not gone, but they're quieter, as if someone turned down the volume on the horror film that's been my life.

Two weeks pass, and the doctors talk about stabilisation. But what's stable about a ship that's still rocking from the storm? I'm not fixed, I'm just less broken. The urge for a hit hasn't left; it's there, a constant craving that I've pushed to the background while survival takes centre stage.

When they tell me I'm ready to leave, the sunlight is too real, the sounds of the city too immediate. I'm not being released into freedom; I'm stepping out into a battlefield unarmed, every day a war where victory is just making it through to the next.

As I walk out of the hospital, it's not a march towards recovery; it's a tentative step into a cease-fire that could break at any second. I'm not walking toward hope, I'm just walking away from despair. And for now, that's enough.

An Angel 2006

I was teetering on the brink again, my mind a tumult of shadows and whispers, when Brendan and Theresa came to see me. It had been ages since we'd last spoken; life had a way of stretching gaps into chasms. But there they stood in my cramped London flat, the city's grey light spilling across their concerned faces.

The moment Theresa's eyes met mine, I saw the dam break, her tears a silent testament to the state I was in. It was a mirror I couldn't look away from, her sorrow reflecting the depths I had sunk to. I wanted to tell her not to cry, that I was alright, but the lie tasted too bitter, even for me.

Brendan's voice cut through the haze. 'I know a place you can go now, but you have to go as you are. I'm gonna phone up the place, I'm gonna sort it out for you, but you've got to go right now or the deal's off.'

His words were a lifeline, but I was too scared to reach out and grab it. I followed them, my steps as heavy as my heart, all the way to the train, spewing every excuse my frantic mind could muster. 'I don't need to go,' I protested. 'It's a bad thing to just up and leave. It won't work.'

Their reassurances were a distant hum against the clamour of my fears. As we sat on the tube, the world outside blurring past, I felt trapped in my own spiralling thoughts, a carousel of denial and desperation.

Then he spoke, a black man sitting across from me, his voice a calm anchor. 'All these things you are saying are excuses.

Listen to your brother; he is trying to help you. You must go to this place.'

His words struck a chord, a note of truth in the discord of my life. I looked at him, really looked at him, wondering how he could see so clearly what I was trying so hard to blur. I turned away, a mix of defiance and fear, and when I looked back, he was gone.

In that moment, I felt something shift inside me. Was he an angel? I couldn't be sure. But in his words, I found a clarity I hadn't realised I was searching for. My brother was reaching out, not to pull me back, but to guide me forward.

As the train pulled into the station, I knew it was now or never. The angel's words echoed in my ears, a melody of hope amidst the cacophony of my doubts. 'You must go to this place.' And so, I stepped off the train, into the unknown, carrying with me the possibility that someone, maybe even God, still believed I was worth saving. At that point there was no future only decline and death.

Rehab 2006

We were all in the old, great hall at Haines Clinic, a place of high moulded white ceilings and a grand stone fireplace that was used for main meetings and checking-in in the mornings and afternoon. Where the clients of the rehab could build confidence, share a feeling or problem and the councillors could give feedback and pivotal interventions and gauge the progress of the day.

One of two specialist addiction Councillors, a light skinned, highly skilled slight man in his early forties who held in his hands a thick stack of polaroid photographs, told us to spread out around the room. There were twenty-six of us. A real mixture, from young men and women to the old and incontinent. I moved back towards a wide window behind me. Out there was the large rolling grass garden and grounds that belonged to the old main building. It housed, in its well-kept landscape stone statues, quiet places of reflection, paths that led into the forest lands that surrounded the property, and a square paved area with stone columns and benches that were formed in a square to sit on.

By the window, with the morning sun spreading soft light through the burnished glass, I watched the councillor as he walked around the room throwing the polaroid pictures everywhere around us on the rich red carpet.

I liked it here. The Bedfordshire countryside, the quiet and peace and seclusion of the place. I had been here two weeks. Fourteen days, since my brother, Brendan by chance having a business meeting near the east end, had met me for a rare coffee and seeing how thin I had become and how bad I looked had broken down, researched, paid and personally driven me here. On the way, having left behind everything I was and owned, a dangerous life of serious villainy that closed-in and a progressive addiction to drugs that raced me towards an untimely death, I had looked out of the window as we left London. At the rolling hills and countryside and I realised I was on deaths door and he had saved my life.

The councillors, two men who themselves had beaten a long life of battering and painful addiction, had a serious look in their eyes, a sober countenance on their faces.

The light skinned one, fifteen years sober who had moved from London full time years back to pursue his crusade to save as many addicts as possible, said, 'Right, I want you to look at the photographs on the floor. Walk around and look closely at all the faces in the photographs.

We obeyed. I wandered. My body was starting to shiver, my stomach tightened in a knot of striking cramps. Slight tremors were appearing in the nerve-endings of my feet, legs and hands as withdrawal started hitting again. My mind, again emotionally shattered, was trying desperately and slowly to repair itself.

The faces in the photographs stared back at me. Pale, thin, with translucent skin, unhealthy, sad and lost faces, framed with the look of desperation and holding a glazed look that projected a kink or flaw of the soul. Old, young, men with hats and coats ruffled and with tussled demeanours, women without makeup and uncombed hair. Vacant eyes that stared and showed a yearning to imbue freshness into their lives.

I walked. Slowly, I looked and pondered over them.

Striding amongst us, for effect and in a no-nonsense voice, one of the councillors said,' Take a good look. All of the people in the photographs, the polaroid's were taken on their arrival here like yours were taken. All these people are now dead!'

The solitary photo of a young twenty-three old man with blond hair was in his hand.

It was held high.

'…This was, James. He was the latest to die. I remember James. He stood here where you are now not nine months ago doing this same exercise. He was extrovert, the life and soul of the party. When he was younger he went to private schools. He had one of the best educations' money could buy. He had dreams of becoming a famous anthropologist, was a talented cricketer and was nearly picked one year to be on the rowing team for Oxford…We got him clean here. He left through that door out the front that you all came in with those dreams. When he got to the train station where his family were due to pick him up he went into the toilet and injected a hit of heroin that was too strong for his recovering body to take. He died right there in the toilet alone and took the dreams of his future with him…'

We stood and the impact of the story tore at us. The room was silent. I had known great adversity and danger but a lump had formed in my throat and the aches and pains of my body were ignored for a moment as a dryness claimed and formed in my mouth. I could see it in the eyes that hung and lingered and gathered and tried to hide. Contemplation, horror, pain, denial, guilt and shame.

We were told to form a circle.

'Right, I want you to look at the person next to you. First to your right, have a good look, and then the person to your left…'

The first week for me had been horrendous here. It was a beautiful place that had been built by a tobacco baron in the early nineteen hundreds. A maze of hidden corners and twisting landings with fine décor, comfortable bedrooms, places to sit and do your written work, and the finest of healthy and attentively cooked foods. But it was structured and succinctly regimented. Everything, the meetings, the timings, the many daily chores and written work given, the attitudes that challenged and poked and prodded were staged and focused towards people's recovery.

'Take a good look everyone. Within a year, out of the three of you. One will be clean, one will be using and one will be dead…You really are in the fight of your life here…Now if you can follow us into the other meeting room it's time for group therapy…'

I could feel it as we formed a group towards the door. The minds that were deep in thought. Solitary islands that wrestled desperately to remove inner demons and understand their guilt and shame. We walked down the corridor that had white panelled walls, past the fine architraves and into a room with a circle of chairs. The mood was grim, the feeling sullen, the energy dull and stagnant. It was hard not to think of the young man who was a fine rower, who was vibrant, and who had met a final end alone in a grubby urinal. It hit my nostrils, a nauseating smell that was beautifully cooked vegetables, a choice of meats and hams, mashed potatoes, pastas and a mixture of fresh cakes. Pulling a chair back to sit on I drew back.

It came and went. The waves of sickness that were hot and cold flushes, painful limbs, clenching stomach cramps, fluctuating pains, crushing headaches, emotions that rose and fell. Some were constant, some intermittently fanning out through every cell in my body.

For the first week I had twisted and turned in agony in sweat-soaked sheets and no sleep had found me. I felt the darkness cling to my soul and had fought for it to lift. My mind and emotions were a storm that threw me around like debris in a strong hurricane and through the solitary, quiet darkness I had repeatedly screamed and winced internally. On the deck of that ship my addictions had laughed and flung and tossed me under growling waves whilst I held on refusing treatment. I had fought the good fight night after night as the narcotics slowly left my system, the recuperating nerve-endings in my brain and body healing and reconfiguring as my limbs jolted and jumped uncontrollably.

Sitting within the circle of chairs, in the wide room that had soft settees and tables with magazines, rich blue curtains and a library of books, we faced each other uneasily as the main group therapy session of the day was about to open up. People shifted, moved uneasily and fidgeted, as the counsellors took their seats and looked around the group. It was a safe place to share, a sharp, uncomfortable, challenging arena where denial was smashed and unhealthy ways of thinking and feeling were pushed, pulled, opened to the light, destroyed and righted.

The counsellors' experienced eyes searched, stopped at me, and in a calm but pointed tone, 'Stephen, would you open the group today?'

Feeling the flush of my waning physical pains move to my knees and legs, my addled mind found a clearing between the clouds of my gripping and turbulent racing emotions. Steadying myself, and slowly, clearly, I said,' Hi, my name is Stephen and I'm an addict...'

I was sitting with Gordon, one of the therapists and he turned to me, 'You know Stephen, you only have to change one thing, in order to get better and to live your life.'

I looked at him, scepticism clear in my eyes, 'One thing, and what's that?'

He smiled, 'Everything.'

Post Rehab 2006

Stepping out of the private facility's gates, I felt the sun on my face like a gentle affirmation. The place had been a sanctuary, a reprieve wrapped in comfort, where the demons that once danced in my head had been called out into the light and named one by one. Rehab wasn't a sentence; it was a lifeline, pulling me from the depths to which I'd sunk. And in that time, I found something I hadn't felt in years: peace.

Two months of therapy, group sessions, and quiet reflection had stripped away the grime of my addiction, revealing the man I could be. The Twelve Steps had given me a path to walk on, a way through the minefield of my own past. I learned about triggers and trauma, about surrender and acceptance. I learned how to live without the crutch of cocaine or the escape of any high. I had begun the Twelve Step Programme and I finally felt in control of my own destiny.

I knew from this point onwards I would never stop moving forward.

Seeing Maria again was like seeing colour after a lifetime of grey. She was vivid, vibrant, but with a softness to her now, a roundness that spoke of the life growing inside her. Our child was a symbol of hope, a new beginning that was both exhilarating and terrifying.

Back to the grind of the building site by day, and by the nascent glow of a desk lamp at night, I laid the foundations for a business that was all mine. But it wasn't just about the work. It was about proving to myself, to Maria, to our future, that I could be the man I saw in those quiet moments at rehab – strong, capable, whole.

'I've got this second chance, Maria. It's not just for me; it's for us and this little one.' I placed a hand gently over her belly, feeling the promise beneath.

Maria looked down at his hand, her expression a mix of wonder and uncertainty. 'I'm glad you're better. But it's a lot, you know? You coming back like this... it's different.'

'I know it's a change, but it's a good one. It's like... like I've been asleep for years, and I'm finally awake. And I want nothing more than to be the best for both of you.' My voice fervent, a testament to my resolve.

Maria snubbed out her joint, and sighed, a sound that seemed to carry the weight of her apprehension. 'I want to believe that, Stephen. I do. But it's hard. It's like I don't even know who you are anymore.'

I'm still me, Maria. Just a clearer version. And I'm asking you, just give me the chance to show you. To show our kid what it means to rise above. I can't erase the past, but I can build a future. With you.'

But her eyes, they were the same hazel that had seen me at my worst, and I couldn't help but wonder if she was ready to see me at my best.

I was back on the building site by day, dirt and sweat a testament to the life I was building, brick by literal brick. By night, I was plotting out my future business, the blueprints of ambition spread out on the kitchen table while Maria watched from the couch, a joint dangling from her fingers.

I looked at Maria with the cautious optimism of a man who'd crossed through fire and didn't want to get burned again. 'Maria, love, we need to talk about... about everything. About the baby, about us.'

Maria took a pull of her joint, the smoke curling around her like a shield. 'Talk then. You've been doing a lot of that lately.'

I sat across from her, my hands steady, my eyes clear. 'I can't be around the weed, Maria. It's not just about me anymore – it's about our kid too. I want to be better for you both.'

Maria laughed but there was an edge to it, a discordance. 'You come out of the loony bin and now you're preaching? You think you're better than me now?'

'It's not about being better. It's about being present, being alive for our family. The stuff I've learned, it's given me a second chance. I want you to be a part of that.' I said firmly but gently.

Maria's eyes narrowed and she became defensive. 'I've been part of it, haven't I? I've been here while you went off the rails. And now what, you want me to change?'

I reached across the table, trying to bridge the chasm that had opened between us 'I want us to grow, together. To build something real. This child, our child, deserves parents who are there, really there.'

Maria put the joint out, something like realisation dawning in her gaze. 'And what about what I want? What about my life?'

I nodded, acknowledging her struggle. 'We'll figure it out, one day at a time. But we've got to do it together. I can't go back to who I was, and I don't want to go forward without you.'

Working For Myself 2007

Fresh out of rehab and feeling like a man reborn, I wasn't sure what to expect from the world I'd left behind. But there was Brendan, my brother, again with an offer that had the sweet scent of redemption – a job at his construction firm. It was legit, a far cry from the shadows we both knew too well, but old reputations die hard. The council officials were quick to judge, eyes narrowed, whispers of intimidation tactics that weren't too far off from the life I'd vowed to leave behind.

But Brendan, he had a way with words, a humour that could disarm the most suspicious of minds. At one meeting with the council, after our competitors had tried to discredit our work, by saying we were driving around with slicked back hair threatening the men. 'We aren't intimidating them,' he'd say with a grin, 'we're threatening to kill them if they don't work quickly enough!' And just like that, the room would erupt in laughter, the tension dissipating amongst the top council officials like smoke on the wind. They knew the game, knew it was other competitors trying to slander us and take the work, and that our swiftness, attention, management and finishing of such big and complicated projects, like town centres, were second to none.

Respect is currency in our line of work, and I earned mine the only way I knew how – by being better, working harder. I was shoulder to shoulder with the lads, showing I wasn't just some ex-con with a sob story. I ran gangs of men, directed them with a firm hand and a fair word, and they followed because they saw their respect reflected in my eyes.

But family and business, they're a cocktail that'll either warm you or burn your throat. For me and Brendan, it was a bit of both. I needed to make my own mark, free from the protective shadow of my brother. So, I took the leap, went full pelt into my own ventures. The family wasn't pleased; they wanted to keep me close, keep me safe. But safety felt too much like stagnation, and I wasn't about to let the past dictate my pace.

I got my own flat, a place that was mine alone. My routine was a relentless race against the clock – working for Brendan by day, racing home for a quick change, then out again to price up jobs or bury my head in engineering books. I was chasing a dream that was just mine, and I could almost taste it.

The big break came like a storm – £¼ million worth of work landed on my desk, a chance to prove that I wasn't just part of a family successful in construction but Stephen, a name to be reckoned with on my own terms. I'd pay out of my pocket whenever I had to, hire people to cover my shifts at the family company, because this was bigger than a day job – this was the future.

Brendan's smile didn't reach his eyes when I told him. He'd pulled me from the mire, and now I was reaching for skies that seemed to stretch beyond his horizon. I was the oldest, the one who'd always been first, first to wed, first to have a child and equally, the first to fall. When I was inside, the weight of expectation had shifted to his shoulders, and he'd borne it, grown powerful in ways neither of us had imagined.

Money and power though, they're funny things. They can bring you together or slice through bonds like a knife through silk. We'd always been close, but as Brendan grappled with his own rise and fall, as he headed for that wall at five hundred miles per hour, our paths diverged.

Deep down, I knew he was scared. Scared that if I got my wings, I'd soar too high, out of reach. So, he held me down, gave me just enough rope to climb but never enough to swing. It was a mix of love and jealousy, a cocktail that left a bitter taste. But he had much to manage, and it was his way not just with me but how he coped and worked with all of us in the family, who were at times, hard work. He was a good brother who had flown the flag properly and, like I had done for him, saved my arse many times.

Brendan was healing in his own way, fighting ghosts I couldn't see. And in his eyes, I saw the reflection of his struggle – he saw me getting everything he needed, too. He was my brother, my blood, but the road we walked was splitting beneath our feet, I had to take flight and hope he'd understand that the sky was big enough for both of us. We each had to have our part of it, there was enough for everyone.

A place of Solace 2007

The sun had long set by the time I'd walk down Mile End Road, the neon signs and streetlamps casting shadows that danced just out of step with the passers-by. There was a church there, an old building with a spire that seemed to pierce the darkness, a beacon for the lost and the weary. I wasn't much for religion although I knew that God walked with me, but there was something about that place that felt like coming home.

Inside, the pews were pushed back to make room for beds and tables, a makeshift sanctuary for those with nowhere else to turn. I found solace in the rhythm of setting up those rooms, in the echoes of 'thank you' and 'God bless' that filled the air like a chorus. Pastor Ken ran the show, a man whose faith was as much in the people he served as the God he preached about.

He and I, we'd sit and talk long after the last tray of food had been served, our conversations meandering through the realms of philosophy, religion, and the cutthroat world of business. Ken had a way of speaking that made you want to listen, a wisdom that seemed to come from a life lived in many shoes.

'Stephen,' he'd say to me, his eyes twinkling with a mix of mirth and sincerity, 'you find your soul in the service of others. There's no ledger keeping score; there's just what you put into the world.'

And so, I poured myself into the work, two nights a week, setting up beds, serving meals, and talking. Talking to people who had stories etched into their faces, tales of loss, of bad luck, or bad choices. In those hours, I was no one and everyone – not an ex-con, not a brother in the shadow of another, just a man with hands ready to help.

I never talked about myself; that wasn't the point. Instead, I listened, and in their stories, I found fragments of my own. Each person I met, each life that crossed mine, they gave me back pieces of my humanity, chipping away at the walls I had built around my heart.

It was food for the soul, Pastor Ken said, and he was right. With every bed I made, every conversation I had, I felt more grounded, more real. It wasn't redemption – that was too grand a word for what was happening. It was simpler than that, purer. It was connection, a shared existence, a collective healing.

In that church, with the stained glass looking down on us, I found a community that asked for nothing but accepted everything. They were, in many ways, the best people I'd ever known – not because their lives were perfect, but because they understood the imperfection of existence and still found reasons to smile, to laugh, to keep moving forward.

Pastor Ken would often say, 'The greatest gift you can offer is your presence.' And so, I offered mine, fully and without expectation. In the echo of prayers and the silence of the night, I was learning, growing, healing. And for the first time in a long time, I was hopeful about the days to come.

My Beautiful Children 2010

The moment Lucia was born, the universe contracted into a single, sharp point of pure love. Holding her, with her fierce new-born cry and flailing arms, I understood redemption. Stevie's entrance into this world was no less miraculous, his tiny fingers grasping at life with an innate curiosity that took my breath away. They were my heart and soul made manifest, the most profound parts of me living and breathing outside my body.

And for all the mistakes I'd made, the years lost and roads wrongly taken, here was something pure and right.

Being there for their births, cutting the cords and wrapping them in their first embrace, I felt a promise settle in my chest. This time, I was here, really here. Not on borrowed time, not with the spectre of a cell hanging over me, but genuinely present.

Missing Sid's early years had left a void nothing could fill, a chasm of lost moments and milestones I could never get back. My past, with all its shadows, had taught me the value of presence. I was there for every heartbeat, every first word, every tentative step. Sid's absence in my life had been a wound that never quite healed, a silent echo of lost years. With Stevie and Lucia, I was given a second chance, and every day with them was a day reclaimed.

But life has a way of testing you, throwing you curveballs that you can only hope to catch. Maria, with her chaotic beauty, her laughter that could fill a room and then some, was struggling. The partying, a holdover from a life less complicated, sometimes spilled over into the daylight hours. I saw how the revelry and the weed were not just indulgences but escapes. We were a juxtaposition, she and I, where the very thing that helped her unwind tangled me up in worries for our future, for our children.

My business was growing, a media venture that brought me into the orbit of influential clients. It was a delicate ecosystem, one where professionalism and private life had to maintain a careful balance. I tread carefully, always mindful of the tightrope I walked. I couldn't save Maria from herself; I'd learned that the hard way. But I could save Lucia and Stevie from the fallout. I built my business with them in mind, a legacy, a safety net. And every time Maria's struggles threatened to spill over, I was there to catch them, to keep them insulated from the chaos.

In the quiet moments, when the children slept and the world seemed to hold its breath, I'd allow myself to feel it all - the love, the fear, the frustration. Lucia's laughter, Stevie's curious gaze, they were my anchors, my reasons to keep the ship steady through the storm.

The love for my children was simple, uncomplicated by the messiness of adult grievances. They were my second chance, my opportunity to do it right. And no matter what the future held, no matter the struggles with Maria or the shadows of my past, that love was a beacon that would guide me through. For them, I was not just Stephen; I was Dad, the fixer of toys, the soother of nightmares, the audience to every school play. And in their eyes, I found a hope and a purpose that outshone any darkness from my own youth.

Maria's journey was her own, and I stood by her with the patience that love demands, with the understanding that life's dance is sometimes a solo. For Lucia, Stevie, and yes, for Sid, I was the constant, the promise of tomorrow.

And that was enough. More than enough.

Reflection

Reaching the brink of one's mental limits can be life-altering. My own brush with death, a dance with danger and chaos that lasted too long, brought about a psychological crisis. Being sectioned under the Mental Health Act was the culmination of persistent trauma. Losing grip on reality, plagued by hallucinations and voices, was a descent into terror. The path to recovery was long and secluded, but in the wards of Whitechapel, I found respite and healing.

Emerging from that dark chapter, I was transformed. A switch had been flipped, dulling the edge of my rage, tempering my wildness. It was a pivotal moment, the beginning of a journey towards clarity and a more constructive future.

CHAPTER 10

Building a Life

"In the midst of chaos, there is also opportunity"

— Sun-Tzu, A Arte da Guerra

New Foundations 2012

The West End's winds cut through the city's towering skyline, churning the afternoon's grey haze with the street's exhaust. In the corner of our usual deli, the three of us settled into an afternoon of talks and tepid coffee.

Tony, with his incessant grin and a suit that screamed 'salesman', pitched his spiel across the table. 'You'll see, Stephen, it's gonna be huge. I've got followers, and I teach 'em to talk the talk. Just need you to boost my channel, get the word out. That's your gig, right?'

Bruno's sceptical glance said it all. We'd crossed paths in his phone repair shop, two blokes with big plans, and he wasn't one to be easily sold a dream. Tony's voice was all New York hustle – smooth, persuasive, but with that edge that set off alarm bells if you listened long enough.

'I'm telling you, we're talking big fish here, guys. We could be a powerhouse. You help me out, I'll get you on stage. Scratch my back, I'll scratch yours,' Tony said, his eyes alight with the pitch.

The deli buzzed around us, but in the background noise, there was a silent conversation between Bruno and me. We knew the score.

'What's your take, Bruno?' I asked, already knowing his mind.

He nodded, cautious. 'It's promising, but we're talking about a serious grind. We've put blood, sweat, and code into this business. We've cracked the algorithm; that's worth its weight in gold. You want in, we need to talk payment upfront.'

Bruno's words hung in the air, a clear signal to Tony, who squirmed in his seat. His eyes flickered, the gears turning as he weighed his pitch against our hard-line.

'I get it, Bruno, I do. It's just that funds are tight right now...' Tony tried to hedge.

The coffee's warmth spread through me as I observed their back-and-forth. I was half-listening, half-lost in the grind of my own making. Muscles sore from manual labour, mind racing from nights spent chasing down leads, crafting strategies, always pushing the past further away with each new deal.

'Tony, we'll come back to you with our terms,' I told him, marking a deliberate pause in the conversation. It was time to put a pin in the deal, to step back and reassess.

We got to our feet, Bruno giving me a sidelong glance, his face etched with concern. Tony rose too, a hulking figure crowding into our space uninvited, his smile stretched too thin to hide the self-serving glint in his eye.

'Great meeting you fellas. Give me a bell, we'll talk, yeah?' Tony boomed, overplaying the camaraderie.

We watched his back as he shuffled out the deli, his departure leaving a slick trail in his wake.

'He's a slippery one,' Bruno muttered, echoing my own instincts.

Out on Mile End Road, the bustle of the city was a living, breathing thing. Colours and sounds mingled with the dissonance of life in East London.

Bruno broached the subject again as he adjusted his bag. 'We might have to consider his offer,' he said, stress lining his voice.

I felt the weight of his worry mirroring my own. Our start-up was scrappy, and my side gig in construction, along with raising two kids, meant the financial squeeze was relentless.

'We're running on fumes here, Stephen. We need gear, staff, marketers, film crews... we can't keep up,' Bruno's voice trailed off, the 'rent' hanging between us like a four-letter word.

I met his gaze squarely, forcing a grin. 'Don't sweat it,' I said, my resolve firm despite the madness of our predicament. The delays, the subpar work - it was a familiar chaos, one that I now understood as a killer of dreams for many start-ups.

'I'm not relying on these people anymore. It's a slow death. The marketing, the filming, the advertising, learning the IT, the research for the documentaries, the editing and everything else we need - we'll do it all ourselves!'

'That's crazy. We have so much that we need to learn. We don't have the time!'

I walked away from him, down towards the tube station and through the moving crowd of people, but I knew his face was folded and creased with frustration and concern.

I turned, shouted back,' Bruno We don't need them. We'll do it ourselves!'

'You're mad. One mad fucker!'

I called back, 'We don't need them. We're enough!'

'Madman!' His voice chased after me, but there was a grin behind it, I could tell.

I wove through the crowd, the little bracelet in my pocket a tangible reminder of the stakes. The fatigue of endless work, the clash of frayed nerves, the relentless drive - it was all there in the rear view. But ahead? There was a path we could carve out ourselves.

'You're off your rocker, Stephen!' Bruno's shout was a mixture of exasperation and admiration.

I didn't look back. I felt the vibrant animals of the bracelet between my fingers, my daughter's craft anchoring me. A smile played on my lips; determination set in my stride. I pushed through the human tide with the street-honed skill of a man who'd danced with darker shadows, now moving with a purpose that was unshakable. It was only me that could do it for me, it always was, but the people you populate your life with are pivotal. They can elevate and lift you up, or bring all you've built crashing down in a moment. One of the biggest skills was managing this and people.

My Beautiful Children 2014

Sitting down with Lucia and little Stevie, their eyes wide with the endless curiosity of childhood, I shared a story, a little tale of their beginnings, designed to fill the room with laughter and love.

'Kids, did I ever tell you about the day each of you were born? Right there in Whitechapel, in the heart of London, something magical happened. Lucia, when you arrived, the doctors and nurses stopped in their tracks you had a head full of beautiful black hair. And Stevie, when it was your turn, the same wonder struck them all over again.'

Lucia, ever the protective older sister, looked at Stevie with a mixture of pride and a hint of that sibling superiority only an older sister can have.

'You see, you two were so breathtakingly beautiful that the whole hospital stopped and gasped when you were born. The buzz of the hospital hushed, and for a moment, it was like you were the royalty gracing us with your presence. They stared, not quite believing their eyes, completely enchanted by the two of you.'

Stevie's giggles bubbled up, his four-year-old mind delighted by the imagery.

'And do you know what they did next?' I continued, my voice dropping to a conspiratorial whisper, drawing them in. 'They all wanted to say hello, to be blessed by your charm. Nurses, doctors, even the man who delivers the post; they all lined up for a peek at the wonders who'd just entered the world.'

Lucia leaned in, her eyes shining with the magic of the story, embracing the wonder of her little brother's laughter mingling with her own.

'It's true,' I affirmed with a nod, basking in their joy. 'Because you two are my stars, lighting up my life more brilliantly than anything in the night sky. And that's why, wherever we go, we spread a bit of that magic around, just like we did on the day you were born.'

The room filled with their laughter, a sound that was my favourite melody, a reminder of the beauty and innocence that life could hold. Those moments, those stories, they were my way of showing Lucia and Stevie just how much they meant to me, that their very existence was a marvel that transformed every space they entered.

London School of Business 2010

Juggling the growth of my business with academic pursuits, I embarked on a degree in business management at the London School of Business. The classroom was a world away from the harsh realities I'd navigated, yet here I found another arena in which to prove myself. When I graduated with honours, it wasn't just a personal victory; it was a declaration that my past would not define my capabilities nor my future.

As I sat among my peers during lectures, I couldn't help but notice the stark contrast in our experiences. Many were on the cusp of their business journeys, armed with theory but lacking the scars of practical warfare in the commercial battlefield. In contrast, I had not only weathered storms but had also navigated Brendan's business through tumultuous waters and built my own venture from the ashes of my previous life.

It was this unique blend of real-world experience and academic achievement that caught the attention of the university's faculty. I was chosen to represent the institution in a project that brought together top business executives - titans of industry who handled deals and investments that dwarfed anything I had previously been involved with.

The initial meetings were intimidating. Here I was, a man who had learned the hard truths of business in the crucible of life's harshest lessons, now seated at tables with individuals whose decisions shaped economies. Yet, as the discussions unfolded, a realisation dawned on me: despite our different paths, we spoke the same language. The acumen required to navigate the complex waters of business was a trait we shared, and I found that not only could I keep up with their strategic discussions, but I could also offer insights forged in the fire of my own experiences.

This realisation was a watershed moment. My confidence, previously buoyed by necessity and survival, now found a new foundation in the recognition of my peers and mentors. I understood that my journey, though unorthodox, had equipped me with a perspective both unique and invaluable. My entrepreneurial mindset, tempered by the trials of building something from nothing, offered a fresh lens through which to view challenges and opportunities - a stark contrast to the more conventional, corporate paths many of them had taken.

The project with the university was more than just an academic exercise; it was a gateway to a world I had once viewed from the outside. The contacts made and the conversations had during this time were stepping stones to my next venture. The executives, once figures of an unreachable echelon, became mentors and, in some cases, valuable connections.

As I moved forward, leveraging these new and rewarding associates, I carried with me the lessons of the past and the insights of the present. My path had shown me that while the worlds of academia and high-stakes business might seem worlds apart, the bridge between them was built on the foundation of hard-earned wisdom and the relentless pursuit of growth.

In navigating these new waters, I was no longer just a survivor of my circumstances but a creator of my destiny, armed with the knowledge that my entrepreneurial spirit, honed by experiences both bitter and sweet, was my greatest asset.

Networking and a new direction 2011

The clink of glasses and the low hum of conversation filled the air of the upscale London hotel where the business networking event was being held. I was an outsider here, a man with a past that read like a cautionary tale, now clean and steering my own ship in the form of a burgeoning business. The irony wasn't lost on me; just years ago, I couldn't have imagined being in such a place, among these people.

I found myself in conversation with one of the organisers, a sharply dressed woman named Claire, who had the keen eye of someone always looking for the next big thing. Our chat started casually, with the usual pleasantries exchanged between potential business contacts. But as my story unfolded - the raw, unvarnished truth of where I'd come from and how far I'd managed to climb - her interest piqued.

'Stephen, your journey is nothing short of remarkable. Have you ever considered sharing your story more widely? There's a power in authenticity that this crowd could really benefit from.' Claire smiled at me encouragingly.

The suggestion struck me like a bolt from the blue. Me, speaking in front of an audience? The very thought sent a wave of imposter syndrome crashing over me. I was a man who had fought tooth and nail to rebuild his life, yes, but to stand up and present myself as a beacon of motivational insight? It seemed a stretch too far.

'I appreciate the kind words, Claire, but I'm no speaker. My story is... it's not what people come to these events to hear.'

'On the contrary, Stephen. It's exactly what they need to hear. Success isn't just about profits and market share; it's about overcoming obstacles, something you know all too well. I'd like to invite you to speak at our next meeting. No polish needed - just be yourself.' I could tell that she had the bit between her teeth and was used to getting her own way.

The weeks leading up to the event were a blur of anxiety and second-guessing. The thought of baring my soul to a room full of strangers, of business professionals who had navigated a very different world from mine, was daunting. I grappled with feelings of inadequacy, the fear that my past, my very essence, would be deemed unworthy by those who had never faced the darkness I had.

But as the day arrived and I stood at the podium, looking out at the expectant faces before me, a calm settled over me. This was my story, my truth, and no one could tell it better than me. I began to speak, my voice steady, recounting the days of despair in prison, the battle with addiction, the hard-won fight for redemption, and the unexpected path to entrepreneurship.

As I spoke, the room was rapt, the air charged with an electric silence that spoke of minds being opened and perspectives being shifted. I realised then that authenticity was my greatest asset. My lack of polish didn't matter; it was the raw, unfiltered honesty of my journey that resonated.

Afterwards, the feedback was overwhelmingly positive. People approached me, thanking me for my candour, sharing their own struggles and aspirations. In that moment, I understood the true power of my story. It wasn't just mine anymore; it had become a beacon of hope for others, a testament to the resilience of the human spirit.

The imposter syndrome that had once threatened to undermine me had been replaced with a sense of purpose. I had found my voice, not as a polished speaker, but as Stephen, a survivor, a fighter, a man who had traversed the depths and emerged into the light. And that was more than enough – for now.

Stepping into Media 2014

The digital world was a frontier I knew I needed to conquer, but my expertise lay in the tangible, in streets and deals, not bytes and online presence. That's where Bruno came into the picture. He wasn't your typical tech kid, but he had a knack for computers that couldn't be ignored. At fourteen he was taking apart computer viruses and sending them back to their originator. His wealth in blockchain was a recent victory, a testament to his savvy in the ever-evolving tech landscape.

Our meeting was happenstance, two different worlds colliding in a coffee shop where the aroma of fresh espresso was as strong as the buzz of ideas. Bruno was Romanian and down to earth, his intelligence matched by a humility that was refreshing. I knew nothing of IT or social media - my understanding was rudimentary at best. But Bruno had an approach that demystified the digital domain.

We talked, and as we did, an idea began to form, a fusion of his technical prowess and my burgeoning media aspirations. It was a partnership of complementary skills, with Bruno's digital literacy amplifying my message and my stories providing compelling content.

The formation of our media company was a natural progression. I had started to carve a name for myself as a motivational speaker, taking to stages with a raw authenticity that resonated. My narrative, once a source of personal torment, had become my most valuable asset. I was sharing it not for accolades, but to offer hope, to guide others away from the pitfalls I had stumbled into.

'I've got stories, Bruno. Real, hard-hitting tales that need a platform. You've got the tech know-how. Together, we can create something powerful.'

'Your experiences are unique, Stephen. They carry weight.' Bruno said 'I can help you bring them to a wider audience. Let's harness the power of digital media, share your journey, and maybe change some lives along the way.'

Our collaboration was grounded in mutual respect and shared ambition. We weren't just business partners; we were two individuals who believed in the power of storytelling, of the influence that honest, lived experiences could have in the virtual world.

In those early days, our media company was little more than an idea fuelled by determination and a shoestring budget. We were two men with a vision, armed with nothing but our skills and the drive to be heard. For me, it was a new kind of hustle, learning the ropes of documentary making, piecing together narratives that had the weight of lived experience behind them. Bruno's editing skills were unmatched, and together we had the makings of something potent.

We started small, setting up shop in a lock-up unit that was more echo chamber than studio. I remember recording voiceovers with the rumble of trains overhead, the vibrations a constant reminder of the movement and life beyond our walls. Our setup was makeshift, a hodgepodge of second-hand equipment and a patchwork of software - but it was ours.

'We've got something here, Bruno. We can really make a go of this.' I was buoyed by the idea.

'Absolutely. It's raw, but that's the beauty of it. People want authenticity, and that's exactly what we're going to give them.' Bruno got it, he understood what we were creating.

We poured our energy into building a YouTube channel, a platform where I could lend my voice to the stories we wanted to tell. Each video was a labour of love, hours of footage distilled into narratives that felt immediate and real. Bruno would work his magic on the edits, transforming our rough cuts into pieces that, while lacking polish, had heart.

I reviewed the footage. 'This is it, mate. It's not just about getting heard; it's about saying something that matters.'

Bruno focusing on his screen said, 'Definitely. And with each video, we'll get better. This is just the beginning.'

Money was tight, and every view, like, and subscriber was a small victory, a sign that we were on the right track. We didn't have the luxury of advertising or fancy studios. Our growth was organic, each new follower a person who connected with our message, with the gritty reality we presented.

'I don't mind the trains, you know. It's like... they're part of our story. The grind, the noise, it's all part of where we've come from.' I mused.

Bruno laughed 'Yeah. It keeps us grounded. Reminds us that we're building this from the ground up.'

In those early days, every challenge was an opportunity to learn. When the lighting wasn't right, we improvised. When the sound was off, we adapted. We were creators in the most fundamental sense, crafting content that spoke to the resilience and fortitude of the human spirit.

It was this spirit, this unwavering commitment to telling stories that mattered, that slowly began to draw attention. Our YouTube channel became a beacon for those seeking something genuine, something that cut through the noise and spoke to the realities of struggle, survival, and hope.

Bruno and I, we were an unlikely pair, but our partnership was founded on the belief that our voices could make a difference. As we watched our channel grow, as we engaged with an audience that saw value in what we offered, we knew we had tapped into something special. It was the start of a journey neither of us could have fully anticipated, but one we were ready to embrace with all the tenacity we had honed over the years.

As the business grew, so did our separate paths. Bruno found success in blockchain, his acumen shining through in a market that was as volatile as it was lucrative. We drifted apart, not through any dramatic fallout, but through the natural divergence of personal journeys.

London 2016

I had held the project in my mind for a year now. The fascinating and inspirational journeys, the twists and turns of the world's billionaires as they built their empires. Like a coder constructing binary code, I observed and unravelled their business frameworks, stories, achievements, characters, and innovations. I tapped the keys of my computer, delving deeper into research.

Beside me, Bruno was editing our latest documentary on Walmart - a fast-paced and riveting thirty-minute piece on the lives of Sam and Bud Walton. Their incredible ascent from nickel-and-dime backwater salesmen in Arkansas to the world's largest retail giant was nothing short of remarkable.

In the back sitting room of our little house in Stepney, East London, with the silky grey curtains drawn at the back window shielding us from the approaching dawn, we persevered. Tiredness had settled upon us, and the signs of great mental, physical, and emotional fatigue, which we had so far managed to control, were nearing a tipping point.

People called us mad, foolish, saying it would never work and that all this toiling was a waste of time. It was our second consecutive day and night of work. Another of our essential, gruelling marathons.

I surveyed the scattered papers on the table before me - a scrawled and categorised collection of companies, dates, pivotal moments, victories, defeats, and tragedies. It was the stuff of life, and I was set to unravel these wonderful stories of the world's most formidable empires. With careful skill, I would delve into the persona at their inception, exploring with diligent wonder. By uncovering their tragedies, loves, and losses, I aimed to discover the real person, what truly made them unique. From this modest set of rooms, I would reveal their paths to success and embark on the remarkable journeys these unique individuals had taken.

The late hours ticked by unnoticed.

In our individual enclaves of creativity, we strained every sinew to honour our impending deadline.

Giving Back 2018

I rushed through Mile End Park in the early evening chill, the snowfall intensifying and a bustling wind sweeping across Mile End stadium, scattering the winter leaves. Gripping the hands of my son, Stevie, and daughter, Lucia, a little tighter, we braved the thickly falling snowflakes. Bundled in hats, scarves, and gloves, we pressed on past the tall, wired fence of the football field, following the winding track towards the new church on Burdett Road.

We left the park, navigating the slowing traffic. The tall, modern-looking brick church loomed ahead.

'Daddy, is it hard for the homeless people at this time of year? Do they get presents, and can we help them?' Lucia's voice was tinged with concern.

She was nine and had recently gifted me an animal bracelet, crafted with love. We had sat on her bed, going through the colours and animals, and I had felt an overwhelming warmth fill me, bringing tears to my eyes.

'Yes, Lucia, we are going to help them. Good girl. And you, Stevie, do you want to help the homeless?' I asked.

His smile was bright in the dimming light. 'Yes, Daddy.'

They were my world, two little souls, fresh to life and always seeking my attention.

'Where are their mummies and daddies?' Stevie's question, his brown eyes peering from under his woolly hat, hit me with a weight that stole my breath.

'They're coming, son. One day they will come...' I assured him, though my heart felt the uncertainty of my words.

Pressing the intercom at the glass doors, I glanced at those huddled against the snow, their lives carried in backpacks. My heart ached with the pity I felt for the challenges they faced. We entered the church, descending the stairs into a room where twenty makeshift beds awaited in the church crèche.

'Oh, I see you've brought the little ones,' greeted Margaret, a sweet, grey-haired Scottish woman with square glasses and a long floral dress. As the senior volunteer, she and her husband had been the backbone of the shelter for eight years, collaborating with other East End churches to provide refuge and support during the winter months.

The children's wide eyes followed me as we set about our tasks in the creche adorned with modest decorations and a small Christmas tree twinkling with warm lights. Stevie distributed pillowcases while Lucia and I made the beds, her small hands eagerly assisting.

'Daddy, why are people homeless?' Lucia's question came as we smoothed out sheets.

'Life is tough, darling. Sometimes, unexpected things happen. We should always be thankful and think of others,' I explained.

'But why, Daddy?' Stevie chimed in; his voice muffled by the hat.

'We're all equal, son. Life's got this way of balancing out. What we give, we often receive... And remember, the darker the night, the brighter the stars shine.'

They nodded, a sign of understanding dawning in their young eyes. Together, we finished making the beds, tidied the room, and returned the spare linen to storage.

Now the homeless were arriving, shouldering their bags, their faces etched with relief to escape the cold. We greeted each person at the dining hall door with smiles, sharing in their simple joy of finding warmth.

In the adjacent room, where volunteers were bustling around the kitchen hatch, carols played softly. The children and

I set the long blue table in preparation for the meal, their small hands working diligently.

As I sat watching them place cutlery and fold napkins, a sense of profound contentment enveloped me. Here, amid the festive decorations and the soulful strains of 'Ave Maria', I reflected on the journey that had brought me from darkness into light.

Stevie returned from the hatch, arms laden with extra cups, while Lucia meticulously arranged napkins. This was my hope: that they would understand the world and contribute to its goodness.

Walking away from my past, I'd answered the call of my better nature. Now, settled in the chair, surrounded by the warmth and the soft glimmers of tinsel, I listened as the soprano's voice soared, the children gathering close.

Shooting Star 2018

I was sitting at a quiet corner table of a lovely restaurant in Knightsbridge, a setting I hoped would appeal to Daphne. Mutual friends had spoken of her with a blend of reverence and affection, painting the picture of a woman whose spirit was as vibrant as her design portfolio. When she agreed to meet, I felt that familiar flicker of opportunity, the same one that had driven me through countless ventures. But with Daphne there was something more, deeper, as if we'd known each other in a past life.

Daphne arrived with an air of someone who owned every second of her time, her presence commanding yet not imposing. She scanned the room, her gaze landing on me with a recognition that spoke of research done, of curiosities piqued.

'Stephen? I have heard quite a lot about you, it would seem fate has been conspiring to put us together.' She took a seat at the table, watching me, as though she was looking something in me. 'However,' she continued, 'I'm extremely busy, so I'll get straight to the point. What do you want from me?'

Her directness was refreshing, a trait I had come to value above most.

I looked at her straight in the eye and said 'Everything.' I paused and realised how that sounded so I smiled and continued 'I want your eye for design on my board, your creativity steering our brand. Shooting Stars Events isn't just about getting celebrities heard; it's about creating a platform where substance meets style, where stories are told with the elegance they deserve.'

She assessed me then, her eyes searching, perhaps for the catch, for the sales pitch. But smiled gently.

'I can give you one day a week - Saturdays. That's my offer.'

A smile broke across my face, both at her guarded commitment and the challenge she presented. 'I'll take it, Daphne. You'll be my Saturday girl, the highlight of my week.'

The phrase was a gamble, a bit of humour to bridge the formality. Her raised eyebrow and the hint of a smile told me it had paid off.

As we delved into the details over lunch, the connection between us was undeniable. Daphne was unlike anyone I had ever met, strong, grounded, spiritual, and fiercely independent. She was a breath of fresh air, a gust that threatened to turn the embers of my ambition into a wildfire.

Our Saturdays together became a crucible for creativity and a foundation for something more profound than business. As we worked to streamline Shooting Stars Events, it became clear that the business, heavy with the weight of directors not pulling their weight, was struggling to take off.

One late Saturday, as we were tallying numbers and facing the stark reality, I found myself sharing the analogy that had been turning over in my mind.

'Building a business... it's like launching a rocket. It starts off heavy, laden with all these parts that you think you need. But as it climbs, as the pressure mounts, bits start to fall away. It's only when it's streamlined that it can really shoot for the moon.'

Daphne listened, her head tilted, considering the metaphor.

'And what part are we at, Stephen, in this rocket launch of yours?'

I leaned back, the weight of the situation settling in my chest. 'We're at the critical stage. It's getting lighter, but not because we're shedding what we don't need... We're losing parts that should've held us together. It's make or break, and I refuse to break.'

Her hand found mine across the table, a silent vow of solidarity.

'Then we streamline. We focus on what's essential, and we push forward. If parts need to drop off for us to reach the stars, then so be it.'

The business might have been haemorrhaging money, but in those moments with Daphne, I felt the pulse of something new, something vital. She was more than a Saturday girl; she was a partner in the truest sense, one who might just help me steer this faltering ship back on course.

In the end, we decided that Shooting Star Events needed to crash and burn, but from its embers arose RMC Studios.

Now, as I stand at the helm of RMC Studios a multi-award winning business, I see a reflection of my journey in the fabric of the company. From branding to advertising, and from creative sound to influencer broadcasting, we are a team that thrives on creating impactful narratives. We're more than a business; we're a collective on a mission to innovate and inspire across London, Zurich, Toronto, Vancouver, and Los Angeles. Our ethos is etched in every project - challenging, nurturing, and celebrating the strength in every story. Here I am, years down the line, channelling my past into a force for change, building not just a business, but a legacy. For more on where I stand today with Roar Media Creative, visit our website.

Snapshots from the journey 2019

The week had unfolded in its usual flurry. Our office buzzed with activity, more strategy sessions etched across the whiteboard by senior staff than was typical. We were on an upward trajectory, our business initiatives propelling us with a momentum that translated into tangible progress. Our media outreach was gaining steam. Through relentless engagement with global social platforms, we were carving a substantial niche for our marketing and advertising efforts. Our ventures spanned multiple markets – filmmaking, event management, public relations, pharmaceuticals, technology, design, and the crafting of bespoke business ventures. The drive to maintain our leading edge was incessant. Yet, amidst this hive of industry, my mind was adrift.

'Are you ready for a catch-up?' Daphne, my partner in both business and life, her career luminous with achievements. An international designer and branding guru, her resume boasted significant media accomplishments, including a stint as personal assistant and gate-keeper to none other than Tom Jones.

'Give me two minutes, just wrapping this up,' I replied, casting a glance through the window at the nondescript light of an average afternoon.

I was blissfully unaware of the impending news.

Glancing at my phone, I noticed persistent text messages from Caroline Heward, the Harley Street stress expert – messages that now seemed urgent. Caroline's words were rapid and assured when I finally responded.

'Stephen. Stephen, can you hear me?'

She broke the news: I was being considered for the Sunhak International Peace Prize from South Korea, a highly prestigious accolade. As a UK Peace Ambassador for the Universal Peace Federation, she had put my name forward, supported by the Secretary-General Robin Marsh & UK

Director Margaret Ali. My story, my past work and current endeavours, she believed, made me an exemplary candidate to represent Britain. There was optimism in her voice that this year, the UK could clinch the prize.

I was silent as she continued. They had discussed my life's extraordinary turnaround, my journey from being involved in high-level organised crime, with over a decade spent in Category A maximum security prisons, to becoming a beacon of hope. My narrative was not just unique but inspirational, touching lives across the globe. To Caroline, I was the epitome of transformation.

From the UPF headquarters at Lancaster Gate, closely aligned with the United Nations, the question had been raised: 'Is this someone we should nominate?'

'...Absolutely,' came the unanimous agreement.'

'We're on a tight schedule, Stephen,' she added hastily. 'I've been trying to reach you for two days. Tomorrow is the cut-off for nominations!'

Surrounded by the familiar hum of the office, in my open-plan, brightly lit room with pristine white walls, cream furnishings, and polished wooden floors, I absorbed her words, the phone still pressed to my ear.

She was already sending the details. 'There's a form that needs your attention, Stephen. Once filled, it requires the Secretary-General's final sign-off. Remember, only a thousand people worldwide have the privilege to nominate for the Sunhak Prize.'

'I understand, and Caroline, thank you.'

Setting the phone aside, the full impact of Caroline's announcement hadn't quite sunk in, nor had the emotional odyssey that awaited me over the next two weeks began to unfold.

My thoughts wandered back to the earlier part of the conversation in the bathroom, where Caroline had first caught me thirty minutes prior. She had unfolded her vision with enthusiasm, detailing my role as a UK Peace Ambassador and my affiliation with the Universal Peace Federation. She had discussed me at length with the Secretary-General and the UK Director, painting a picture of my transformation from a high-security prisoner to an influential figure who had made significant strides within the prison system. She praised the transformative impact of my work in the media and my ventures across various business sectors, including my contributions as a keynote motivational speaker spreading messages of wisdom, strength, and hope.

She had spoken passionately about my endeavours in the pharmaceutical industry in Africa, particularly my involvement in the open wound sector aimed at saving lives. She highlighted the exceptional individuals around me, all united in the pursuit of shared goals, and how my personal journey was particularly inspiring.

Caroline had explained that the Sunhak Award was akin to a Nobel Prize, complete with a million dollars in prize money to be shared between two recipients. Only a thousand people in the world had the authority to nominate someone for it. Presidents had been recent winners. It was a great honour to be nominated. The news was so unexpected it barely registered.

The award covered multiple categories, including one for conflict resolution.

Daphne emerged from the adjoining office, a vision of elegance in a white dress, her blonde hair resting perfectly at shoulder length, and those soft, knowing green eyes that seemed to understand without words. Her intuition was uncanny, her ability to read people unparalleled.

I found myself unusually silent until my usual brisk, direct manner took over as I shared the news of the phone call with her.

'Wonderful,' she said, her smile carrying a hint of pride and certainty. 'You truly deserve this, Stephen. I see the effort you put in. This could change everything.'

I turned to gaze out the window, over the meticulously maintained trees and the expanse of the private estate. My eyes drifted towards the tranquil blue sky to my left. In that moment, I felt the truth of Daphne's words resonate within me.

For days, I found myself adrift in an emotional maelstrom, an experience so surreal it felt almost like an out-of-body occurrence. There was a distinct sensation of change within me, as if an inner force was stirring, reshaping my very essence. I was treading uncharted territory, facing a new echelon of responsibility that marked another significant ascent in my personal evolution. The way my emotions swirled within was unexpected, a stark reminder that personal growth is a relentless journey. Yet, in this whirlwind, I knew I was precisely where I was destined to be. On one of my reflective walks, a practice I took to for mental clarity, the realization dawned upon me.

Back in the office, with the view of the skyline just beyond the large window, Daphne's words jolted me from my introspection.

'You're sabotaging yourself again. It's apparent, written all over you!'

She was right, of course. My heightened anxiousness, the mercurial thoughts, the erratic actions, and my terse responses betrayed my inner conflict.

Her insight continued unabated. 'It's a pattern. Every time you're on the cusp of something grand, your old adversary rears its head.'

Leaning against the window ledge, seeking solace, I pondered how such a sentiment was possible for someone who'd endured such a tumultuous and violent past. Memories of the darkness I navigated, the anguish I'd caused, and the moments of weakness when courage faltered – all came flooding back. The sense of unworthiness burrowed deep within, an internal spectre ever-present, ever ready to cast doubt.

For years, I'd grappled with formidable inner demons, constructing mental fortresses to fend off the darkness. These fortifications, meticulously crafted, served to bar external shadows and contain them within. My coping mechanisms assumed archetypal forms: the nemesis, the king, the general, the saboteur. Emotion surged within me, a revelation accompanied by an unbidden welling of tears. In their release, I found equilibrium once more.

The realisation of the profound duty ahead of me crystallised in my mind. The greatest peacemakers, it seemed, were those who had walked the path of warriors – souls forged in adversity, confronting and dispelling unimaginable darkness.

Turning away from the window, I faced Daphne, a newfound understanding lighting up my features.

'Daphne... it's clear to me now. This recognition, this path, it gives my life – all that I've lived through – a profound sense of purpose.'

Opposites Together 2019

The phone call came as the early evening lost its lustre and gave way to a calm late summer encroaching darkness. The two people who communicated in an engaging and positive tone had travelled a long emotive personal internal journey of discovery. A road that had brought them together at this finite point. They had taken different roads in their lives, long winding ones filled with desperate and decisive choices, that dictated for years that they be deadly opposing forces.

Kul Mahay, the ex-high-flying Gold Police Commander, and I a reformed senior criminal continued our phone conversation.

'I've looked at your work, Stephen. Great work in transforming your life and helping others. It is a credit to you...'

'Thank you, Kul. You must be thanked for your great service to humanity also. It is amazing we can talk like this.'

We were at opposite ends of the spectrum, in the past sworn enemies. Two people who took different paths, saw different things. Now joined, we hope to shape a common cause that would improve people's lives for the better.

'I must admit, Stephen at first, when you told me your story, I thought, do I need to be involved with someone who has a history like this? It was the old programming, but your work is amazing.'

'Kul, it was the same for me. But I am far along my journey of transformation. What you see with me, the great work behind me, of going back into prisons to effect change, my progressive work in the business world is the real thing, a true metamorphosis.'

'People can change, Stephen. I have seen it in the great work I do with my events, in leadership training and emotional intelligence for companies. No matter how far we stray or fall, we can find our way back…'

'Thank you, Kul, for your kind words. Maybe we can find a way to bring our knowledge to help people…'

'I would like that, Stephen. Let me think. Well done.'

I held the phone, said, feeling the inspirational innovation fall, 'Thank you, really. Let's talk soon…'

Sunhak International Peace Prize 2019

The morning had seen a steady stream of dignitaries arriving, many of international repute. The Director-General of the Universal Peace Federation, Robin Marsh, and the UK Director, Margaret Ali, were on hand to receive them. Among the guests were a lawyer with close ties to the late Queen Elizabeth and Duke of Edinburgh, a cousin of the President of

Congo, a prominent Queen's Counsel and influential MP, a team instrumental in brokering a ceasefire in Libya, the General Secretary of the PPP and former Deputy Speaker to the National Assembly for Pakistan, and a former Director-General of the Global Bank. These individuals, along with other activists, converged on the tall white Grade II-listed stucco building in Bayswater, just north of Kensington, which served as the bustling headquarters of the UPF in Lancaster Gate.

After navigating the lively mid-afternoon traffic of the West End, we parked the car and stepped into the typical London greyness. The grand white concrete pillars of the building's front entrance beckoned from across the road. We made our way across the square.

'We've made good time, Daphne… That traffic was dreadful,' I remarked, adjusting the cuffs of my pink shirt, the silver and gold cufflinks catching the light.

At the roadside, Daphne paused to perfect my appearance with her impeccable eye for detail. After fastening my top shirt button and straightening my collar, she deftly arranged my burgundy-striped tie.

'There you are,' she said, stepping back to survey her handiwork. Dressed in a silk, grey-blue patterned dress, her elegance was effortless. Her cultivated blonde hair framed her face, and her striking turquoise eyes gave me another thorough once-over. 'Much better. The colours suit you,' she observed, her gaze approving my blue suit, black shoes, and the tie that added a pop of contrast.

As we approached the building, a diverse crowd gathered outside, heralding the wide array of activists attending from around the globe. Their causes were varied, from feeding the poor and aiding the homeless to engaging in green climate projects, collaborating with the Red Cross to distribute supplies, and negotiating ceasefires in conflict-ridden regions. Their unified aim was the pursuit of peace and equality for all.

Ascending the small step beneath the lofty porch, we crossed the glossy black-and-white tiled foyer to the large door, pressing the intercom to announce our arrival.

'Hello, Stephen, Daphne,' greeted Robin, extending his hand. Clad in a light suit and red tie, his demeanour was gentle and inviting, with soft facial features, piercing blue eyes, wavy blond hair, and an effortlessly welcoming air. 'It's wonderful to see you both. Please, come in.'

'The traffic was a challenge, Robin, but we managed to arrive promptly. It's a pleasure to see you,' I replied. 'Is Margaret around?'

The Secretary-General, a longstanding friend and peace activist of over twenty years, ushered us into the lively reception area, his eyes sparkling with a warm smile. 'She's here somewhere, Stephen. I look forward to catching up later,' he said softly before disappearing back into the crowd, resuming his duties with grace and congeniality.

The room was a hive of activity, its former grandeur still evident beneath the white and soft blue decor, with tall ceilings giving way to an impromptu meeting space furnished with an eclectic array of chairs and tables. Conversations ebbed and flowed as attendees mingled, some congregating around the refreshments counter, laden with plated food and beverages.

Amidst the dynamic assembly of small groups, a tapestry of conversations ebbed and flowed, weaving a vibrant tableau of engagement and exchange.

We made a beeline for the tea counter, a strategic move to allow us to settle after a busy day, get refreshed, find space and to prepare. Amidst the friendly nods and handshakes from acquaintances wishing to exchange pleasantries, a figure caught my eye. A young, promising diplomat, embodying the essence of European youth with neatly tailored black hair, dressed in a crisp blue suit, white shirt, and matching tie. Clasping a coffee cup, he was deeply engrossed in his conversation, but upon noticing me, his face brightened with a healthy glow, his eyes conveying a thoughtful intensity, and a genuine smile graced his lips.

'Hi brother,' he greeted warmly. 'Great to see you,' we exchanged handshakes, two comrades united in a global crusade for change. Kirk Vanderplas, a tireless peace advocate and entrepreneur, had inherited a formidable legacy from his European parents - a legacy he now channelled into innovative avenues for peace. Engaged in significant work with global leaders, he was instrumental in the Global Equality Initiative, championing peace and unity across all divides.

'Brother, we need to talk. The pharmaceutical company, the board appointment we discussed, the Global Equality Initiative - how we can step up our involvement, offer more support?' I proposed amidst the room's lively hum, a cacophony of diverse voices weaving a rich tapestry of dialogue.

With a reassuring hand on my shoulder, he replied, 'Absolutely. Let's find time for that.'

She navigated the throng with determined grace, her presence unmistakable. The short, resolute figure of Margaret, clad in a flowing blue patterned dress, was a wellspring of strength and clarity. Her grandchildren had much to be proud of.

Taking our elbows in a firm yet gentle grip, she implored, 'Stephen, Kirk, I'd be grateful if you'd both speak on peace later. Just a few words... about peace.' Her eyes, alight behind round glasses, and her neatly styled brown hair complemented her open, welcoming smile.

Standing with an air of gentle authority, she was not one to be easily declined. We nodded, our broad smiles sealing the agreement.

'Of course, Margaret. It would be an honour. When?' I inquired.

'After the Doctor's address, if that's alright. I'll signal you,' she confirmed, then promptly disappeared back into the crowd, as purposeful in her departure as she had been in her approach, a nurturing force within our midst.

I caught sight of Daphne engaging with an elderly gentleman at the back of the room. Standing tall, his grey hair neatly trimmed and glasses framing a determined face, he was the accountant who had approached us months earlier with a vision to combat suicide rates through the arts. 'I've written a play,' he had said, 'and I want your help to bring it to the Royal Albert Hall to raise awareness.'

Excusing myself through the crowd, I navigated the sea of shifting bodies with tactful agility. Soon, we would ascend to the main hall, and I needed a moment of fresh air to clear my thoughts.

I stepped out the front door, the clamour of the crowd inside dimming behind me. There I was, standing at the threshold of a building that felt worlds apart from the life I once knew. The London air, cool and bracing, greeted me like a challenge. On this ordinary spring afternoon, I found myself wrestling with a familiar turmoil, a mix of old ghosts and newfound purpose swirling within.

The journey from my past - marked by violence, confinement, and chaos - had been steep. And here I was, climbing a different kind of mountain, one where battles were fought with words and ideas, not fists and fury. The cloud-streaked sky overhead mirrored the tumult of my inner landscape, a testament to the hard truths I'd faced down. Peace, I'd come to learn, was as real and hard-fought as any war I'd ever known.

Pacing the pavement, my steps were measured, echoing the quiet rhythm of a sea far calmer than any I'd sailed before. But even in this moment of reflection, I couldn't escape the weight of my history, the drag of a name once synonymous with fear now seeking redemption. The path of change had forced me through the gauntlet of public scrutiny, with only my grit and a newfound sense of gratitude as my shield. Yet, the scars of disdain and mockery lingered, a reminder of debts I was still paying off.

A gentle breeze brushed against my skin, a fleeting comfort against the hard truths I carried. It was these truths that had grounded me, that had become my touchstones: gratitude, tenacity, humility, and the courage to forge a new vision out of the ruins of my past. This was the work ethic, the discipline that had guided me through the darkest corridors of hell. There were times when I raced through its choking darkness, desperate for an exit. And when I finally faced the reality that I was still human, still needed, I came to understand that a man is moulded by experience, not defined by his past.

Looking back at the building, its grandeur felt both imposing and distant. In my earlier days of struggle, I was hollowed out, directionless, a man left to wrangle the formidable beast within.

The breeze shifted, and my gaze followed, upwards to the patchwork sky, then across the stark whiteness of the surrounding architecture. The war within wasn't over; it had just changed battlefields. My past was a wreckage I'd left behind, but the present, that was a canvas still being painted. The hard truth was that I had stripped myself down to nothing but the will to push forward, to build, to give, to evolve without end.

Kirk joined me outside, his expression carefully neutral but his smile unable to hide the sharpness of his mind.

'Kirk... Hey,' I greeted him.

He sidled up beside me, phone in hand, his eyes reflecting the weight of our shared mission. 'Stephen, good to see you. Let's get down to it, shall we? Tell me what's going on.'

As he listened, I laid it all out - the board position at the pharmaceutical company, the 'miracle' product making waves in Africa, the years of R&D behind it, the lives already being saved. The conversation shifted to funding, to strategy, to the network of influence we needed to tap into. With Kirk's connections, we had a shot at getting this life-saving treatment out to those who needed it most. The question hung in the air between us: could he be the ally we needed to make this happen?.

We retraced our steps towards the building, Kirk affirming his commitment to collaborate. He'd recently set up a venture that was channelling vital medical aid to secluded villages in Cambodia. Our conversation was straightforward, no frills – just the nodding of heads, the exchange of smiles, the promise to meet and discuss further.

'Brother, there's so much more we can do in the world,' Kirk said, conviction in his tone.

'It's crucial work,' I agreed, recalling the video he'd sent, showcasing his efforts. The strides he was making towards meaningful change were not lost on me.

Kirk delved into his recent travels, detailing the network of leaders he'd rallied from across the globe. His meetings with prominent figures like Vice President Dick Cheney and Prime Minister Deve Gowda were steps toward a global mission for peace, leveraging education, sports, arts, and media.

As we paused, his hands punctuated his vision of equality and access to education, his passion tangible. I nodded, my own thoughts turning to the power of trade and investment as tools for improvement.

'Only the other day, I addressed a room with four finance ministers,' Kirk added. 'We're getting attention.'

Approaching the entrance, I lightly touched his arm. 'The mark of the great is persistence, Kirk. To lead with integrity and grasp the future with certainty.'

I saw in him the type of individuals I sought in my life – dedicated, inventive, with a strong compass aimed at bettering lives. These were people of substance, not of pretence, with clear minds and loyal hearts.

He pressed the intercom, a hopeful gleam in his eyes. 'I'm off to New York in December for a UN meeting. Come with me, dear brother. Will you?'

'I'd be honoured. I'll check my schedule. Just let me know the details,' I replied.

As he disappeared through the door, he left behind an air of optimism, a shared vision of the future we were both striving towards. It was a future carved by those who recognized their kind – resolute, charging ahead with courage and a clear plan.

Turning back inside, I was ready for the discussions ahead, including the chance to speak. But in that brief pause, I sensed a steely resolve within me, built upon layers of resilience and clarity. I'd traversed a long journey back to find myself. The echoes of a past life, another self, seemed distant now – locked away, the key thrown out.

In my pocket, my fingers found the small plastic figures of the bracelet my daughter Lucia had crafted – a tangible reminder of innocence and love. Holding it, I felt its significance, especially in moments that called for calm and decisive thought.

I stepped up and pressed the intercom, ready to re-join the fray, the little colourful animals in my grasp grounding me – a simple token, yet one of my most treasured possessions, embodying the pure love of a child for her father.

London, 2019

The richness of his life had been hard to translate into meaningful memories with the painful burdens he had carried against the long years. Now, in the later twilight years of his life he had learned that his journey, arranged in his mind and heart as a compartmentalized book of emotive pictures and woven feeling of people, places and times, had become a fine wine that had concentrated and wizened with the growing years.

He had been in England, his mind tinged with nostalgia and a weathered heart that secluded and held wistful feelings, for a week. He had watched them shopping in the West End today, eating at the Ritz at Green Park and walking close together in tender conversation and, as the scattered city daylight had transformed into a shining glitz of gleaming night lights, he had followed them through Leicester Square towards Trafalgar and St Martin-in-the-Fields where they now stood about to go in to listen to Vivaldi's 'Four Seasons' by Candlelight.

Back behind the black railings of the church, with the National Gallery closing its doors behind him, in a new tweed hat and a green Barbour coat, he looked up into and through the milling crowd to where Stephen Gillen and, Daphne Diluce hovered by the door. His face had softened over the passing years, and as he looked at the well-dressed couple who shone with the healthy purpose of a successful life, he was happy he had come. In Ireland, as the landscape had heightened, stuttered and balanced to a lingering peace, he had kept a close watch. In the Autumn of his regrets and the guilt that had transfixed his soul to the Winter of his life had exhibited the gripping hold of pain, depression and alcoholism. He had followed the journey of the boy who had ripened as a man and the brightening sun of later years had directed him to a place which he had bolstered his courage to find Summer and the comforting years of acceptance and understanding. He had one last mission to complete.

They were walking in now, holding tickets and taking good seats in the elaborate and ornate high-ceilinged auditorium where the beautiful music would haunt and beguile an audience.

He felt the slight pain of arthritis in the hand that carried the deformity of three fingers. A wound he had collected as he opened a letter bomb which had been posted through the door of a house where he collected mail long ago. He shuffled forward, he had watched them come here before, a few years back. The Orchestra played. A vibrating and haunting collection of sweet sounds that seduced the senses. From his hidden vantage point, far back behind the packed rows of people as the violins danced and reached a crescendo, he looked at, Stephen Gillen's face far up the hall in the side front row. His eyes were closed, being lost to the music.

The man, who a long time ago was known as the Gardener, smiled. A tight movement that hid his true intent. He knew that death would soon find him, that the years he had remaining were galloping fast. He would not leave this earth until the mission was finished. He would keep going, as long as there was breath left in his body, to finish, to complete the circle that a little boy who had now matured into a man had activated and propelled many years before.

Zurich 2020

Behind the expansive glass windows of Elstree Aerodrome, two men clad in overcoats observed a sleek white private jet as it gathered speed on the runway, then ascended sharply into the azure sky. They watched intently, one man taking a bite from a crisp green apple, as the plane climbed higher, their gaze lingering long after it had vanished into the ether.

The Lear jet, banking gently to adjust its course northward, was a marvel of aviation I admired from the comfort of the cabin. The afternoon sun cast reflective glimmers against the window as the landscape below shrank away. This Lear jet 70/75, a brainchild of founder Bill Lear and a development from the 40/45 models, boasted a cruising speed of 465 knots (535 mph, 861 km/h) and could accommodate eight passengers with its two crew.

'A penny for your thoughts?' Daphne's voice, tinged with curiosity, cut through my reverie. Clad in a blue trouser suit and white blouse, she sat opposite me, her diary in hand.

My attention had been captivated by the cloud formations and, further in the distance, a rare bird. A white stork, resplendent with blue-black tipped feathers, commanded the high thermals with an effortless grace. It dipped and soared towards the sun's golden glare and then disappeared from view.

I adjusted the gold-and-silver cufflinks of my white shirt and settled my grey checked cashmere jacket. A casual stretch of my leg nudged my knees upward, my hand resting atop the seam of my jeans. With a sip of coffee, I mused, 'Did you know I just saw a white stork amidst the clouds? Such elegance.'

She offered a smile, glancing up from her entries in the blue diary. 'We have a two o'clock with Lawrence, the Secretary-General, then an hour to look at emails and the diary for next month. We should allow some time with him. Then at 6 pm, the founder of the global women's movement in Zurich has proposed dinner. Should we accept?'

'The white stork is such a rare sight, Daphne.'

'I could name another rarity,' she replied with a soft, conspiratorial laugh that filled the cabin.

Tony, with his short black hair and glasses, still donned his high-visibility vest from guiding us to the plane. He looked up from his magazine, a wide grin breaking across his face.

'Are you suggesting I'm a rare bird, Miss Diluce?' I jested.

She hesitated, her expression unfolding into one of bemused certainty. 'I'm not just suggesting, Mr. Gillen. I know it. You're unique; they broke the mould with you – a mould they must have cobbled together in the first place.'

A thin smile played upon her red lips, and I pondered the sentiment.

It had taken a long time for me to embrace the narratives spun by others, by the press about me. Yet, as my life's events unfolded, the possibility that they might be right had become increasingly undeniable.

My gaze drifted to the cream leather interior above. Life was a complex game of realities, offering not what you wanted but what you became.

'The founder of the global women's group?' She poised the pencil above the open diary.

'Women's empowerment? Let's consider it...' I leaned back thoughtfully.

'Perhaps it's the men who need empowering,' Daphne mused, a playful smile on her lips.

'Absolutely. Let's pencil it in tentatively and decide later.'

Daphne's focus returned to our latest project. 'Today, my main task is to refine our new product, to distil it into its purest form, its design, its authentic essence...'

'Excellent. Once you've crystallised the concept, I can position it strategically, and we'll move to scale and automate...'

Coffee cups clinked gently, the ambient hum of high altitude filling the cabin as the plane roared onwards. Through breaks in the clouds, we levelled off.

Our trip to Switzerland, specifically Zurich, was business-oriented, tied to a media client. We'd recently launched a global digital marketing platform, an extension of our innovative film and music business, RMC Studios. Our client, a prosperous property magnate with connections to the German Ambassador and stars like Madonna and U2, awaited our arrival. Time spent with him promised to be invaluable, with pivotal initiatives on the agenda. He expected us at a private airfield near Zurich, where dinner arrangements had been made.

As the plane dipped and veered into the dazzling sunlight, Daphne turned her gaze outward. I knew her thoughts were with her son, who lived just outside Zurich, a successful banker known for his daredevil escapades, from snowboarding to racing superbikes through the Alps.

'We'll make time to see him, Daphne,' I assured her.

'Yes... I know,' she replied, her voice tinged with anticipation and a contented half-smile on her face.

My focus returned to the vast expanse of clouds below and the boundless sky. Peering out the window, my mind raced with excitement for the future.

Opposites Together 2020

The programme was entitled 'Two Extremes' – a unique and authentic portrayal of two men who had lived hard and succeeded in their chosen paths. Despite being at opposite ends of the spectrum, they had unravelled profound truths about their purpose and destinations. United in a global mission of positive change, they were embarking on a national tour across the UK, with one city visited each month. The events, designed to empower and effect positive social change, were already attracting significant media attention and were booked to occur in Parliament, sharing the stage with the Lord Chancellor and Secretary of Justice, one of the highest-ranking ministers in the UK.

In the expansive theatre in Derby, the audience was captivated as Kul Mahay and I, now bound in brotherhood and a commitment to fostering improvement, delivered our talks.

A gentle smile graced my face. As the event drew to a close in the vast auditorium, with cameras poised and lights casting their glow, the enormous projected image of Kul Mahay and myself behind us basking in the radiance of its illumination, I felt a profound sense of coming home to myself, reaching out to become the individual I was destined to be.

Daphne, resplendent in a striking red dress, her blonde hair impeccably styled, still held the microphone from hosting the Q&A session.

'...Stephen, let me introduce you to Delia and her grandson.'

Delia offered a warm smile, a middle-aged Asian lady, her fourteen-year-old grandson at her side.

'I just wanted to say thank you. We've been having some challenges with my grandson here. We sat back in the audience, and what you said was remarkable. He listened, and he's told me that hearing you speak has truly helped him. Thank you...'

Gratefully, I placed a gentle hand on her arm. Her grandson, a tall, slender youth, stepped forward tentatively, a boy straining against the world on the cusp of manhood. In that instant, I was reminded of my own mother, her image imprinted with care, radiant in gleaming white, smiling with the love of pride.

In a soft, hesitant voice, he asked, 'If you could sum up your best piece of advice in one sentence, what would it be?'

I returned the smile warmly, appreciating the depth and thoughtfulness of his question.

'That's easy,' I responded. 'Keep doing the next right thing, no matter how difficult it may be, and I guarantee you'll end up somewhere good...'

The Gardner, London 2020

We sat in the National Gallery before the 1565-1570 masterpiece, 'The Family of Darius before Alexander'. On a modest wooden bench, we beheld the depiction of Stateira, wife of King Darius, and her mother, captured post-Issus where the last Achaemenid emperor had narrowly avoided capture. Together, we absorbed the vivid colours and layered drama infused within the painting.

He was known to me as the Gardener among other monikers, but mostly, he was a silhouette woven with questions, accompanying my quietest moments with whispers of ancient histories.

With the forefinger of his gnarled hand, he gestured towards the canvas. 'Alexander showed mercy in triumph,' he said, his voice soft yet clear. 'Here, King Darius's wife implores for her husband's life in defeat. Despite her famed beauty, Alexander, deeming self-control more regal than conquest, did not seek closeness with his captives...'

Years had passed in silence, punctuated by my questions. 'All these years, you've been a presence. Who are you?'

Seated together in our seclusion, the bustling tourists and the gallery's crowd milling around us, he persisted. 'The beauty of this painting lies in her mistaking Alexander for Hephaestion, his counsellor and lifelong confidant... It's wondrous, profound. What do you think, Stephen? It speaks volumes of the man, does it not?'

He had been the enigma at critical crossroads of my existence, his clandestine steps echoing alongside the uneven path of my life.

'...Why have you lingered in the shadows of my life for so long?'

Because of a boy, Stephen. Bright and brave and full of the exuberance of a life to come'.

'A boy?'

'Yes. A boy who was full of vigour. Whom I begged to stay at home one night while riots raged and a street war was fought, while the night coldness cut and a place that ached for peace mourned'.

I pulled back. In my mind it was surfacing, dots were joining, a picture was forming.

'…The boy was my son, Stephen. My beautiful nineteen-year-old who I had sworn to protect like any parent and couldn't…'

'You mean?' I questioned.

'It was the times. Where we were all trapped by the times and the history and pain of our sufferings and sacrifices. When he was young, Stephen I tried to get peace in Belfast, tried to lead an example that would show us to put our differences behind us. That together we could live in peace…'

'I don't understand…'

'The boy, Stephen. The one shot before your eyes as you hid beneath the hedge all those years ago. That boy was my son. I was known in Belfast for founding a youth club open to all, Catholics and Protestants alike. You weren't born then, but my son was just a child when the letter bomb came through our door and I opened it.'

'My God, I'm so sorry. It's all coming back to me.' The painting before us transported me to a time of anguish, where I clutched the cold earth, my body wracked with fear. The acrid smell of smoke and cordite filled the air, mingling with the stench of gasoline. I gasped, and among the shifting throngs of the Gallery, it

was as if only the two of us existed, isolated, our focus traversing back to a distant, tumultuous past.

'My son got involved. I did everything, but the constant reminder of my deformity and the hardness of our existence was a daily stick that beat him. He found hard to take that at the beginning as I struggled.'

Our eyes met, and a broad smile spread across his face.

'You understand boys, Stephen. They need to be boys, particularly at that pivotal stage. I was there that night, shadowing him as I was prone to, hoping that when the crucial moment arrived, I could somehow intervene, alter the course, protect him.'

'Thank you.'

'For what?'

'For your bravery.'

'But after all these years, why have you followed me, throughout my life?'

'Because you were like him, Stephen. My son's name was Sean. Sean, Stephen... And I watched you that night as he lay dying, his life ebbing away on the pavement. As young and terrified as you were, you reached out to him when he needed it, and I couldn't.'

His words burrowed deep, unearthing a pain I had long contained, releasing it into the light. Tears welled in my eyes, recalling the night where tracer rounds streaked the sky, people scattered in panic, gunfire resonated, and I hid, petrified. The grandeur of the masterpiece before us captured the ambiguity of a moment long past with pictorial eloquence.

'Sean passed away despite our efforts. I vowed, Stephen, to shadow you until I could repay that debt. Knowing your family made it easy to keep abreast of your life. The years have been tough

on you. You possess so much of him - the 'devil-may-care' spirit, the resilience, the zest for life. Over the years, I've come to think of you, to carry you in my heart, as my own...'

'I'm sorry I couldn't save him...'

'My name is Declan, Stephen. Declan Brown.'

'If only I could have made a difference, Declan...'

'I know, Stephen. I know. You did everything a child in that frightful night could. I wanted to thank you, for me and in loving memory of Sean's brief life... Thank you...'

His hand rested on my elbow, signalling it was time to depart. 'I have never forgotten your kindness, Stephen, throughout these challenging years. My promise to Sean's memory, to watch over you until you became the man you were meant to be, has been fulfilled. You've become a man of substance and your aunt would be proud. And Sean, well, he's surely smiling down on us... I won't pretend though that there weren't times I worried for you!'

Enveloped by the majesty of the old masters and the vibrant thrum of the gallery, I found myself momentarily speechless, as the weight of his revelation compartmentalised the memories within me.

Declan Brown, known to some as the Gardener, now approaching his twilight years yet never relinquishing hope, stood once more before the painting. With a contemplative half-smile, he mused, 'What I cherish about this piece is the depiction of nobility, the way it intertwines humility with immense power. Alexander, a commander destined to conquer much of the known world, is garbed in influence yet veiled in enigma. To embody such presence and yet remain unseen when necessary is a rare skill. There's one final thing I need to know.'

'Yes…Anything?'

'…As my son lay dying, I saw his lips move. After all these years, Stephen. What were his last words…?'

His gaze, piercing green, laden with the rare airing of deep-seated memories, held a depth born of profound experience and hardship.

'He spoke of his love for you, for his mother. He called out for you. He was enveloped in the love you gave him.'

That moment struck him with the force of a blow, and he stood rigid, then turned away. Amidst the gallery's historic masterpieces and the bustling crowd, he stood to walk away.

'Thank you, Stephen, you have granted me peace today.' And with that, he departed, taking a swath of history in his wake.

Retreating into the enigmatic corridors of the gallery, as swift and unobtrusive as his entrance, I reflected on the painting where Alexander extended his arms. Standing there, with the prospect of a new life chapter before me and the name on the paper signalling the advent of my future glory, I felt the profound symbolism of the greatness that enveloped me. My experiences, wrought from adversity and refined over time, had prepared me for what lay ahead. With a final glance at the painting, I merged into the sea of moving figures that filled the room, my presence as transient as the fleeting moment I had shared with Declan.

Reflection

Throughout my life, I've learned from a series of mentors. The key lesson has been the importance of remaining open to learning. Acknowledging the potential within oneself is the first step; realising that boundless possibilities await is the next. Surrounding oneself with individuals of the highest calibre, and emulating their virtues and methods, accelerates personal growth.

Maintaining a clear vision of who you aim to become is essential, drawing inspiration from the successes of those you admire. The journey towards this ideal self is punctuated by consistent effort, strategic action, and sacrifices. Over time, the person you aspired to be becomes a reflection in the mirror, often surpassing the initial image you held in your mind's eye.

Giving Back 2024

"Reflect upon your present blessings - of which every man has many - not on your past misfortunes, of which all men have some."
— Charles Dickens, A Christmas Carol

Venturing into prisons and speaking directly to inmates, I share the hard-earned truths about conflict resolution. I draw from the depths of my own experiences to offer a glimmer of understanding and a path to a new chapter. My efforts stretch to the inner city, where I meet with gangs, aiming to divert energy from violence to peace, a mission that saw my work recognised with a nomination for the Sunhak International Peace Prize.

My heart extends across the globe; in Africa, I'm deeply involved in supporting medical aid for those enduring the aftermath of amputations, attempting to bring solace and solutions to the suffering.

Being the charity ambassador for initiatives like Flo Coin, a new accountable decentralised currency, that aligns with my goal to impact lives, positively lifting up people who need opportunity. It's not just about charity; it's about enabling empowerment and fostering sustainable growth.

My aim in life is simple yet ambitious: to help and touch hundreds of millions of people across the world. Whether it's a handshake or a shared story, every connection is a step towards that goal - a chance to plant the seeds of peace and prosperity. It's a journey of a thousand miles, and each step is taken with the hope of leaving a trail of harmony and opportunity in my wake. I am happy to say we are well on our way to completing this great mission.

Daphne is by my side, continuing to support me and my family. She asked me how I thought I might be able to make it happen, to be able to help hundreds of millions of people, my answer is that I'd like to give them hope. That in reading my story, if you are going through what I have, or are feeling that you cannot change the path you're on, you'll see that there is always a possibility and opportunity for change.

It would be wrong of me to say that I have come through this unscathed. I have not. I carry with me scars and my demons and PTSD can sometimes rage at me day in and day out. I am not an easy man, a big picture person, and I am driven to succeed, to make up for the time that I lost and to challenge myself. I consider myself a person of integrity, who has had to muster immense courage and wield a sharp sense of timing, coupled with the necessary skills and clear opportunities to navigate back to my true self against overwhelming odds. My focus is on generosity, committing to significant and consistent strides towards change, not solely within myself but extending to others, to the environments I inhabit, and beyond to the wider world. I am acutely aware that we are merely custodians of the material world, and it is in the imprints we leave on the lives around us and the positive changes we forge in the world that will stand as a lasting legacy, truly enduring beyond our time. At the very core of myself, it the desire to always do the next best thing.

I asked Daphne to give her perspective on living with someone who has had a traumatic past and this was her response, '*Stephen is a good man, trying to do good things, he is a work of art in the making, BUT like all works of art, in order for it to be beautiful, there must be shadow mixed with the light, darkness to offset the bright colours. If you are supporting someone going through trauma it is not a path for the meek and mild, you must be strong, for there will be times when their demons rampage. But if you love that person, then you can be there, help them to find the peace that they're searching for.*'

True success isn't about stumbling upon one good choice or passively waiting for a lucky break. It's not even about making a handful or a thousand wise decisions. Real progress, the kind that leads to lasting happiness and success, is crafted through a series of deliberate choices. It's about aligning with the right people, acting at the right time, and moving in a direction that's been thoughtfully chosen. Consistent, extraordinary actions over time pave the road to achievement.

It's this discipline, this commitment to excellence in every small act, that forges a successful life.

I've seen how the wrong environment, the wrong influences, can set a person on a path of ruin. Yet, I've also seen transformation - how, with the right system and the right support, change is possible. It's about seizing the moment, harnessing opportunity, and having the strength and planning to forge a new path.

Change needs a confluence of factors: timing, circumstances, intervention, opportunity, strength, and strategy. When all these elements align, that's when you can start to move forward. Small steps become great strides, and a new course is charted.

I've come to understand that even with a few of these elements in place, without the full combination, progress can falter. That's why, despite strength and intervention, without opportunity, clear goals, and precise timing, efforts can fall short. But when everything aligns, that's when real, meaningful change takes root. That's the method I've applied to my life and intend to share in my next book - the keys to not just turning a life around, but to achieving levels of success and wealth beyond the ordinary. It's a complex formula, but at its core, it's about setting a direction and taking the steps, however small, towards a greater future.

People, in all their complexity, fall under what I've come to know as the human condition. It's become clear to me that despite our diverse backgrounds, teachings, and lifestyles, we're all essentially striving for similar outcomes. Our paths may differ, but the core issues that drive us often converge.

Leadership, for example, is a skill that transcends context. Whether you're navigating the underworld or steering a corporate giant, it boils down to innate qualities: strength, intuition, vision, and the capability to inspire others to follow. It's about aspiring to achieve more and to be more. The key is to start at what we can give, how can we add value and not take.

Experience is the crucible that shapes an individual. The calibre of their thoughts and the company they keep forge their character. The situations they face bring to light the specific challenges they must tackle. At the core, it's the quality of a person's heart that dictates whether they construct or destruct.

We exist within a framework of boundaries, a matrix that subtly directs our choices and actions. This structure posits that given 'A' set of circumstances, a human is likely to exhibit 'B' behaviour. It's this framework, alongside our nature, that propels and confines us. It's a simple yet profound truth, a divine coding that governs our existence. Life is a tapestry of multiple realities, numerous guides, and varied roles we embody throughout our journey.

I hope that you have enjoyed my story, that it may have helped you in some way. If you feel that you need help, do not be afraid to ask.

Coming Soon - The 9 Laws of Transformation

"*The 9 Laws of Transformation*" is the riveting new book from Stephen Gillen, a man who has journeyed from the depths of criminality as a Category A prisoner to the heights of global business leadership. In this ground-breaking work, Stephen divulges the personal methodology that fuelled his radical metamorphosis. With raw authenticity, he distils his hard-earned wisdom into nine transformative steps, charting the course from profound adversity to unparalleled success.

This book a powerful guide that promises to catalyse change in anyone. Whether emerging from challenging backgrounds or already on the ladder of success and aspiring to reach higher rungs, readers will discover pioneering insights for exponential personal growth. Stephen's compelling narrative is a testament to the potential for change in all of us, underscored by his own dramatic life transformation which now finds him as a CEO, TV presenter, author, and a nominee for an international peace prize.

In "*The 9 Laws of Transformation*," Stephen shares not only his journey overcoming poverty, criminality, mental health struggles, and addiction but also the actionable steps anyone can take towards a full 360-degree turnaround.

This book is an invitation to embark on a journey of meaningful and expansive change, offering the keys to unlock potential and achieve a transformation that's both far-reaching and deeply personal.

FIND OUT MORE

To book Stephen for Speaking Events, interviews or Company training: stephen@stephengillen.com

For merchandise and further free content and information, go to Stephen's personal website at www.stephengillen.com

For exclusive coaching services, contact his PA at hello@stephengillen.com

To work with Stephen Gillen & his team for Business Development, to upscale, Global or National PR, Profile Development, Branding, Marketing and or Filmmaking and other Media Services email: stephen@stephengillen.com

For collaboration or to offer services or donate to humanitarian work Hello@stephengillen.com